21世纪高等学校专业英语系列教材

教育学专业英语教程
（第2版）

English for Pedagogy
(Second Edition)

主　编　董晓波
副主编　董德馨　叶　霞
参编者　边　君　蒋　菲　曾鸣玥

清华大学出版社
北京交通大学出版社
·北京·

内 容 简 介

本教程在内容编排上力图反映当代教育学的发展趋势与新特征,注重教育学专业知识与英语学习的有机结合,所包括的课文涉及当代教育学的主要方面,不仅注重英语能力的培养,也强调教育学专业知识的传授和技能的训练。

本教程除适合高等师范院校本科生、研究生使用外,也可供各级各类教育学院教育学、教育心理学、英语教学法等专业的本科生和研究生学习教育学专业英语之用。此外,对于大、中、小学教师了解教育学理论知识,提高教育学专业英语水平也是难得的参考书。

本书封面贴有清华大学出版社防伪标签,无标签者不得销售。
版权所有,侵权必究。侵权举报电话: 010-62782989 13501256678 13801310933

图书在版编目(CIP)数据

教育学专业英语教程/董晓波主编. —2 版. —北京:北京交通大学出版社 :清华大学出版社,2023.11
ISBN 978-7-5121-5096-6

Ⅰ. ①教… Ⅱ. ①董… Ⅲ. ①教育学-英语-教材 Ⅳ. ①G40

中国国家版本馆 CIP 数据核字(2023)第 214310 号

教育学专业英语教程
JIAOYUXUE ZHUANYE YINGYU JIAOCHENG

责任编辑:田秀青	
出版发行:清 华 大 学 出 版 社　邮编:100084　电话:010-62776969　http://www.tup.com.cn	
北京交通大学出版社　邮编:100044　电话:010-51686414　http://www.bjtup.com.cn	
印　刷　者:北京鑫海金澳胶印有限公司	
经　　　销:全国新华书店	
开　　　本:185 mm×243 mm　　印张:18　　字数:404 千字	
版 印　　次:2015 年 2 月第 1 版　　2023 年 11 月第 2 版　　2023 年 11 月第 1 次印刷	
印　　　数:1~2 000 册　　定价:49.00 元	

本书如有质量问题,请向北京交通大学出版社质监组反映。对您的意见和批评,我们表示欢迎和感谢。
投诉电话:010-51686043,51686008;传真:010-62225406;E-mail:press@bjtu.edu.cn。

Preface 前言

以中国式教育现代化助推中华民族伟大复兴

习近平总书记在党的二十大报告中明确指出:"从现在起,中国共产党的中心任务就是团结带领全国各族人民全面建成社会主义现代化强国、实现第二个百年奋斗目标,以中国式现代化全面推进中华民族伟大复兴。"在中国式现代化的历史进程中,教育现代化至关重要。中国式教育现代化是中国式现代化的重要组成部分,更是实现中国式现代化的基础性、战略性支撑。面对新时代强国建设战略部署与中华民族伟大复兴的历史重任,迫切需要以中国式教育现代化助推中华民族伟大复兴。

习近平总书记指出,"现代化的本质是人的现代化"。新时代教育发展不仅仅是为了满足民生需求,更是经济社会发展的内在生产性要素,教师教育要整体谋划服务各级各类教育的现代化,使其更好促进经济社会发展。党的十八大以来,党中央坚持把教师队伍建设作为基础工作。习近平总书记心系广大教师,对教师队伍建设作出系列重要指示批示,强调教师是立教之本、兴教之源,号召广大教师坚持"四个相统一",做"四有好老师""四个引路人",做学生为学、为事、为人的大先生。

近年来,我国政府十分重视教师队伍建设。中共中央、国务院颁布了《关于全面深化新时代教师队伍建设改革的意见》《教师教育振兴行动计划(2018—2022年)》《新时代基础教育强师计划》等一系列政策。各省市也陆续发布了相关政策,为中国式教师教育现代化提供了政策指引。这些政策立足国家或地方全局,从实际问题出发,坚持系统观念,积极推动新时代教师教育守正创新。尽管如此,我国教师教育发展仍然存在不少挑战,比如不同地区教师供需和师资配给依旧不均衡、不充分,教师职业吸引力和发展后劲不足,职前教师人才培养理念与社会发展需求未能有效衔接,入职和职后教师培训质量不尽如人意,政府、高等院校、中小学校及家庭协同育人机制不健全等。

在学习贯彻落实党的二十大精神过程中,我们应该充分认识到,建设教育强国、实现教育高质量发展,以中国式现代化推动实现中华民族伟大复兴,离不开一支师德高尚、业务精湛、结构合理、充满生机活力的高素质专业化创新型教师队伍。

首先，坚持党对教育工作的全面领导，落实立德树人根本任务。

中国式教育现代化是党领导下的伟大实践。坚持党的领导是教育现代化的政治保证和组织保障。"党政军民学，东西南北中，党是领导一切的"，这个"学"就是教育，凸显加强党对教育工作的全面领导。坚持党管办学方向、管改革发展、管干部、管人才，把党的领导贯穿教育工作的各方面各环节，使教育领域成为坚持党的领导的坚强阵地。习近平总书记多次强调，人无德不立，育人的根本在于立德。这是人才培养的辩证法。办学就要尊重这个规律，否则就办不好学。落实立德树人根本任务，要把立德树人融入思想道德教育、文化知识教育、社会实践教育各环节，贯穿基础教育、职业教育、高等教育各领域。要改革创新思想政治理论课，努力把社会主义核心价值观融入国民教育全过程，积极推进大中小学思政课一体化建设，强化教师使命责任，发挥教师关键引领作用。教师是人类灵魂的工程师，是人类文明的传承者，承载着传播知识、传播思想、传播真理、塑造灵魂、塑造生命、塑造新人的时代重任。落实立德树人根本任务、培养时代新人，最终依靠广大人民教师教书育人的实践与"学高为师，身正为范"的引领。

其次，坚定高等师范教育自信，创新人才培养机制。

我国高等教育整体水平进入了世界第一方阵，但仍存在着人才培养模式相对陈旧、评价标准相对单一、学生培养同构化发展、创新创造能力不足等较为严重的问题和短板。《中共中央关于制定国民经济和社会发展第十四个五年规划和二〇三五年远景目标的建议》提出，要建立高水平现代教师教育体系，推进教师教育资源共建共治共享、互联互通，赋能教师专业发展，探索教师教育数字化治理方式。《新时代基础教育强师计划》提出，到2035年，适应教育现代化和建成教育强国要求，构建开放、协同、联动的高水平教师教育体系。因此，在中国式教师教育现代化进程中，我们需要进一步从体系化、特色化和专业化中加快推进高水平教师教育体系建构，打造服务国家和地方社会发展的多主体、多层级和多功能的中国特色师范新体系。

高校应准确把握好"中国特色"和"世界一流"之间的辩证关系，紧跟世界发展趋势。在体现国际共性和可比性的同时，绝不能把以美国为代表的西方高等教育发展模式奉为圭臬，而是要扎根中国大地，体现中国自主，坚持自己的制度特色、文化特点和价值特性，遵循教育规律和人才成长规律，顺应科技革命、产业革命和世界高等教育格局的深刻变化，打破壁垒和路径依赖，加快中国高等教育的国家化、数字化战略，以"四新"（新工科、新医科、新农科、新文科）建设，创新人才培养机制，不断提升中国高等师范教育对国家经济、社会、科技文化的服务力、支撑力、引领力、感召力、塑造力和国际影响力，力争在新领域、新赛道作出更大的全局性、先导性贡献。

再次，全面推进各级各类教育现代化，优化调整教师队伍建设布局。

中国式现代化是社会各领域全方位而均衡的现代化。中国式教育现代化作为中国式现代化的重要组成部分或衍生概念，自然也绝对不是碎片式的、点状的、单独某一类教育的中国式现代化。全面推进中国式教育现代化，必须要坚持统筹兼顾和全面协调，促进各级各类教育中国式现代化的均衡发展与齐头并进。

根据新型城镇化战略、乡村振兴战略的总体部署，适应以县城为重要载体的城镇化建设和城乡融合发展的需求，优化教师队伍建设整体布局，将素质提升、结构优化摆在教师队伍建设的优先位置，推动教师队伍建设由规模扩展走向质量提升。

加强乡村教师队伍建设，补齐教师队伍薄弱短板。深入落实加强新时代乡村教师队伍建设的意见，在乡村教师培养培训、职称、待遇、表彰宣传等各方面给予政策支持，为乡村学校打造"下得去、教得好、留得住"的教师队伍。

面向基础教育，建设培养卓越之师的教师教育体系。推动师范教育发展，将办好师范教育作为第一职责，实施好师范教育协同提质计划，强化区域教师发展机构建设，加快健全以师范院校为主体、高水平大学参与，本科和硕博士一体化培养的中国特色教师教育体系。

面向职业教育，发展培养高质量工匠之师的教师教育体系。优化职业教育类型定位，推进职普融通、产教融合、科教融汇。首先，支持高水平理工科大学、行业企业、职业院校等多主体共同参与职业院校教师培养培训。其次，支持高水平学校和大中型企业共建"双师型"教师培养培训基地和企业实践基地，启动实施职业学校教师学历提升行动、名师（名匠）名校长培养计划。最后，突出"双师型"导向的教师考核评价改革，优化职业院校教师队伍结构。

推进高校教师队伍改革，打造高素质专业化创新型教师队伍。高等学校的教师队伍是我国教师队伍中学历水平和职称等级最高的部分，但是相对于创新驱动发展战略所需的创新型教师还有很大距离。因此，深化高校人事管理及教师考核评价改革，激发教师队伍创新活力，加强校级教师发展机构建设和院系教师发展共同体建设，支持高校教师教育教学创新和专业素质能力提升尤为重要。

最后，加快推进教育数字化，大力提升教师信息、数字素养与综合能力。

中国式教师教育现代化不能只通过教师学历比例、师生比例等量化指标来衡量，更为重要的是"质"的提升，需要在技术理性、终身学习与文化传承中回归育人本真价值。党的二十大报告首次把教育、科技、人才进行"三位一体"统筹安排、一体部署，并首次将"推进教育数字化"写入报告，赋予了教育在全面建设社会主义现代化国家中新的使命任务，明确了教育数字化未来发展的行动纲领，具有重大意义。教师是改革的实施者，要加强数字时代教师队伍建设，多层次开展教师数字化能力培训工作，积极应对教育信息化、数字化挑战，大力提升教师信息、数字素养与综合能力，主动应用教育数字化、智能化工具，创新教育教学方法与实践，为教师职业发展赋能，为教学改革升级。

总之，党的二十大指引着教育改革方向，为中国式教师教育现代化提供了基本思想和实践方略。建设中国式教师教育现代化，加快建成教育强国，是新时代、新征程的目标和使命。面对百年未有之大变局，各级教育部门要把握好习近平新时代中国特色社会主义思想的世界观和方法论，在立德树人和教师专业发展并举中传承中华优秀传统文化，积极推进高水平教师教育体系建设，为党育人、为国育才，努力加快推进中国式教师教育现代化进程，以中国式教师教育现代化助推中华民族伟大复兴。

本教程是为高等院校教育学专业的本科生和研究生编写的，旨在通俗、系统地介绍教育学学科理论和教学实践的专业英语教材。

基于历史和现实的原因，英语作为国际语言，适用范围广、影响大，能更好地促进各个领域的交流和实践，尤其是在教育教学改革不断深入的当今社会，教育学作为一门研究人类教育现象和问题、揭示一般教育规律的社会学科，是广泛存在于人类生活中的社会现象，是有目的地培养社会人的活动。随着现代社会的进步以及现代教育实践的发展，为了有效地进行教育活动，人们对教育学研究以及教师教育提出更新、更高的要求。就教育学课程体系构建和教材建设而言，教育学专业英语教程的编写既需结合我国教师教育实际，又需满足基础教育改革对师资需求，进而有效地推动我国高等师范院校改革和发展新型的教师教育模式。因此，《教育学专业英语教程》将学习英语与了解教育领域内一些常见学科理论及教学实践，提高解决实际教育问题的能力紧密结合，即在学习英语的同时，使学生系统地了解教育学科学理论、专业知识和教学实践；在认识和走进教育领域的同时，学习和了解教育学科中一些常见的教育理论、观点（包括专业词汇、术语等）的英语表达，在巩固一般语言知识和运用能力的基础上进一步扩展学生的语言知识，提高学生的语言应用能力，将语言教学和专业教育融会贯通。

本教程是在第1版基础上的修订完善版，选材广泛，信息量大，基本包含了当代教育学的主要方面。本教程文字浅显，结构严谨，行文流畅，语言地道。在编排体例方面，为了方便读者提高阅读能力，本书增加了文章背景知识介绍，言简意赅地介绍文章基本线索，便于读者快速阅读和理解文章主旨；注释力求简单明了，方便读者了解教育学知识。词汇接近大学英语四六级难度，主要汇集教育学专业词汇，以降低阅读难度。书后附有练习答案，便于读者自学，自测学习效果。

本教程除适合高等师范院校本科生、研究生使用外，也可供各级各类教育学院教育学、教育心理学、英语教学法等专业的本科生和研究生学习教育学专业英语之用。此外，对于大、中、小学教师了解教育学理论知识，提高教育学专业英语水平也是难得的参考书。

在整个编写过程中，我们力求完美，但是限于水平及一些不可避免的因素，定不乏偏颇和疏漏，恳请广大读者朋友和同行不吝指正。

董晓波

2023年7月于南京仙林

Contents
目 录

Unit 1　Origin & History of Education　教育的起源和历史·················· 1
　　Text A　The History of Compulsory Education in Europe················ 1
　　Text B　A History of American Higher Education···················· 6
　　Useful phrases and expressions······························ 13

Unit 2　Education & Social Development　教育与社会发展················ 16
　　Text A　Open and Distance Education: a Better Way of Competence Building
　　　　　 and Sustainable Development···························· 16
　　Text B　Higher Education within a Knowledge-based Society············ 23
　　Useful phrases and expressions······························ 30

Unit 3　Education & People's Overall Development　教育与人的全面发展
　　　·· 33
　　Text A　Role of Education in the Developmental Process············· 33
　　Text B　Social Skills Development in Primary Education············· 38
　　Useful phrases and expressions······························ 45

Unit 4　Educational System & Educational Law　教育制度与教育法·········· 47
　　Text A　E-learning and Evaluation in Modern Educational System········ 47
　　Text B　Legislation and Equality in Basic Education················ 52
　　Useful phrases and expressions······························ 58

Unit 5　Educational Justice　教育公平···························· 60
　　Text A　Educational Justice in Schools························· 60

I

  Text B Efficiency and Equity of European Education and Training
      Policies ·· 65
  Useful phrases and expressions ·· 71

Unit 6 Educator & Educational Thoughts 教育家与教育思想 ················ 74
  Text A Disciples of Confucius ··· 74
  Text B Educational Thought and Teaching ······································ 79
  Useful phrases and expressions ·· 85

Unit 7 Educational Objectives 教育目的 ·· 87
  Text A Aims and Objectives of Education ······································· 87
  Text B Education, Basics of Education and Educational Objectives ············ 96
  Useful phrases and expressions ·· 104

Unit 8 Teacher & Student 教师与学生 ··· 107
  Text A The Teacher, the Student and the Classroom ························· 107
  Text B Teacher-Student Attachment and Teachers' Attitudes towards
      Work ··· 117
  Useful phrases and expressions ·· 127

Unit 9 School & Family 学校与家庭 ··· 129
  Text A School and Family Cooperation Models for Reducing Social
      Problems ·· 129
  Text B The Effects of Family, School, and Classroom Ecologies on Changes
      in Children's Social Competence and Emotional and Behavioral
      Problems in First Grade ··· 139
  Useful phrases and expressions ·· 146

Unit 10 Moral Education 道德教育 ··· 149
  Text A Education as a Moral Enterprise ··· 149
  Text B Moral Education of Youth in the Information Age ···················· 154
  Useful phrases and expressions ·· 161

Unit 11 Extra-curricular Activities 课外活动 ······································ 163
  Text A Extra-curricular Activity and the Transition from Higher Education to

     Work ·········· 163
  Text B Extra-curricular Physical Activity and Socioeconomic Status in
     Italian Adolescents ·········· 171
  Useful phrases and expressions ·········· 180

Unit 12 School Management 学校管理 ·········· 183
  Text A What is School-based Management? ·········· 183
  Text B Comparative Case Study on School Management Practices in Two
     Schools in the United States and Türkiye ·········· 192
  Useful phrases and expressions ·········· 201

Unit 13 Teaching Methods 教学方法 ·········· 204
  Text A Refuting Misconceptions about Classroom Discussion ·········· 204
  Text B Brainstorming: a Creative Way to Learn ·········· 212
  Useful phrases and expressions ·········· 219

Unit 14 Materials & Test 教材与考试 ·········· 221
  Text A Materials and Media ·········· 221
  Text B In Defense of Teaching "Outdated" Material ·········· 229
  Useful phrases and expressions ·········· 236

Unit 15 Educational Evaluation 教育评价 ·········· 238
  Text A Integration of Technology and Educational Assessment ·········· 238
  Text B Sustainable Assessment and Evaluation Strategies for Open and
     Distance Learning ·········· 246
  Useful phrases and expressions ·········· 253

Keys to Exercises 练习答案 ·········· 255

References 参考文献 ·········· 265

Unit 1 Origin & History of Education
教育的起源和历史

Text A The History of Compulsory Education in Europe

导读：义务教育，是根据法律规定，适龄儿童和青少年都必须接受的，国家、社会、家庭必须予以保证的国民教育。其实质是指政府有义务运用公共资源保障所有适龄儿童接受的教育。义务教育又称强迫教育和免费义务教育。义务教育具有强制性、免费性、普及性的特点。凡是适龄儿童都有强制接受教育的义务，并且教育对象没有阶级或是出身的限制，此外还必须是免纳学费的。1717年，普鲁士王国开始实施义务国民教育，是全世界第一个实施义务教育的国家。《世界人权宣言》第26条第一款指出："人人都有受教育的权利，教育应当免费，至少在初级和基本阶段应如此。初级教育应属义务性质。"现代多数的国家和地区都实施了义务教育，但年数和成效不一。

In the past few years, there has been a high-profile anti-truancy publicity campaign aiming to send out a clear and tough message to the community, particularly the parents of truants—that truancy will not be tolerated. Thousands of press releases from LEA have been fed to the national and local press generating adverse news and stories about the fining and jailing of truants' parents, who are regarded as shamefully irresponsible by failing to stop their children truanting.

Picking up any local newspaper, one would easily find the headlines that slam the "irresponsible parents" whose children are skipping schools. These press headlines on truancy have undoubtedly reinforced the fear that truancy levels have reached a crisis point. They have also given people the impression that the perceived newly-emerged "irresponsible parents" are one of the modern day social phenomena that are seriously threatening our compulsory education system and, therefore, our civil society.

However, nearly 500 years ago, in 1530 Luther was already able to observe three equivalent groups of "irresponsible parents" who were most likely to neglect their parental duties in sending their children to school. Most "irresponsible parents" at that time were those who might not understand what Luther thought as their God-given responsibility, others might not be suited for the duty. Luther thought that those parents had learned nothing but how to care for their bellies.

A third group of parents was the ones which did not have the opportunity or the means to educate its children. Luther observed that these parents placed their children's material comfort above their spiritual needs. In 1524 he argued in his address to the lawmakers that the civil authorities are under obligation to compel the people to send their children to school:

Dear rulers... if the government can compel such citizens as are fit for military service to bear spear and rifle, to mount ramparts, and perform other material duties in time of war, how much more has it a right to compel the people to send their children to school, because in this case we are warring with the devil, whose objective is secretly to exhaust our cities and principalities of their strong men.

One of the hallmarks of the Renaissance movement, which was reaching northern Europe in the sixteenth century, was the rebirth of learning. The Christian Reformation activists tirelessly advocated universal education as an important means in producing responsible citizens. In his open letter to the councilmen, in 1524 Luther urged them to have a vested interest in education for a city's best and greatest welfare, safety and strength consist rather in its having many able, earned, wise, honorable, and well-educated citizens than in mighty walls and magnificent buildings.

However, in the early sixteenth century, there was no state education system and most education activities were conducted in monasteries, cloisters and other religious institutions run by the Roman Catholic Church. These institutions very often lacked minimal resources and did not enjoy parents' trust because of the corruption and abuse among the clergy. Many parents were increasingly reluctant to send their children to the training institutions run by the Catholic Church.

In 1530, Luther therefore wrote an open letter to the parents to convince his "beloved Germans" that the spiritual well being of their children was more important than their physical comfort. Luther based his arguments for parental responsibility firmly on the Bible, citing several texts as proof. One quoted by him is Psalm 78: 5-7, on how God commanded our fathers to teach (His laws) to their children; that the next generation might know them...and arise and tell them to their children, so that they should set their hope in God, and not forget the works of God.

Another is Deuteronomy 21: 18-21, the stories of rebellious youths being brought by their parents to the elders for corporal punishment. In Geneva another Protestant reformer, John Calvin in 1536 was similarly making a case for compulsory schooling where all children were to be instructed in the "true faith" and "in the languages and worldly sciences" which served as a necessary preliminary for such instruction. Like Luther, Calvin was supremely confident that his possession of "the truth" gave him warrant to override the wishes and desires of parents who did not share his beliefs.

As a result of a Protestant reformers' campaign in the state of Gotha, the world's first primitive form of state schooling was established in 1524. It soon spread to Thuringia, Saxony, Wurttemberg and other German Protestant states. In 1559, the duchy of Wurttemberg ordered the introduction of a school attendance register and for the first time in educational history, levied fines on the parents whose children truanted.

However, the elaborate version of compulsory education as we see today did not emerge until the beginning of the nineteenth century when the Kings of Prussia established a system of state-controlled compulsory schooling and forcefully discouraged voluntary education. A minister of the interior was appointed to supervise the running of state schools. In 1810, state certifications of teachers were instituted and in 1812 children were prohibited from leaving school until they had passed a compulsory examination.

Regarded as a successful way of making every citizen useful to the state, the Prussian schooling system soon spread to most Western countries in the nineteenth century, including the USA and the UK.

1. **LEA=Local Education Authority**（英国地方教育局）: LEA is a local authority in England and Wales that has responsibility for education within its jurisdiction. Since the Children Act 2004 each local education authority is also a children's services authority and the responsibility for both functions is held by the director of children's services.

2. **Luther—Martin Luther**（马丁·路德）: Martin Luther was a German priest and professor of theology who initiated the Protestant Reformation. He strongly disputed the claim that freedom from God's punishment of sin could be purchased with money. He thought that

salvation is not earned by good deeds but received only as a free gift of God's grace through faith in Jesus as redeemer from sin. His theology challenged the authority of the pope of the Roman Catholic Church by teaching that the Bible is the only source of divinely revealed knowledge and opposed sacerdotalism (祭司制度，僧侣政治) by considering all baptized Christians to be a holy priesthood. Those who identify with Luther's teachings are called Lutherans.

3. **Psalm** [诗篇（《圣经·旧约》中的一卷）]: Psalm is a book of the Hebrew Bible and the Christian Bible. Its current, most commonly used form consists of 150 songs and prayers referred to individually as psalms and referenced by chapter and verse, which "express virtually the full range of Israel's religious faith".

4. **Deuteronomy** [申命记（《圣经·旧约》中的一卷）]: Deuteronomy is the fifth book of the Hebrew Bible, and the fifth of five books of the Jewish Torah/Pentateuch. The book consists of three sermons or speeches delivered by Moses, a recounting of the law (thought to be the Book of the Covenant found in Josiah's time), and supplementary material, including an account of Moses' death.

5. **John Calvin** (约翰·加尔文): John Calvin was an influential French theologian and pastor during the Protestant Reformation. He was a principal figure in the development of the system of Christian theology later called Calvinism. His writing and preaching provided the seeds for the branch of theology that bears his name. The Reformed and Presbyterian churches, which look to Calvin as a chief expositor of their beliefs, have spread throughout the world.

6. **Prussia** (普鲁士): Prussia was a German kingdom and historic state originating out of the Duchy of Prussia and the Margraviate of Brandenburg. For centuries, the House of Hohenzollern ruled Prussia, successfully expanding its size by way of an unusually well-organized and effective army. Prussia shaped the history of Germany, with its capital in Berlin after 1451. After 1871, Prussia was increasingly merged into Germany, losing its distinctive identity. It was effectively abolished in 1932, and officially abolished in 1947.

New words and expressions

1. compulsory [kəm'pʌlsəri]   *adj.*   强制的，势在必行的，义务的
2. truancy ['truːənsi]   *n.*   逃学，旷课；玩忽职守
3. slam [slæm]   *v.*   砰地关上，猛放，猛烈攻击

Unit 1 Origin & History of Education 教育的起源和历史

	n.	砰然声，猛烈抨击
	n.	满贯
4. rampart ['ræmpɑːt]	n.	垒，壁垒，城墙
	vt.	用壁垒围绕，防卫，守卫
5. principality [ˌprinsi'pæliti]	n.	封邑，公国，主权
6. hallmark ['hɔːlmɑːk]	n.	纯度标记，标志，特征
	vt.	标纯度
7. monastery ['mɔnəsteri]	n.	修道院，寺院
8. cloister ['klɔistə]	n.	修道院，寺庙，隐居地
	vt.	远离尘世，隐居，用环廊环绕
9. clergy ['klɜːdʒi]	n.	[总称]牧师，神职人员
10. reluctant [ri'lʌktənt]	adj.	不情愿的，勉强的
11. corporal ['kɔːpərəl]	adj.	肉体的，身体的
	n.	（陆军或空军）下士
12. preliminary [pri'liminəri]	adj.	初步的，预备的
	n.	初步行动，准备，初步措施

I Vocabulary.

Fill in the blanks with the most suitable words. Change the form when necessary.

reluctant	compulsory	preliminary	slam	principality
corporal	hallmark	rampart	truancy	monastery

1. A teacher should not give students _____ punishment.
2. The plan has all the _____ of being a total failure.
3. A _____ is a building or collection of buildings in which monks live.
4. He closed the door with a _____.
5. The schools were fighting endlessly to combat _____.
6. Ministers have shown extreme _____ to explain their position to the media.
7. Perhaps the tower is part of the _____ of the city.

8. A _____ talk on the future of the bases began yesterday.
9. Attendance at evening prayers is not _____.
10. I've been to the _____ of Monaco.

II Translate the following words and phrases into English.

义务教育　　　　　　　_____
说服，使信服　　　　　_____
物质享受　　　　　　　_____
精神需求　　　　　　　_____
监督，管理，指导　　　_____

III Comprehension of the text.

Decide whether the following statements are true (T) or false (F) according to the passage.

1. National and local press have generated adverse news and stories about the fining and jailing of truants, who are regarded as shamefully irresponsible.　(　　)
2. A third group of parents placed their children's material comfort below their spiritual needs.　(　　)
3. In the early sixteenth century, there was only one state education system and most education activities were conducted in monasteries, cloisters and other religious institutions run by the Roman Catholic Church.　(　　)
4. As many parents were reluctant to send their children to the training institutions run by the Catholic Church, Luther wrote an open letter to them to convince the importance of spiritual well being of their children.　(　　)
5. The elaborate version of compulsory education as we see today emerge at the beginning of the nineteenth century when the Kings of Prussia established a system of state-controlled compulsory schooling.　(　　)

Text B　A History of American Higher Education

导读：高等教育（Higher Education）广义上是指一切建立在中等教育基础上的专业教育，是培养高级专门人才的社会活动。高等教育是大学、文理学院、理工学院和师范学院等机构所提供的各种类型的教育，包括专科教育、本科教育和研究生教育，其基本

Unit 1 Origin & History of Education 教育的起源和历史

入学条件为完成中等教育，学完课程后授予学位、文凭或证书，作为完成高等学业的证明。高等教育的发展历史可以追溯到中世纪的大学，后来历经发展，主要是英国、德国、美国的大学的不断转型，形成了高等教育的三项职能，即：培养专门人才；科学研究；服务社会。作为一种教育方式，高等教育是人生存方式的一个阶段，从时间上说，是人生存过程中的终身学习选择阶段，从空间上说，高等教育是人进入完全社会生活的最后一个准备场所。高等教育还是高深文化知识传播创新的社会组织机构；在传播高深文化的同时，还复制或者再制了社会的价值、行为模式和道德规范。

Higher education in the United States has been molded and influenced by a variety of historical forces. On one hand, there are the patterns and traditions of higher learning which have brought over form Western Europe. On the other hand, we find the native American conditions which have affected and modified the development of these transplanted institutions. Out of the interaction of these two essential elements and, most "importantly", out of the growth of democracy in every area of American life, America has developed a truly unique system of higher education.

English influences

Oxford and Cambridge furnished the original model which the colonial colleges sought to copy. The prototype for the first English-American college was Emmanuel College, Cambridge University. As we read the explicit statements left by Harvard's founders, we find that the earliest Harvard College statutes were taken directly from the Elizabethan statutes of the University of Cambridge; that the phrase *pro modo Academiarum in Anglia* ("according to the manner of universities in England") is to be found in the first Harvard degree formula; that early Harvard, like Elizabethan Cambridge, welcomed "fellow commoners" as well as serious degree students, "gentlemen" who paid double tuition for the privilege of residing in the college and dining with the Fellows; that even the names of the four college classes—freshman, sophomore, junior sophister, and senior sophister—were borrowed directly from England. In other points involving student discipline, curriculum, administrative regulations, and degree requirements, Harvard followed English college precedents as closely and faithfully as she could; and Harvard, in turn, became the great prototype for all the later colleges of English America.

As late as the middle of the eighteenth century, President Clap of Yale prepared himself for his administrative duties by borrowing histories of Oxford and Cambridge and seeking information from Americans who had secured English college degree. When

Clap waged his campaign of 1745 to secure a new Yale charter, he based it on a careful and detailed study of administrative practices at Oxford and Cambridge.

Even at William and Mary, English influence soon challenged an earlier Scottish trend. From 1729 to 1757, eight of thirteen faculty members were Oxford men, and of these eight, Queens College. After 1757, a battle raged almost continuously between this Oxford-bred faculty and the native Virginian Board of Visitors. By 1766 the Visitors "had rid the college of the last of that band of able Oxford graduates, ministers all of them, whose chief fault had been that their ties with English were too close, that they looked too blindly to their homeland".

In almost every case, however, the English colonists eventually found that the unique conditions of the American physical and social environment produced unexpected changes and modifications in their academic institutions. Some of these were destined to be of great importance for the later development of higher education in the United States.

It was soon discovered that it would be impossible to erect in English-America any great university collection of colleges such as existed at Oxford or Cambridge. For one thing, it was doubtful that the Crown would ever grant the required royal charter for such an American university. Besides, the land was too vast and the people too poor. The narrow fringe of British settlements which faced the broad Atlantic on one side and trackless forests on the other represented what for that time was far western frontier of English civilization. All that could be done under these circumstances was to establish a number of scattered, widely separated degree-granting colleges, thus diffusing educational effort.

After a time, still another colonial divergence from the English norm made an appearance. Because of the heterogeneity of the American population, collegiate boards of control were established which were interdenominational in make-up and at least one of which was completely secular. Nothing like this had yet been seen in the home country, although the University of Leyden in the Netherlands already followed this pattern.

Scottish influences

Other modifications were due mainly to Scottish influence. The post-reformation Scottish university, unlike Oxford or Cambridge, was nonresidential, professionally oriented, and under the control, not of the faculty, but of prominent lay representatives of the community. At the college of William and Mary some of these Scottish ideas seem to have been influential from the very founding. Commissary James Blair, founder and first president, was a graduate of Marischal College, Aberdeen, and the University of Edinburgh. Reverend William Smith, graduate of Aberdeen, exercised a great influence, as we shall see, over the curricular planning of both King's College in New York, later Columbia, and the College of Philadelphia. John Witherspoon, Scotch theologian who came to the New World in 1768 to become president of the College of New Jersey, later Princeton, exerted an important influence over American higher education.

Although even Harvard was not immune to Scottish university influence, it was at William and Mary that it was felt most directly. The charter Blair obtained for the Virginia school resembled that of a Scottish "unicollege" institution. Like Aberdeen, Glasgow, King's, and Marischal, it incorporated both a university and a degree-granting college by a single letter-parent. At the same time, a governing board was created, made up of members of the nonacademic community; this was, in characteristic Scottish fashion, to have real administrative authority over the college. Even William and Mary's architecture reflected Scottish influence, as did Blair's early plans for a course of study.

Spanish and French influences

As an afterthought on how different the development of higher education in the United States might have been if Continental rather than English precedents had been dominant, we might look for a moment at the institutions of higher learning founders by the Spanish and French in America. Originally, the English and Continental European universities had a somewhat similar type of organization. Nevertheless, Oxford and Cambridge very early began to follow a largely independent line of development. By the time of the Renaissance, these English universities were changing into loosely federated associations of residential colleges. The Continental universities, on the other hand, were becoming nonresident graduate school providing specific types of post-baccalaureate training.

The French and Spanish universities in America represented the later Continental type of university. When Charles V of Spain in 1551 founded "the Royal and Pontifical University" of Mexico and the University of San Marcos in Lima, Peru, he accorded them all "the privileges, exemptions, and limitations of the University of Salamanca." This meant that they were definitely to follow the Continental model, because Salamanca was essentially a collection of graduate faculties in arts, theology, law, and medicine. Besides Mexico and Lima, eight other universities were chartered and opened for instruction before a single college appeared in English America. In all, the Spanish-Americans established twenty-three such institutions.

In contrast, higher education in New France developed more slowly. It was not until the 1660s that Bishop Laval developed at Quebec a "great seminary" for advanced theological training. Although modern Laval University developed from this nucleus, in colonial times the Quebec institution never covered as broad as had the Spanish-American universities.

1. **Oxford**（牛津大学）: (informally Oxford University) Oxford is a public university in Oxford, United Kingdom. It is the second oldest surviving university in the world and the oldest in the English-speaking world. Although the exact date of foundation remains unclear, there is evidence of teaching there as far back as the 11th century. The University grew rapidly from 1167 when Henry II banned English students from attending the University of Paris. In post-nominals, the University of Oxford was historically abbreviated as Oxon. (from the Latin *Oxoniensis*), although Oxf is nowadays used in official University publications.

2. **Cambridge**（剑桥大学）: (informally Cambridge University) Cambridge is a public, research university located in Cambridge, United Kingdom. It is the second-oldest university in both England and the English-speaking world and the seventh-oldest globally. In post-nominals the university's name is abbreviated as *Cantab*, a shortened form of *Cantabrigiensis* (an adjective derived from *Cantabrigia*, the Latinised form of *Cambridge*).

3. **Harvard**（哈佛大学）: Harvard is a private Ivy League university located in Cambridge, Massachusetts, United States, established in 1636 by the Massachusetts legislature. Harvard is the oldest institution of higher learning in the United States and the first corporation (officially *The President and Fellows of Harvard College*) chartered in the country. Harvard's history, influence, and wealth have made it one of the most prestigious universities in the world.

4. **Yale**（耶鲁大学）: Yale is a private Ivy League university located in New Haven, Connecticut, United States of America. Founded in 1701 in the Colony of Connecticut, the university is the third oldest institution of higher education in the United States. Yale is widely considered one of the most prestigious and selective universities in the world.

5. **Renaissance**（文艺复兴）：Renaissance was a cultural movement that profoundly affected European intellectual life in the early modern period. Beginning in Italy, and spreading to the rest of Europe by the 16th century, its influence affected literature, philosophy, art, politics, science, religion, and other aspects of intellectual inquiry. Renaissance scholars employed the humanist method in study, and searched for realism and human emotion in art.

6. **Quebec**（魁北克）：Quebec is a province in east-central Canada. It is the only Canadian province with a predominantly French-speaking population and the only one whose sole official language is French at the provincial level. Quebec is Canada's largest province by area and its second-largest administrative division.

New words and expressions

1. prototype ['prəutətaip]   n.   原型，范例，雏形
2. explicit [ik'splisit]   adj.   明确的，清晰的，清楚的，露骨的
3. formula ['fɔːmjulə]   n.   配方，公式，规则，代乳品
      adj.   方程式的，（赛车）级的
4. commoner ['kɔmənə]   n.   平民，自费学生，有共用权的人
5. erect [i'rekt]   vt.   使竖立，建立，建造
      adj.   直立的，竖立的，笔直的
6. fringe [frindʒ]   n.   流苏，边缘，次要，额外补贴
      vt.   用流苏修饰，镶边
7. heterogeneity [,hetərədʒi'niːəti]   n.   多相性，异质性
8. interdenominational ['intədi,nɔmi'neiʃənəl]
      adj.   派系间的，宗派之间的
9. secular ['sekjulə]   adj.   世俗的，现世的，不朽的，非宗教的
      n.   牧师，凡人
10. commissary ['kɔmisəri]   n.   代表；委员；（部队，学校，矿场等的）杂货商店
11. baccalaureate [,bækə'lɔːriət]   n.   学士学位，告别训辞
12. exemption [ig'zempʃən]   n.   免除（税）

I Vocabulary.

Match the word in Column A to the correct definition in the Column B.

Column A	
1. commissary	2. erect
3. exemption	4. secular
5. explicit	6. commoner
7. formula	8. prototype
9. interdenominational	10. baccalaureate

Column B
A. standing/sitting straight up
B. an original model on which something is patterned
C. of or relating to the worldly or temporal
D. a particular method of doing or achieving sth.
E. a shop that provides food and equipment
F. clear and easy to understand
G. shared by different religious groups
H. official permission not to pay sth.
I. a person without noble rank or title
J. the degree of bachelor conferred by universities and colleges

II Translate the following words and phrases into English.

（大学）新生，一年级学生　　　　_____

（大学）二年级学生　　　　　　　_____

（大学）三年级学生　　　　　　　_____

（大学）四年级学生　　　　　　　_____

学术机构，学院，研究所　　　　　_____

行政规章　　　　　　　　　　　　_____

未预料到的变化　　　　　　　　　_____

注定的，注定要　　　　　　　　　_____

不受……影响的，对……有免疫力的　_____

Unit 1　Origin & History of Education　教育的起源和历史

寄宿制大学，寄宿学院　_____

III　Comprehension of the text.

Decide whether the following statements are true (T) or false (F) according to the passage.

1. The earliest Harvard College statutes were taken indirectly from the Elizabethan statutes of the University of Cambridge.　(　)
2. Harvard followed English college precedents closely and faithfully in terms of student discipline, curriculum, administrative regulations, and degree requirements, and in turn it became the great prototype for all the later colleges of English America.　(　)
3. From 1729 to 1757, eight of thirteen faculty members were Oxford men, from Queens College.　(　)
4. Only in some cases, the English colonists found that the unique conditions of the American physical and social environment produced unexpected changes and modifications in their academic institutions.　(　)
5. It is impossible to erect in English-America any great university collection of colleges such as existed at Oxford or Cambridge and there are two reasons mentioned in the article.　(　)
6. The post-Reformation Scottish university, was professionally oriented, and under the control, of prominent lay representatives of the community, which was as like as the system of Oxford or Cambridge.　(　)
7. In characteristic Scottish fashion, it was possible to have real administrative authority over the college.　(　)
8. Originally speaking, there were somewhat slightly different types of organization in the English and Continentals European universities.　(　)
9. The Spanish-Americans established twenty-three such institutions which were chartered and opened for instruction before a single college appeared in English America.　(　)
10. It was not until 1660 that Bishop Laval developed at Quebec a "great seminary" for advanced theological training.　(　)

▶▶ Useful phrases and expressions ◀◀◀◀◀—

科教兴国战略 the strategy of rejuvenating the country through science and education
建设教育强国 make the country an educational powerhouse
人才强国战略 the strategy of rejuvenating the country through talent pooling

担当民族复兴大任 shoulder the responsibility of national rejuvenation
办好人民满意的教育 ensure that education meets the expectations of the people
精深厚重的中国文化底蕴 the richness of Chinese cultural heritage
教育改革发展历史经验 experience in education reform and development
中华民族崇文重教的优良传统 the finest Chinese traditions of respecting culture and education
中国特色社会主义教育发展道路 new trails in developing socialist education
发展具有中国特色、世界水平的现代教育 build a world-class, modern education system

As China marches forward, our demand for scientific knowledge and exceptional talent will intensify in parallel with our expectations for equitable and higher quality education.

时代越是向前，国家对科学知识和卓越人才的渴求就越发强烈，人民群众对更加公平、更高质量教育的期待就越发迫切。

Our education system must inherit and pass on China's splendid cultural heritage, and continue to enrich its soft power while learning from other civilizations.

中国教育必须传承和弘扬中华优秀传统文化，吸收人类文明有益成果，不断增强国家文化软实力。

Education will serve this purpose of becoming an economic power by developing the appropriate human and talent resources.

中国正加快实现向经济强国的跨越，这就要求教育必须充分发挥人力资源和人才资源开发的长效作用。

China will prime our education programs to be founded on an unswerving commitment to understand and practice the core socialist values.

中国教育必须充分发挥在坚持社会主义核心价值体系、培育和践行社会主义核心价值观中的基础作用。

In this new era, our education programs will promote exchanges between peoples, countries, and civilizations. China will thus contribute to a brighter future for humanity in new and greater ways.

进入新时代，中国教育必须加强对外交流，促进民心相通和文明交流互鉴，为创造人类美好未来作出新的更大贡献。

In establishing the world's largest education system, China has blazed new trails in developing socialist education, which has contributed significantly to its economic and social growth.

中国建成了世界最大规模的教育体系，走出了一条中国特色社会主义教育发展道路，为经济社会发展作出了重要贡献。

The CPC Central Committee has implemented the strategy of rejuvenating the country through science, education, and talent pooling.

党中央坚定不移实施科教兴国战略和人才强国战略。

It has given priority to educational development through reform, investment, and modernization efforts, and has sought to raise education to a new level.

坚持优先发展教育,大力推进教育领域综合改革,持续加大教育投入,加速推进教育现代化,不断推动教育发展迈上新台阶。

From the founding of the People's Republic of China in 1949, through reform and opening up in 1978, to the present day, the great strides made in reforming and developing China's education have attracted worldwide attention.

新中国成立以来特别是改革开放以来,我国教育改革发展取得了举世瞩目的伟大成就。

We need a future-ready education program that can nurture a new generation of highly adaptable and innovative talent that enables China's strategic transformation from a follower to a competitor, and then a pacesetter in science and technology.

教育必须着眼未来,抓紧培养能够适应和引领未来发展的一代新人,特别是培养集聚大批拔尖创新型人才,加快实现我国整体科技水平从跟跑向并跑、领跑的战略性转变。

Unit 2　Education & Social Development
教育与社会发展

Text A　Open and Distance Education: a Better Way of Competence Building and Sustainable Development

导读： 远程开放教育是当今信息时代的发展趋势，它以一种新型的、多元化的、互动的方式传播教育。远程开放教育包括两层含义：一是远程教育（也叫远距离教育），二是开放教育。远程教育是一种现代化教育形式，它包括函授教育、广播电视教育、多媒体远程教育等，是利用媒体技术进行教学的各类教育。开放教育是实行不同程度开放入学政策，放宽或取消各种入学条件限制，教育技术上采用多媒体技术的教学方法，教学场所上突破了以课堂教学为主的传统教育限制，学生可以自学，可以利用计算机网络、电视、电话等多种媒体接受或反馈教学信息。两者关系密切，互不可分。远程开放教育是以学生为主体，在教师的指导下利用多媒体进行自学的教学模式。这种模式体现了以学生为中心的现代教育思想，适应了学习社会化的需要。

　　Globalization as a phenomenon influences all the disciplines of life, also education. Still increasing demand for higher educated people is the cause for permanent education. It also forces newer, better, faster and more convenient ways of learning. There is fast progress in information technology, and fulfilling this demand is possible by open and distance education. Distance education is a system where teacher and students are separated by physical distance and where they use technology like print, voice, data and video to convey the learning material through postal services, countries, Internet, and CDs etc. Open and Distance Learning (ODL) system comes into existence where a student cannot go to the traditional institution due to distance, resource limitation, time constraint, physical disability, age etc.

Competence building

Competence building considers the aspects such as strengthening the identity and foundation of emotional stability and self esteem. It is necessary to improve the human capital. Competence includes the education and skills acquired through technical related to social behavior, an aptitude for team work and of initiative and a readiness to take risk. Competence building is important for the physical, mental, financial and legal power for the best performance. So competence building should be viewed in much comprehensive and deeper way.

In the present era of globalization, there is much need of sustainable development and competence building process. Sustainable development is a pattern of resource use that aims to meet human needs while preserving the environment, so that these needs can be met not only in the present, but also for future generation. Sustainable development was formally defined for the first time in the "Brundtland Commission report" published in 1987 as "development that meets the needs of the present without compromising the ability of future generations to their own needs". This definition encompasses that the ideas of limitations imposed by the state of technology and social organization on the ability of the environment to meet present and future needs. Sustainable development suggests that the needs of the future depend on how well we balance social, economic and environment objectives or needs when making decisions today. Sustainable development ties together concern for the carrying capacity of natural system with the social challenges facing humanity.

Education for sustainable development

Important prerequisite to sustainable development is the issue of equity—equity for future generation and equity for those of the present generation, who have little or no access to natural resources and economic goods. Education plays an important role for human sustainable development. Education and training appear to be determinant factors for increasing creativity and rational thinking, problem solving capacities and competitiveness needed to foster the increasing complex cultural, social and technological decision involved in sustainable development. Education and training for sustainable development is not only a social issue but also a matter of economic policy. Decision makers today face two major challenges in reshaping education for sustainable development. One is devising institutional educational strategies and programs, taking into account all the educational actors and communication channels available. The other is increasing the quality and usefulness of the various educational and training processes, aimed primarily at citizens, economic partners and young people.

Strengthening worldwide co-operation in education should help each country devise the most effective ways and means of enabling its people to contribute to improving the material and spiritual living conditions of the present generation without denying life for future generation. Education for sustainable development stresses the achievement of continuous well-being by searching for an optimal balance in the formation and use of different resources and capital types—human capital, physical infrastructure and tools, natural resources, financial means, technology and decision system, the world of work and that of the media. Open and distance learning (ODL) system plays a very important role in achieving these goals regarding sustainable development and competence building.

The role of ODL in sustainable development and competence building

The role of ODL in sustainable development and competence building is mainly to develop human capital and encourage technical progress, as well as fostering the cultural conditions favoring social and economic changes. This is the key to creative and effective utilization of human potential and all forms of capital ensuring rapid and more equitable growth. Empirical evidences demonstrate that education is positively correlated with productivity and technological progress, because it enables companies to obtain and evaluate information on new technologies and economic opportunities.

ODL is especially well suited to deliver learning outcomes consistent with sustainability goals. Its emphasis on access, the service of personal needs and the supporting life long learning mirrors the way in which environmental values are best inculcated into personal and professional life. ODL plays a very important role in environmental sustainability. Technologies in e-learning distance education are helping the environment. Online courses showed a 20% reduction in energy and 12% reduction in CO_2 emission compared to printed based courses. There is less carbon pollution in on-line delivery in ODL system, so it truly results in "dematerialization". In ODL system, students have to travel less for going to their study centre because study centers are mostly near to their residence, so consumption of petroleum oil becomes less. Built structure is also very economic in ODL system. These factors help in environmental sustainability and encourage for sustainable management. Thus it can be called as "Green Distance Education".

ODL is very helpful in "inclusive education" which is based on the aspects of human rights, equal opportunities, social justice and participation. It has multiple interpretations. Poverty, ethnicity, disability, gender or membership of a minority group may limit access to or marginalize. Within education, inclusive education appreciates every learner's fundamental rights to learn and know that each child has unique abilities and needs. If given the right opportunity, all children can develop their potential. Inclusive education considers difference in the learning and physical abilities of children. ODL is very helpful in achieving these goals of inclusive education.

Authorities of the universities running distance education courses should sharply ensure that distance education centers do not get reduced to degree distribution institutions. So universities and distance institutions higher authorities keep ensure that only quality education should be provided through ODL. Proper library, laboratory and required study materials, essential equipment: and materials for students should be in coordination with other related universities running similar courses located in the same area. Open and distance learning has been improvised upon by integrating various other methods which are successfully followed in other countries such as Virtual Education, Alternative Education and E-learning.

The need of the hour is to pool such innovative experience and disseminate the same effectively. The exchange of experiences within and between the countries would surely help to promote and transfer knowledge to the masses and benefit the society in the long run.

1. **Open and Distance Learning**（远程开放教育）: Open and Distance Learning is a field of education that focuses on teaching methods and technology with the aim of delivering teaching, often on an individual basis, to students who are not physically present in a traditional educational setting such as a classroom. It has been described as "a process to create and provide access to learning when the source of information and the learners are separated by time and distance, or both". Its courses that require a physical on-site presence for any reason (including taking examinations) have been referred to as hybrid or blended courses of study.

2. **Brundtland Commission**（布伦特兰委员会）: Brundtland Commission, formally the World Commission on Environment and Development (WCED), known by the name of its

Chair Gro Harlem Brundtland, was convened by the United Nations in 1983. The commission was created to address growing concern "about the accelerating deterioration of the human environment and natural resources and the consequences of that deterioration for economic and social development". In establishing the commission, the UN General Assembly recognized that environmental problems were global in nature and determined that it was in the common interest of all nations to establish policies for sustainable development.

3. **Inclusive Education**（全纳教育）：Inclusive Education is an approach to educating students with special educational needs. Under the inclusion model, students with special needs spend most or all of their time with non-disabled students. It is about the child's right to participate and the school's duty to accept the child. A premium is placed upon full participation by students with disabilities and upon respect for their social, civil, and educational rights.

4. **Virtual Education**（虚拟教育）：Virtual Education refers to instruction in a learning environment where teacher and student are separated by time or space, or both, and the teacher provides course content through course management applications, multimedia resources, the Internet, videoconferencing, etc. Students receive the content and communicate with the teacher via the same technologies. This term is primarily used in higher education where so-called Virtual Universities have been established.

5. **Alternative Education**（选择性教育）：Alternative Education, also known as non-traditional education or educational alternative, includes a number of approaches to teaching and learning other than mainstream or traditional education. It is often rooted in various philosophies that are fundamentally different from those of mainstream or traditional education. While some have strong political, scholarly, or philosophical orientations, others are more informal associations of teachers and students dissatisfied with some aspects of mainstream or traditional education. Alternative Education, which include charter schools, alternative schools, independent schools, and home-based learning, varies widely, but often emphasizes the value of small class size, close relationships between students and teachers, and a sense of community.

6. **E-learning**（在线学习，电子化学习或网络学习）：E-learning comprises all forms of electronically supported learning and teaching. The information and communication systems, whether networked or not, serve as specific media to implement the learning process. The term will still most likely be utilized to reference out-of-classroom and

Unit 2　Education & Social Development　教育与社会发展

in-classroom educational experiences via technology, even as advances continue in regard to devices and curriculum. E-learning is essentially the computer and network-enabled transfer of skills and knowledge. E-learning applications and processes include Web-based learning, computer-based learning, virtual classroom opportunities and digital collaboration. Content is delivered via the Internet, intranet/extranet, audio or video tape, satellite TV, and CD-ROM. It can be self-paced or instructor-led and includes media in the form of text, image, animation, streaming video and audio.

New words and expressions

1. aptitude ['æptitju:d]　　　　　　　n.　　天资；自然倾向；适宜
2. initiative [i'niʃiətiv]　　　　　　　n.　　主动权；首创精神
　　　　　　　　　　　　　　　　　adj.　主动的；起始的
3. comprehensive [ˌkɔmpri'hensiv]　　adj.　综合广泛的；有理解力的
　　　　　　　　　　　　　　　　　n.　　综合学校
4. compromise ['kɔmprəmaiz]　　　　vt.　　妥协；危害
　　　　　　　　　　　　　　　　　vi.　　妥协；让步
　　　　　　　　　　　　　　　　　n.　　妥协；折中
5. encompass [in'kʌmpəs]　　　　　　vt.　　包含；包围，环绕；完成
6. optimal ['ɔptiməl]　　　　　　　　adj.　最佳的；最理想的
7. empirical [em'pirikəl]　　　　　　adj.　经验主义的，完全根据经验的
8. inculcate ['inkʌlkeit]　　　　　　 vt.　　教育；谆谆教诲；教授；反覆灌输
9. interpretation [inˌtə:pri'teiʃən]　　n.　　解释；翻译；演出
10. marginalize ['ma:dʒinəlaiz]　　　vt.　　排斥；忽视；使处于社会边缘
11. integrate ['intigreit]　　　　　　vt.　　使……完整；使……成整体；求……的积分；表示……的总和
　　　　　　　　　　　　　　　　　vi.　　求积分；取消隔离；成为一体
　　　　　　　　　　　　　　　　　adj.　整合的；完全的
　　　　　　　　　　　　　　　　　n.　　一体化
12. disseminate [di'semineit]　　　　vt.　　宣传，传播；散布
　　　　　　　　　　　　　　　　　vi.　　散布；广为传播

Exercises

I Vocabulary.

Fill in the blanks with the most suitable words. Change the form when necessary.

| aptitude | comprehensive | encompass | integrate | interpretation |
| initiative | compromise | optimal | inculcate | disseminate |

1. He was educated at the local _____ school.
2. How can local communities work with planners and decision-makers to find some _____ solutions for the future?
3. If a child shows any musical _____ or interest, get an instrument into her hand early.
4. These so-called solar-energy zones _____ about 680,000 acres of land owned by the federal government.
5. It's hard for a state-run program to _____ ideals like thinking out of the box.
6. I wanted to go to Greece, however, my wife wanted to go to Spain. After a little talk, we _____ on Italy.
7. Can we _____ his silence as a refusal?
8. It has been very difficult to _____ all of the local agencies into the national organization.
9. This publication has been prepared to _____ the lessons learned to a wider audience.
10. Charles is shy and does not take the _____ in making acquaintances.

II Translate the following phrases into English.

人力资源　　　　　　　　_____
可持续发展　　　　　　　_____
自然资源　　　　　　　　_____
理性思维　　　　　　　　_____
考虑；重视；体谅　　　　_____
生活条件；居住环境　　　_____
基础设施建设　　　　　　_____

符合；与……一致 _____
终身学习 _____
社会公正 _____

III Comprehension of the text.

Decide whether the following statements are true (T) or false (F) according to the passage.

1. Distance education is a system where teacher and students are integrated by physical distance and where they use technology like print, voice, data and video to convey the learning material through postal services, countries, internet, and CDs etc. ( )

2. Sustainable development was formally defined for the first time in the "Brundtland Commission report" published in 1978 as "development that meets the needs of the present without compromising the ability of future generations to their own needs". ( )

3. Education and training for sustainable development is not only a social issue but also a matter of economic policy. ( )

4. Online courses showed a 12% reduction in energy and 20% reduction in CO_2 emission compared to printed based courses. ( )

5. Proper library, laboratory and required study materials, essential equipments and materials for students should be in co-ordination with other related universities running similar courses located in the same area. ( )

Text B Higher Education within a Knowledge-based Society

导读：知识社会是一个以创新为社会主要驱动力的社会，知识社会环境下的创新推动了创新民主化。知识社会也是一个大众创新、共同创新、开放创新成为常态的社会，知识、创新是知识社会的核心。在知识社会里，每个人都要学会在信息海洋里来去自如，培养认知能力和批评精神，以便区分有用信息和无用信息，拥有新知识；它也使得创新不再是少数科技精英的专利，而成为更为广泛的大众参与，推动了创新的民主化进程。知识社会更加关注全球问题：通过国际合作和科学协作，环境破坏、技术风险、经济危机和贫困等问题有望得到更好的解决；知识共享是知识社会的拱顶石，以大众创新、共同创新、开放创新为特点的创新是知识社会的实质，而知识社会是人类可持续发展的源泉。

Research in higher education is a quite new field of interest and can be seen as a multidisciplinary subject. Researchers from different fields of study are interested in learning about the complexity of higher education. They are looking on higher education from different angles as for instance, educational or political sciences, psychology, sociology, history, economy or law—different fields of research are interested in bringing light into the complex system of higher education (educational, management and social science approach). Nevertheless the term higher education is relatively new and became popular in the 1970s because universities lost their exclusive right to provide higher education. From the middle age to the 60s the main and often the only post secondary institution have been the university. After that time other forms of tertiary education emerged and higher education came up to include universities as well as vocational and professional institutions.

Until World War II university education was a domain of the elite but this changed dramatically. The following figure illustrates phases of higher education developments with a clear tendency towards more diversification and mercerization of higher education in a knowledge driven economy. In the last phase especially research in higher education is emphasized "as primary differentiator of higher education institutions" in the 21st century.

Figure 1 Phases of higher education developments

Today's university is facing great strain and tension because of ongoing societal developments. Knowledge changed to a factor of production and theoretical knowledge gains more importance as source of innovation and basis for political decisions in highly industrialized societies. The Nobel Prize winner Joseph Stiglitz stated that knowledge is a global public good though the source of brainpower is limited by genetic distributions of talent and cultural disadvantages. The nature of education is bound to change and will become a continuing life-time affair for the professional and technical person. In this context Daniel Bell articulated that we need especially postdoctoral universities where new knowledge and new techniques can be passed along.

The arrival of knowledge-based societies, of course, has a great importance according to the development of universities. One could say that they are the first institutions to benefit from this increasing usage of information. These days' universities compete with other institutions as, for instance, vocational colleges, research institutions and high-tech companies in popularity to cope with the increasing importance of knowledge. Universities cannot handle all these new forces and demands of the knowledge society which means that they are in an unstable situation and loose their position of high status and power. They have to be powerful and successful but loose at the same time their clear position (success vs. uncertainty). There is an intrinsic relationship between universities and knowledge societies but the future consequences are not foreseeable. One sees a future of knowledge as strategic resource for universities. Others see a world of academic capitalism. Thus, academia goes together with the knowledge society where "competition with other institutions and a loss of the monopoly of universities" prevails (virtual universities, corporate universities, media organizations, consortia, strategic alliances, private and public institutions).

The new mode of knowledge production effects academic research and brings new opportunities because entrepreneurial activities emerge. It must be kept in mind, however, that the basic stable function of the university is to educate researchers and to generate the cultural norms of a society. Nevertheless, an epistemic dimension in this development of academic knowledge production to societal knowledge production brings new practices though also uncertainty for today's knowledge-based society. Good practices are needed from traditional science with "the heterogeneity of knowledge and the importance of new stakeholders" to combine either academic or economic functions of the academia.

Therefore different mechanisms and practices of quality assurance are needed. A (internationally and nationally recognized) quality assurance system should be able to guarantee transparency and control of higher education programs and that diplomas and degrees of students are approved. Although nearly all over the world international and national quality assurance agencies have been developed, there are different approaches to ensure quality (internal or external procedures, accreditation vs. evaluations, quality audits etc.). While some countries established only one national agency (e.g. Finland) others have separate agencies with different responsibilities (e.g. Germany), which shows the political and cultural diversity of the countries all over the world. Furthermore the initiative to establish international qualification frameworks helps small countries to set up a regional quality assurance system or assist different global quality assurance initiatives.

Tertiary education has to cope with lots of new challenges due to enormous changes (globalization, ICT, socio-political transformations, lifelong learning and knowledge-based society) but faces also new opportunities as playing the key role in today's society. Santiago et al. recommend some practical arrangements for a functioning quality assurance system:

• Avoid fragmentation of the quality assurance organizational structure
• Avoid excessive costs and burdens
• Improve quality information base
• Improve information dissemination

With these suggestions, current quality assurance systems, which vary among countries in their scope and emphasis, could be improved. Quality assurance schemes have to be developed as necessary instruments to adjust higher education institutions to the ongoing transformation processes. As the different systems are most of the time newly developed, they should be able to adapt to changes and try to act quickly to the needs of our knowledge-based society. Quality assurance in higher education is not fully developed but still under construction!

1. **World War II**（第二次世界大战）：World War II or the Second World War, was a global military conflict lasting from 1939 to 1945, which involved most of the world's nations, including all of the great powers: eventually forming two opposing military alliances, the Allies (同盟国) and the Axis (轴心国). It was the most widespread war in history, with more than 100 million military personnel mobilized. In a state of "total war", the major participants placed their entire economic, industrial, and scientific capabilities at the service of the war effort, erasing the distinction between civilian and military resources. Marked by significant events involving the mass death of civilians, including the Holocaust (大屠杀) and the only use of nuclear weapons in warfare, it was the deadliest conflict in human history, resulting in 40 million to over 70 million fatalities. The war ended with the

Unit 2 Education & Social Development 教育与社会发展

total victory of the Allies over Germany and Japan in 1945. World War II altered the political alignment and social structure of the world. The United Nations was established to foster international cooperation and prevent future conflicts. The Soviet Union and the United States emerged as rival superpowers, setting the stage for the Cold War, which lasted for the next 46 years. Meanwhile, the influence of European great powers started to decline, while the decolonization of Asia and Africa began. Most countries whose industries had been damaged moved towards economic recovery. Political integration, especially in Europe, emerged as an effort to stabilize postwar relations.

2. **Joseph Stiglitz**（约瑟夫·斯蒂格利茨）: Joseph Stiglitz, born February 9th, 1943, is an American economist and a professor at Columbia University. He is a recipient of the Nobel Memorial Prize in Economic Sciences (2001) and the John Bates Clark Medal (1979). He is also the former Senior Vice President and Chief Economist of the World Bank. He is known for his critical view of the management of globalization, free-market economists (whom he calls "free market fundamentalists") and some international institutions like the International Monetary Fund and the World Bank.

3. **Quality assurance**（质量保证）: Quality assurance or QA for short, is the systematic monitoring and evaluation of the various aspects of a project, service or facility to maximize the probability that minimum standards of quality are being attained by the production process. QA cannot absolutely guarantee the production of quality products. Here QA refers to the guarantee of the higher education.

4. **Tertiary education**（高等教育或第三级教育）: Tertiary education, also referred to as third stage, third level, and post-secondary education, is the educational level following the completion of a school providing a secondary education, such as a high school, secondary school, and university-preparatory school. Higher education is taken to include undergraduate and postgraduate education, while vocational education and training beyond secondary education are known as further education in the United Kingdom, or continuing education in the United States. Colleges, universities, institutes of technology and polytechnics are the main institutions that provide tertiary education (sometimes known collectively as tertiary institutions). Tertiary education generally culminates in the receipt of certificates, diplomas, or academic degrees.

5. **ICT**（信息通信技术）: ICT, also known as Information and Communication Technology, is often used as an extended synonym for information technology (IT) but is usually a more general term that stresses the role of unified communications and the integration of telecommunications (telephone lines and wireless signals), intelligent building management systems and audio-visual systems in modern information technology. ICT consists of all

technical means used to handle information and aid communication, including computer and network hardware, communication middleware as well as necessary software. In other words, ICT consists of IT as well as telephony, broadcast media, all types of audio and video processing and transmission and network based control and monitoring functions.

New words and expressions

1. exclusive [ik'sklu:siv]　　　　　　*adj.*　独有的；排外的；专一的
　　　　　　　　　　　　　　　　　　n.　独家新闻；排外者
2. tertiary ['tə:ʃəri]　　　　　　　　*n.*　第三纪；第三修道会会员；第三级教士
　　　　　　　　　　　　　　　　　　adj.　第三的；第三位的；三代的
3. elite [ei'li:t]　　　　　　　　　　*n.*　精英；精华；中坚分子
4. mercerization [,mə:sərai'zeiʃən]　　*n.*　［纺］丝光作用；碱化
5. differentiator [,difə'renʃieitə]　　*n.*　［自］微分器；微分电路；区分者
6. articulate [ɑ:'tikjulət]　　　　　　*vt.*　清晰地发（音）；明确有力地表达；用关节连接
　　　　　　　　　　　　　　　　　　vi.　发音；清楚地讲话；用关节连接起来
　　　　　　　　　　　　　　　　　　adj.　发音清晰的；口才好的；有关节的
7. postdoctoral [pəust'dɔktərəl]　　　*adj.*　博士后的；博士学位取得后的
8. capitalism ['kæpitəlizəm]　　　　　*n.*　资本主义
9. monopoly [mə'nɔpəli]　　　　　　　*n.*　垄断；垄断者；专卖权
10. epistemic [,epi'sti:mik]　　　　　*adj.*　知识的；认识的，与认识有关的
11. transparency [træns'pærənsi]　　　*n.*　透明，透明度；幻灯片；有图案的玻璃
12. accreditation [ə,kredi'teiʃən]　　*n.*　达到标准；鉴定合格

I Vocabulary.

Match the word in Column A to the correct definition in the Column B.

Unit 2 Education & Social Development 教育与社会发展

Column A

1. exclusive
2. elite
3. articulate
4. capitalism
5. accreditation
6. epistemic
7. postdoctoral
8. monopoly
9. transparency
10. tertiary

Column B

A. of or relating to knowledge or knowing
B. belonging to or used by only one person or a group
C. to give official authorization to or approval of
D. controlled by one company
E. the most powerful, rich, or talented people within a particular group, place, or society
F. an economic and political system in which property, business, and industry are owned by private individuals and not by the state.
G. third in order, third in importance, or at a third stage of development
H. expressing oneself readily, clearly, or effectively
I. being beyond the doctoral level
J. something especially transparent

II Translate the following phrases into English.

知识社会   _____
阐明   _____
专有权   _____
第三级教育   _____
必然，必定   _____
高职院校，职业学院 _____
文化规范，文化准则 _____
质量保证，品质保证 _____
品质监察   _____
文化多样性   _____
适应   _____

III Comprehension of the text.

Decide whether the following statements are true (T) or false (F) according to the passage.

1. In the 1970s, universities lost their exclusive right to provide higher education, therefore the term higher education is relatively new and became popular.   (   )
2. Before World War II, university education was a domain of the elite, but after that, this situation changed dramatically.   (   )
3. Although as source of innovation and basis for political decisions in highly industrialized societies, knowledge changed to a factor of production and theoretical knowledge gains less importance.   (   )
4. As Daniel Bell articulated that, we postdoctoral universities are especially need so that new knowledge and new techniques can be passed along.   (   )
5. All these new forces and demands of the knowledge society can be handled by universities. In other words, universities are in a stable situation and tighten their position of high status and power.   (   )
6. The only basic stable function of the university is to generate the cultural norms of a society.   (   )
7. Two dimensions should be guaranteed in a quality assurance system: one is the transparency and control of higher education programs, the other is the diplomas and degrees of students are approved.   (   )
8. In terms of the quality assurance agency, all the countries have separate agencies with different responsibilities, which show the political and cultural diversity of the countries all over the world.   (   )
9. Due to enormous changes, tertiary education has to not only cope with lots of new challenges, but also faces new opportunities as playing the key role in today's society.   (   )
10. In some countries, quality assurance in higher education is fully developed but in others it is still under construction.   (   )

▶▶ Useful phrases and expressions ◀◀◀◀◀

立足时代 keep abreast with the times
融通中外 building bridges connecting with foreign lands
思想政治教育 moral and political education

Unit 2　Education & Social Development　教育与社会发展

优先发展教育 given priority to educational development
教育必须着眼未来 a future-ready education program
多位一体的育人格局 a multi-dimensional education model
加快推进教育现代化 accelerate education modernization
扎根中国大地办教育 run education with a firm footing within China
以人民为中心发展教育 a people-centered approach throughout educational development
思想道德素质持续向好 a stronger moral framework

Education in China must reflect the unique characteristics of China and be adapted to the country's context.
中国的教育必须按中国的特点和中国的实际办。

Education is a major undertaking of the state and the Party. A nation prospers when its education system flourishes.
教育是国之大计、党之大计。教育兴则国家兴，教育强则国家强。

As the soul of a country and a nation, a burgeoning culture helps a country to thrive, and cultural strength raises a nation into greatness.
文化是一个国家、一个民族的灵魂。文化兴国运兴，文化强民族强。

Education in China has to be rooted in China while building bridges connecting with foreign lands, and it must keep abreast with the times and be forward-looking.
中国的教育要扎根中国、融通中外、立足时代、面向未来。

We must give strategic priority to education to push forward the different undertakings of the Party and the state, and highlight the fundamental, pioneering, and holistic role of education.
要坚持优先发展教育事业作为推动党和国家各项事业发展的重要先手棋，突出教育的基础性、先导性、全局性地位和作用。

We must make sure that benefits of educational development be shared among the people in a more equitable manner as part of our effort to promote social equity and justice.
我们必须不断促进教育事业发展成果更多更公平惠及全体人民，以教育公平促进社会公平正义。

We must strive to ensure equal access to education for all, empowering all to grow and develop, and encouraging all to contribute to society and bring benefits to the people.
我们必须努力让每个人享有受教育的机会，获得发展自身、奉献社会、造福人民的能力。

We must train our students to have strong morals, and create a ready pool of new generations of socialist builders who are developed morally, intellectually, physically, aesthetically, and with a love for labor to shoulder the responsibility of national rejuvenation.

办学质量和水平显著提升，基础教育、职业教育、高等教育等各级各类教育事业全面发展。

We maintain that education must serve the people, serve the CPC in the governance of the country, serve the objectives of consolidating and developing Chinese socialist institutions, serve the objectives of reform and opening up, and serve the modernization of socialism.

我们坚持教育为人民服务，为中国共产党治国理政服务，为巩固和发展中国特色社会主义制度服务，为改革开放和社会主义现代化建设服务。

We need to improve the network where schools, families and society work together for a common goal. Families and society are encouraged to collaborate with schools to consolidate educational outcomes by creating a positive family and social ethos. The three actors working together will create a strong synergy.

要完善学校、家庭、社会三结合的教育网络，引导广大家庭和社会各方面主动配合学校教育，以良好的家庭氛围和社会风气巩固学校教育成果，形成家庭、社会与学校同向同行、携手育人的强大合力。

Unit 3 Education & People's Overall Development
教育与人的全面发展

Text A Role of Education in the Developmental Process

导读：人的全面发展首先是指人的"完整发展"，即人的各种最基本或最基础的素质必须得到完整的发展。人的全面发展从根本上说是指人的劳动能力的全面发展，即人的智力和体力的充分、统一的发展；同时，也包括人的才能、志趣和道德品质的多方面发展，即培养受教育者在德、智、体、美等方面获得完整发展。人的全面发展是全面发展教育的目的，全面发展教育又是实现人的全面发展的教育保障和教育内涵。

With a deep interest in the application of developmental research to educational practice, we are excited by the implications of this work for understanding individual differences in development, as well as the role of the educational environment as a "specialist change agent". We outline an important direction toward which we believe the findings of Kovas et al. point research on development and education: analyzing the role of education in the developmental process.

Dynamic growth modeling allows us to consider the environment as another cluster of variables that affect a child's overall developmental outcomes. Education provides a crucial environment for children's academic development, without which hardly anyone would learn literacy, mathematics, science, or many other skills of modern societies. Considering education as a set of variables within growth equations makes clear that education will not be a distinct and independently acting entity, but rather a set of dynamic influence—both affecting as well as being affected by other environmental and within-child states. Measures of many factors will ultimately need to be combined in dynamic models of school learning, just as they are combined for predicting weather or analyzing the processes in a cell.

Kovas et al. highlight some relevant and intriguing findings such as that the non-shared environment of twins plays a major role in making genetically identical twins achieve to different academic levels. Although non-shared environment remains inadequately understood, we do know that it includes factors such as idiosyncratic experiences affecting one twin only, as well as differential treatment by parents or teachers. These provide an excellent opportunity for building growth models to facilitate analyzing processes of development and learning.

This latter point is vitally important to educators. Educators, by their very role, are an automatic part of a child's developmental "equation" and the extensively documented enormous effects of schools on skills and abilities demonstrate their importance. This means that it is not possible to maintain an extreme view that a child's academic potential is genetically predetermined. Genetics contribute significantly to a child's academic progress, but always as a function of other factors. These may include the "fit" of teaching to a child's individual needs or the presence of an environment that encourages academic engagement. The teaching environment makes possible the realization of a child's genetic propensities.

Teachers should also be aware that those same genetic propensities influence their own "state"; for example, certain personalities or learning profiles within a student can interact both positively and negatively with those of the teacher. Kovas et al. mention the work of Walker and Plomin, which aims to analyze the role of nature versus nurture within a school environment in greater depth. For example, using children from the study, these authors found that perceptions of the classroom environment are driven primarily by child-specific experiences, though such perceptions did not have a strong relationship with school achievement in their study. The perceptions questionnaire probed areas such as teacher helpfulness and peer integration, but this area is ripe for further research. Work exploring more specific experimental factors such as achievement-related motivation and engagement does suggest links to achievement. More focused work in this area will help elucidate these relationships.

In conclusion, the synthesis of Kovas, Haworth, Dale, and Plomin is a landmark in our understanding of the role of genetics and environment in the development of abilities and skills in children who go to school. The finding shows that genes have a significant influence on developmental continuity, while the environment primarily affects change and variation has profound implications. The study lays out this major step in a new kind of developmental analysis that analyzes the dynamics of development of skills and abilities in educational settings. The responsibility is now upon researchers of this generation and the next to take up the challenge to build on these ideas. We have suggested some ways to begin this scientific and educational journey. Returning to our initial questions: How exactly do skills develop and interact? What educational factors cause the most change? What combinations of genes mediate development and change, and how? With a combination of careful research like that of this study with explicit growth modeling of the intertwining processes, researchers can illuminate how students learn and develop the skills they need to thrive in the world of the 21st century.

Genetics（遗传学）: Genetics, a discipline of biology, is the science of genes, heredity, and variation in living organisms. It deals with the molecular structure and function of genes, with gene behavior in the context of a cell or organism, with patterns of inheritance from parent to offspring, and with gene distribution, variation and change in populations. Given that genes are universal to living organisms, genetics can be applied to the study of all living systems, from viruses and bacteria, through plants (especially crops) and domestic animals to humans (as in medical genetics).

New words and expressions

1. cluster ['klʌstə]   n.   群；簇；丛；串
                               vi.   群聚；丛生
                               vt.   使聚集
2. crucial ['kru:ʃəl]   adj. 重要的；决定性的；定局的；决断的
3. equation [i'kweiʒən]   n.   方程式，等式；相等；[化学] 反应式
4. intriguing [in'tri:giŋ]   adj. 有趣的；迷人的
5. idiosyncratic [ˌidiəsiŋ'krætik] adj. 特质的；特殊的；异质的
6. propensity [prəu'pensiti]   n.   倾向，习性；癖好，偏爱
7. profile ['prəufail]   n.   侧面；轮廓；外形；剖面
8. perception [pə'sepʃən]   n.   知觉；[生理] 感觉；看法；洞察力；获取
9. probe [prəub]   n.   探针；调查

	vi.	调查；探测
	vt.	探查；用探针探测
10. elucidate [i'lu:si,deit]	vt.	阐明；说明
11. intertwine [,intə'twain]	vi.	纠缠；编结
	vt.	缠绕；纠缠
12. thrive [θraiv]	vi.	繁荣，兴旺；茁壮成长

I Vocabulary.

Fill in the blanks with the most suitable words. Change the form when necessary.

cluster	perception	elucidate	thrive	crucial
intriguing	probe	intertwine	idiosyncratic	propensity

1. A _____ of stars is smaller than a constellation.
2. The governor appointed a committee to _____ the causes of the strike.
3. We have succeeded in one _____ regard: making this scandal public.
4. The note helps to _____ the most difficult parts of the text.
5. They _____ their fingers.
6. She is a woman of keen _____.
7. A business cannot _____ without good management.
8. He showed a _____ for violence.
9. Some of the members had been _____ to get the secretary dismissed.
10. Her blackboard technique was also extremely _____.

II Translate the following phrases into English.

个体差异   _____
教育环境   _____
成长过程   _____
学术潜力   _____

Unit 3 Education & People's Overall Development 教育与人的全面发展

遗传基因完全相同的　　　　_____
意识到　　　　　　　　　　_____
学习档案，学习历程　　　　_____
展示，摆出，安排，筹划　　_____
应战，接受挑战　　　　　　_____
把……建立于，以……为基础　_____

III Comprehension of the text.

Decide whether the following statements are true (T) or false (F) according to the passage.

1. Education provides a crucial environment for children's academic development, with which anyone would learn literacy, mathematics, science, or many other skills of modern societies. (　)
2. Measures of many factors will ultimately need to be combined in dynamic models of school learning, just as they are combined for predicting weather or analyzing the processes in a cell. (　)
3. Although non-shared environment remains inadequately understood, we do know that it includes factors such as idiosyncratic experiences affecting one twin both, as well as differential treatment by parents or teachers. (　)
4. Educators are an automatic part of a child's developmental "equation" and the extensively documented enormous effects of schools on skills and abilities demonstrate their importance. (　)
5. The teaching environment makes it impossible the realization of a child's genetic propensities. (　)
6. Teachers should also be aware that those different genetic propensities influence their own "state". (　)
7. Perceptions of the classroom environment are driven primarily by teacher-specific experiences, though such perceptions did not have a strong relationship with school achievement in their study. (　)
8. Work exploring more specific experimental factors such as achievement-related motivation and engagement does suggest links to achievement. (　)
9. Genes have a significant influence on developmental continuity, while the environment primarily affects change and variation has profound implications. (　)
10. Although with the combination of careful research like that of this study with explicit growth modeling of the intertwining processes, researchers cannot illuminate

how students learn and develop the skills they need to thrive in the world of the 21st century. ( )

Text B Social Skills Development in Primary Education

导读：初等教育即小学教育，或称基础教育，是使受教育者打下文化知识基础和做好初步生活准备的教育。通常指一个国家学制中第一个阶段的教育，对象一般为 6~12 岁儿童。初等教育的学制为六年，一般为全日制普通小学。这种教育对提高国家民族文化水平极为重要，因此各国在其经济文化发展的一定历史阶段都把它定为实施义务教育或普及教育的目标。

There are four main factors that play an important role in the development of primary school student's social skills: family, school, environment and the personal characteristics of individual students.

Family

The effect of family, which starts in the prenatal period and continues its influence until the end of an individual's life, is of great importance in a child's development. That a child is supported in the primary school period by his parents and spends sufficient and quality time with them is one of the important factors that substantially determine how a person will adapt during the lifelong socialization process.

Unconditional love exhibited by parents, regular care and support develop a child's basic sense of confidence. Positive communication between children and their parents in the primary school period is reflected on the children's social behaviors. Positive social relations and model parental behaviors may set patterns that children can repeat. As stated by the teachers, the children who are accepted by their families as they are can express themselves easier in social environments and develop their social skills. Families should not only focus on the academic successes of their children but also support their social and emotional development. Parents should cooperate with schools and teachers in this area.

School

Primary schools are of great importance in a child's socialization process. Elementary school years constitute the most important period in which children develop attitudes and behaviors. In this period, children learn how to live with others in the same environment, how to share, how to communicate and how to express themselves. Teacher views support the idea that primary school has an important role in the development of young children.

Attaching importance to social activities at schools is one of the sub-themes that educators focus on most. Teachers emphasized that one of the most important aims of primary schools is to prepare children for a healthy social life.

It is also important that activities directed to enabling students to gain social skills are shown in primary school curricula. Educators emphasize that lessons should be prepared in a way that enables an individual to develop his social skills, to realize himself and to actively participate in social activities. Again, the results of research show that the preference of student-centered teaching methods and techniques by the teachers is very important for developing children's social skills.

Primary school is the place where students' tendency to see their teachers role models reaches its highest level. It is known that at these ages the attitudes and behaviors of teachers significantly influence the social development of the child. Teachers also understand that their positive attitudes and behavior in school and the classroom environment will further encourage students to take part in social activities.

The democratic attitudes of teachers in classroom management and positive communication with students can enable students to have more self-confidence and to take part in social activities more voluntarily. According to Küçükahmet, the relationship between teacher and student in the classroom forms the basis of learning and education. Teachers who are conscious of their profession try to furnish their students with the necessary knowledge and skills on one hand; they can be a good model for children with their exemplary characters on the other hand.

It is understood from the teacher views that the exams for passing from primary school to secondary school cause stress on primary school students and therefore students cannot spare time for and be directed to social activities. As the educators, even if it is obligatory to test students for admission to secondary education, the necessary precautions should be taken in order to prevent this situation from negatively affecting the social development of students by way of causing pressure and stress on them.

Environment

According to the teachers, the environment is one of the factors which play an important role in the development of elementary school children's social skills. The environment may be much more dominant than the family and the school in some cases; for example, children may acquire a great deal of information and skills from their close groups of friends. According to Hartup, a child needs to make friends and participate in groups of friends in order to be able to adapt to her social environment. Friendship provides children with the necessary environments and conditions for learning and development, supports children in emotional and cognitive terms and helps them to learn how to take responsibility, how to protect their own rights and how to respect the rights and responsibilities of others. Therefore, children adopt the methods and the rules of social life. Children can develop the skills of working together in a group, struggling for the common goal and group success, obeying rules, leadership and communication thanks to the social and sporting activities in which they participated together with their peers.

One of the most important environmental factors for the social development of primary school students is children's playing games with their peers. Children recognize their own bodies, realize their abilities, get in the habit of taking responsibility and study regularly by way of learning how to share with their peers and help each other.

According to the teachers who participated in this project, some problems may occur in the social development of the children who spend a long time in front of television, computers and the Internet rather than spending time together with their peer groups in their close environments. Moreover, studies show that the children who watch television for a long time, addict to computer games and surf on the Internet for a long time cut off communication with their close environments, exhibit anti-social behaviors and become passive individuals. However, it should be known that the use of these technologies in a controlled manner and relevantly would contribute to the child's social development, knowledge and skill development. For example, some studies emphasize that using a computer plays a quite significant role in the cooperation of primary school students, problem solving, accessing information and the development of primary school students.

Children's personal characteristics

Teachers declared that children's personal characteristics play an important role in the development of their social skills as well as other factors in primary school. The characteristics such as developing language and communication skills in children, building personal characteristics such as self-confidence, self-discipline and expression of personal abilities are actually among the most important aims of primary education.

Language and expression skills play a key role in the development of the social skills such as starting relations between individuals, expressing oneself, giving information and joining a group. The children who have communication skills can easily join groups of friends and improve their self-confidence. According to Cartledge and Milbum, the most important aim of social skill education is to enable individuals to be aware of their feelings and thoughts, express their feelings, deal with undesired behaviors and develop behaviors which allow for positive social interaction.

Consequently, based on the teacher views and the results of research, we learn that family, school, environment and children's personal characteristics play an important role in the development of the social skills of primary school students.

Notes

1. **Social Skills**（社交技能）: Social skills are any skills facilitating interaction and communication with others. Social rules and relations are created, communicated, and changed in verbal and nonverbal ways. The process of learning such skills is called socialization. The rationale for this type of an approach to treatment is that people meet a variety of social problems and can reduce the stress and punishment from the encounter as well as increase their reinforcement by having the correct skills.

2. **Primary Education**（初等教育）: Primary education is the first stage of compulsory education. It is preceded by pre-school or nursery education and is followed by secondary education. In most countries, it is compulsory for children to receive primary education, though in many jurisdictions it is permissible for parents to provide it. The transition to secondary school or high school is somewhat arbitrary, but it generally occurs at about eleven or twelve years of age. Some educational systems have separate middle schools with the transition to the final stage of education taking place at around the age of fourteen. The major goals of primary education are achieving basic literacy and numeracy amongst all pupils, as well as establishing foundations in science, mathematics, geography, history and other social sciences. The relative priority of various areas, and the methods used to teach them, are an area of considerable political debate.

3. **Socialization**（社会化）: Socialization is a term used by sociologists, social psychologists, anthropologists, politicians and educationalists to refer to the process of inheriting norms,

customs and ideologies. It may provide the individual with the skills and habits necessary for participating within their own society; a society develops a culture through a plurality of shared norms, customs, values, traditions, social roles, symbols and languages. Socialization is thus the means by which social and cultural continuity are attained.

4. **Secondary Education**（中等教育）: Secondary education is the stage of education following primary school. Secondary education is generally the final stage of compulsory education. However, secondary education in some countries includes a period of compulsory and a period of non-compulsory education. The next stage of education is usually college or university. Secondary education is characterized by transition from the typically compulsory, comprehensive primary education for minors to the optional, selective tertiary, "post-secondary", or "higher" education for adults.

New words and expressions

1. prenatal [ˌpriːˈneitəl] adj. 产前的；胎儿期的；[医] 出生以前的
2. socialization [ˌsəuʃəlaiˈzeiʃən] n. 社会化，社会主义化
3. elementary [ˌeliˈmentəri] adj. 基本的；初级的；[化学] 元素的
4. preference [ˈprefərəns] n. 偏爱，倾向；优先权
5. exemplary [igˈzempləri] adj. 典范的；惩戒性的；可仿效的
6. obligatory [ˈɔbligətəri] adj. 义务的；必须的；义不容辞的
7. precaution [priˈkɔːʃən] n. 预防，警惕；预防措施
   vt. 警惕；预先警告
8. cognitive [ˈkɔgnitiv] adj. 认知的，认识的
9. peer [piə] vi. 凝视，盯着看；窥视
   vt. 封为贵族；与……同等
   n. 贵族；同等的人
10. addict [əˈdikt] n. 有瘾的人；入迷的人
    vt. 使上瘾；使沉溺
11. access [ˈækses] vt. 使用；存取；接近
    n. 进入；使用权；通路
12. interaction [ˌintərˈækʃən] n. 相互作用；[数] 交互作用

Unit 3　Education & People's Overall Development　教育与人的全面发展

I Vocabulary.

Match the word in Column A to the correct definition in the Column B.

Column A	
1. elementary	2. preference
3. obligatory	4. cognitive
5. precaution	6. peer
7. access	8. interaction
9. addict	10. prenatal

Column B
A. the people who are the same age as you or who have the same status as you
B. the mental process involved in knowing, learning, and understanding things
C. occurring, existing, or performed before birth
D. very simple and basic
E. a way of entering or reaching a place
F. binding in law or conscience
G. mutual or reciprocal action or influence
H. a greater interest in or desire for sb. or sth. than else
I. an action that is intended to prevent something dangerous or unpleasant from happening
J. To cause to become physiologically or psychologically dependent on a habit-forming substance

II Translate the following phrases into English.

社交技能　　　　　　　　　　　＿＿＿＿＿＿＿＿＿＿＿＿＿＿＿
实行，执行；完成，实现　　　　＿＿＿＿＿＿＿＿＿＿＿＿＿＿＿
无条件的爱　　　　　　　　　　＿＿＿＿＿＿＿＿＿＿＿＿＿＿＿
沉溺于，醉心于　　　　　　　　＿＿＿＿＿＿＿＿＿＿＿＿＿＿＿
以学生为中心的教学模式　　　　＿＿＿＿＿＿＿＿＿＿＿＿＿＿＿
觉察，意识到　　　　　　　　　＿＿＿＿＿＿＿＿＿＿＿＿＿＿＿

中等教育　　　　　　　　＿＿＿＿＿＿＿＿＿＿＿＿＿＿＿＿

为……努力　　　　　　　＿＿＿＿＿＿＿＿＿＿＿＿＿＿＿＿

遵守规则　　　　　　　　＿＿＿＿＿＿＿＿＿＿＿＿＿＿＿＿

自律，自我约束　　　　　＿＿＿＿＿＿＿＿＿＿＿＿＿＿＿＿

III Comprehension of the text.

Decide whether the following statements are true (T) or false (F) according to the passage.

1. There are four main factors that play an important role in the development of primary school students' social skills: family, school, environment and the personal characteristics of individual students.　　　　　　　　　　　　　　　　　　(　　)

2. The effect of family starts in the postnatal period and continues its influence until the end of an individual's life and it is of great importance in a child's development.
　　　　　　　　　　　　　　　　　　　　　　　　　　　　　　　　　(　　)

3. Families play an important role in children's development in social skills. Parents should not only focus on the academic successes of their children but also support their social and emotional development.　　　　　　　　　　　　　　(　　)

4. Elementary school years constitute the most important period in which children develop attitudes and behaviors and in which children learn how to live with others in the same environment, how to share, how to communicate and how to express themselves.　　　　　　　　　　　　　　　　　　　　　　　　　　　(　　)

5. Preparing children for a healthy social life is the most important aim of primary schools, according to the teachers.　　　　　　　　　　　　　　　　　(　　)

6. Teachers who are conscious of their profession try to furnish their students with the necessary knowledge and skills on one hand; they may not be a good model for children with their exemplary characters on the other hand.　　　　　(　　)

7. According to the teachers, the stress on primary school students caused by the exams for passing from primary school to secondary school make those children have no spare time for social activities.　　　　　　　　　　　　　　　　　(　　)

8. The environment is one of the factors which play an important role in the development of elementary school children's social skills, which may be much more dominant than the family and the school in some cases.　　　　　　　　　　　　(　　)

9. Although some problems may occur in the social development of the children who spend a long time in front of television, computers and the Internet rather than spending time together with their peer groups in their close environments, it should be

known that the use of these technologies in a controlled manner and relevantly would contribute to the child's social development, knowledge and skill development. (   )

10. The characteristics such as developing language and communication skills in children, building personal characteristics such as self-confidence, self-discipline and expression of personal abilities are actually the most important aims of primary education.   (   )

Useful phrases and expressions ◀◀◀◀

崇德修身 cultivate morality

德才兼备 those with both morals and talent

以德为先 with morality as a priority

战略性转变 strategic transformation

高度的文化自信 a strong confidence in Chinese culture

守公德、严私德 maintains public virtues and practices personal virtues

拔尖创新型人才 highly innovative talent

德智体美劳全面发展 be developed morally, intellectually, physically, aesthetically, and with a love for labor

国无德不兴，人无德不立 morality as the basis for national prosperity and personal success

坚持把立德树人作为根本任务 the fundamental mission of building moral character

Moral integrity concerns the future of our Party and our nation.
立德树人关系党的事业后继有人，关系国家前途命运。

It must be the criterion against which we measure all educational activities.
必须把立德树人成效作为检验学校一切工作的根本标准。

Talents are supportive of virtues, and virtues are guidance to talents.
才者，德之资也；德者，才之帅也。

The Great Learning consists in manifesting one's illustrious virtue, fulfilling the expectations of the people, and engaging in the endless pursuit of moral perfection.
大学之道，在明明德，在亲民，在止于至善。

The CPC leadership in education has never been stronger, nor has moral and political education in schools been keener.
党对教育工作的领导全面加强，学校思想政治工作力度空前。

Students have a stronger moral framework, and stakeholders in education have a stronger sense of confidence.

我们必须努力培养担当民族复兴大任的时代新人，培养德智体美劳全面发展的社会主义建设者和接班人。

Moral integrity is the prerequisite for a successful career and academic life. It is the foundation of a person's life.

做人是做学问、干事业的前提。立德是一个人做人的基础。

Without a noble mind and a strong moral character, young people will not become outstanding even if they are erudite.

青年人没有崇高理想和良好品质，知识掌握再多也无法成为优秀人才。

The greatest virtue is to serve the country and the people and only with great virtues can a person realize a great cause.

要立志报效祖国、服务人民，这是大德，养大德者方可成大业。

There has also been considerable growth in the quality and standards of school operation-in basic education, technical and vocational education, higher education, and various other forms of educational undertakings.

办学质量和水平显著提升，基础教育、职业教育、高等教育等各级各类教育事业全面发展。

Unit 4 Educational System & Educational Law
教育制度与教育法

Text A E-learning and Evaluation in Modern Educational System

导读：网络学习（E-learning）又称数字学习，也译电子化学习、在线学习，它强调的是数字技术，强调用技术来改造和引导教育。E-learning主要通过互联网进行学习与教学活动，它充分利用现代信息技术所提供的、具有全新沟通机制与丰富资源的学习环境，实现一种全新的学习方式。学习的知识不再是一本书，也不再是几本参考书，而是将有关的专业知识建立成数据库。在数据库的支持下，知识体系将被重新划分，学习内容将发生重新组合，学习与研究方法也将发生新的变化。

Implementation of information and communication technologies as well as emersion of new user interfaces and Web 2.0 technologies changes the way of education system, the way of living and business transactions in general. The way we communicate, operate, produce and live is also changing. In accordance with it, the systems of education change from being traditional to being modern. With the development of certain software, students' class attendance no longer represents an important factor, as they can now learn from distance using the mentioned software, taking the learning process one step further.

Confucius, the famous Chinese thinker and philosopher, once said, "I see and I forget, I hear and I remember, I do and I understand." We all know this instinctively, but perhaps Edgar Dale, a U.S. educationist at Ohio State University, explained it the best. He made some study to explain. The results of his study showed a significant deviation between different learning methods. Dale could divide those methods into passive and active learning, and each of them into a nature of enrollment, as reading, looking at pictures, seeing a movie, giving a talk or doing a presentation. The results indicated that the student group that learned from reading remembered only about 10% of what was written, while the student group that learned from watching a demonstration or an exhibit remembered 50%, and the group that actually did the real thing or simulated a real experience remembered an astonishing 90%. Moreover, students who remembered by reading or hearing were able to define or describe the things they remembered. Students who remembered by hearing and seeing were able to apply what they learned, but only those who learned by saying or saying and doing could analyze, evaluate and criticize what they knew.

Science, people and technology are changing too rapidly to follow them using the traditional teaching methods. Thus, only new and innovative learning methods can make a difference. By using E-learning, it is hoped to achieve changes in the way of thinking and learning and to shift from a vertical hierarchy to a horizontal one, where professors and students can call each other colleagues, thus, referring to one another as practically equals, emphasizing the idea of a common goal—innovative learning. Moreover, it is hoped to shift from defined course materials years or even decades ago to an adaptive learning system where students get to choose the topics they would like to explore further. By giving them this option, Dale's cone of learning is being implemented, and doing research by themselves and presenting this research in front of the whole class will help them remember it much better than they would have if a professor just made them learn it. Those implementations would most likely lead to a change in the learning system. Students' knowledge will no longer have to be acquired by merely professors' lectures that will then be expected to reproduce, but by reproducing a knowledge based on experience. It is needless to say, not only this knowledge will be much better understood, but also the students will remember it much longer and much better.

Learning is a process of achieving certain competence that can be defined as a dynamical combination of cognitive and meta-cognitive skills, knowledge and understanding, as well as the development of social skills and growth in ethical values. The target of every educational program should be to enable its participants to have an optimal balance in developing all the above. E-learning enhances the quality of educational process by enabling the practice of new roles in the process of learning. In addition, during this process, lifelong learning technologies are used. There are different forms of E-learning; (1) ICT (information and communication technologies); (2) mixed learning as a combination of classroom teaching and teaching over the system; and

(3) learning at distance. When choosing a form of e-learning, one should have in mind the type of the course it should be applied to as well as the needs and possibilities of students and professors. E-learning should not be seen as an alternative educational system but as an enhancement of the existing one.

Today, we are faced with a new generation of students, and the aberrational characteristics present among them in comparison with the older generations are only going to be more emphasized with the upcoming ones. The new generations of students are capable of fast information adoption and multitasking, and they call for a random access to information ("anytime, anywhere"), as they are accustomed to Google-like informational systems and multiple media operating. They expect to be rewarded at all time. Past educational systems were based on the idea of delivering the knowledge to students who accepted the given knowledge in a passive manner. Professors played the role as keepers of the knowledge. Through E-learning, a new educational environment can be set and an environment can be constructed in the direction of interaction, processing information, researching and problem-solving. The students are asked to actively get involved, and often work in teams. The role of the professor is to design the methods of learning and help the students develop their talents and capabilities.

1. **E-learning**（网络学习）：E-learning comprises all forms of electronically supported learning and teaching. The information and communication systems, whether networked or not, serve as specific media to implement the learning process. It is essentially the computer and network-enabled transfer of skills and knowledge. E-learning applications and processes include Web-based learning, computer-based learning, virtual classroom opportunities and digital collaboration. Content is delivered via the Internet, intranet/extranet, audio or video tape, satellite TV, and CD-ROM.

2. **Web 2.0**（网络 2.0）：Web 2.0 is associated with web applications that facilitate

participatory information sharing, interoperability, user-centered design, and collaboration on the World Wide Web. A Web 2.0 site allows users to interact and collaborate with each other in a social media dialogue as creators of user-generated content in a virtual community, in contrast to websites where users are limited to the passive viewing of content that was created for them. Examples of Web 2.0 include social networking sites, blogs, wikis, video sharing sites, hosted services, web applications, mashups and folksonomies.

3. **Confucius（孔子）**: Confucius was a Chinese thinker and social philosopher of the Spring and Autumn Period. The philosophy of Confucius emphasized personal and governmental morality, correctness of social relationships, justice and sincerity. Confucius' thoughts have been developed into a system of philosophy known as Confucianism.

4. **Xunzi（荀子）**: Xunzi was a Chinese Confucian philosopher who lived during the Warring States Period and contributed to one of the Hundred Schools of Thought. Xunzi believed man's inborn tendencies need to be curbed through education and ritual, counter to Mencius's view that man is innately good. He believed that ethical norms had been invented to rectify mankind. Educated in the state of Qi, Xunzi was associated with the Confucian school, but his philosophy has a pragmatic flavor compared to Confucian optimism. Some scholars attribute it to the divisive times. Xunzi was one of the most sophisticated thinkers of his time, and was the teacher of Li Si and Han Feizi.

New words and expressions

1. implementation [,implimən'teɪʃən]   n.   实现；履行；安装启用
2. interface ['ɪntəfeɪs]   n.   界面；接口；接触面
3. emersion [ɪ'mɜːʃən]   n.   出现；脱出
4. abstraction [æb'strækʃən]   n.   抽象；提取；抽象概念；空想；心不在焉
5. deviation [,diːvi'eɪʃən]   n.   偏差；误差；背离
6. competence ['kɒmpɪtəns]   n.   能力，胜任；权限；作证能力
7. dynamical [daɪ'næmɪkəl]   adj.   动力学的；有生气的；有力的
8. aberrational [,æbə'reɪʃənəl]   adj.   背离真实的；偏离真理的；不正直的
9. in accordance with   依照，与……一致
10. be accustomed to   习惯于

Unit 4   Educational System & Educational Law   教育制度与教育法

I   Read the text and answer the following questions.

1. What is the topic or subject discussed in the text?
2. In your own words, what is the writer's main idea about this topic?
3. What is the Chinese meaning of "I see and I forget, I hear and I remember, I do and I understand."?
4. What is the definition of "learning" in the passage?
5. What is the value of E-learning?

II   Choose the correct letter A, B, C, or D.

1. Different learning methods used in Dale's study are the following except _____.
   A. reading a book   B. listening to music
   C. giving a talk   D. seeing a movie

2. In Dale's study, _____ is the most useful learning method.
   A. looking at an exhibit
   B. participating in a discussion
   C. reading books
   D. doing a presentation

3. Which is the idea of Dale?
   A. I see and I forget, I hear and I remember.
   B. Despite the quicker adapting that is nowadays required, the majority of the learning institutions still rely on the old fashion way of information transmitting.
   C. Doing research by students will be better for them to study than doing by professors.
   D. Students should learn from professors' lectures and produce knowledge based on them.

4. The writer mentioned _____ ways for E-learning.
   A. two   B. three   C. four   D. five

5. The new generations of students are good at _____.
   A. fast information adoption
   B. multitasking
   C. Google-like informational systems and multiple media operating

D. all of above

III Comprehension of the text.

Decide whether the following statements are true (T) or false (F) according to the passage.

1. With the development of certain software, students' class attendance represents an important factor.
2. Learning from reading remembers more than learning from watching a demonstration.
3. New and innovative learning methods can be suitable for science, people and technology.
4. Lifelong learning technologies are used in the E-learning.
5. E-learning should be seen as an alternative educational system.

Text B Legislation and Equality in Basic Education

导读：随着世界经济和社会的进步越来越依靠知识、技术、技能和能力，人力资源将成为国家在全球市场生存中的决定因素。在这种新的社会历史条件下，使所有儿童、青年和成人的基本学习需要真正得到满足，是世界各国旨在缩小差别、促进社会全面进步的一个必要手段，因此基础教育的意义和作用受到了高度的关注，它要满足全民的基本学习需求，要求世界各国在现行基础教育服务范围，保障每一个个体的基本权利。同时，也强调世界各国必须注重基础教育的平等性。

Despite its different meanings and manifestations, the principle of equality has been used to confront social inequalities in a variety of stratified societies and cultures. While the United Nations is striving for universal primary education for children across the globe by 2015, educational inequality persists and has become a significant challenge for educational policy-makers, scholars, and practitioners worldwide. With reference to compulsory schooling legislation, in China, law is used in policy-making as a pragmatic instrument to address specific educational problems, and as a last resort, holds governments of various levels accountable for improving education. In doing so, law can be a device of social justice to promote equality in education by serving as an important mechanism to check and balance the state's power regarding its obligations toward providing basic education, redistributing public resources, reducing disparities, and promoting equality in compulsory schooling. However, using legislation to promote equity in basic education is constrained by economic conditions and other extra-legal factors. Effecting change requires favorable economic, social, and cultural conditions, as well as the cooperation of those who interpret and enforce the law.

Many sociological and educational studies have discussed the relation between equality and education. For example, Horton and Hunt argued that in modern society, people are given status or rewards according to their merits, which are often measured by results of schooling, and in turn can affect individuals' life chances. Dahrendorf considered education as an important vehicle of social mobility in stratified society and equal educational opportunity as a basic right of every person.

Levin expanded the meaning of educational equality to include: equality of educational access, equality of educational participation, equality of educational results, and equality of educational effects on life chances. Equality of opportunity within education, as Bilton argued, needs to be ensured so that opportunities for success in school are the same for everyone with similar abilities, regardless of sex, ethnicity, and socio-economic background. Iannelli and Paterson concluded, however, that the social project of "using education to equalize life chances has been a failure". They even argued that education "cannot be used, on its own, to eradicate social inequalities, and is relatively powerless to counter the middle-class strengths of effective networks, self-confident aspirations and sheer wealth".

Despite the debate, the provision of basic education for all with a minimum period of schooling is still believed to be a vital means for reducing inequality within and between societies. Since World War II, the UN has advocated a rights-based approach to basic education. In the Universal Declaration of Human Rights, the UN declared that "everyone has the right to education" and that education shall be "free" and "compulsory", at least during the elementary and fundamental stages. This right can empower individuals to achieve "the goals of personal autonomy and efficacy" and enable them to determine the course of their lives.

In response to these global aspirations, many countries have adopted strategies to provide basic education for all. Of these strategies, compulsory schooling legislation is a particularly common one. Legislation can compel the state to provide eligible children with free basic education for a minimum period of, for example, six or nine years and compel parents to send their children to school. As a result, despite such problems as gender disparity, the number of children in the world enrolled in primary school increased by 6% to 688 million from 1999 to 2005, and the number of children out of school dropped from 96 million in 1999 to 72 million in 2005. However, providing and legislating compulsory schooling does not necessarily mean the complete eradication of educational inequalities in compulsory schooling. Many studies have shown that inequality in school education continues to exist in many forms. As noted by Coleman, Jencks, Levin, and Ballantine, they include: inequalities in educational input and output, and educational opportunity and life chances for children of different social groups, for boys and girls, and for local and non-local students. Inequality of students' academic performance can be caused by many factors, such as cultural practices, social class, family background, ethnicity, gender, and sexuality. Using legislation as a means to institutionalize equality in basic education is part of an international trend of increasing reliance on legislation to bring about social change.

1. **Basic Education**（基础教育）: Basic education refers to the whole range of educational activities taking place in various settings (formal, non-formal and informal), which aim to meet basic learning needs. According to the International Standard Classification of Education (ISCED), basic education comprises primary education (first stage of basic education) and lower secondary education (second stage). In countries (developing countries in particular), basic education often includes also pre-primary education and/or adult literacy programs.

2. **The Universal Declaration of Human Rights**（UDHR）（世界人权宣言）: The Universal Declaration of Human Rights is a declaration adopted by the United Nations General

Unit 4　Educational System & Educational Law　教育制度与教育法

Assembly on 10 December 1948. The Declaration arose directly from the experience of the Second World War and represents the first global expression of rights to which all human beings are inherently entitled. It consists of 30 articles which have been elaborated in subsequent international treaties, regional human rights instruments, national constitutions and laws.

New words and expressions

1.	manifestation [ˌmænife'steiʃən]	n.	表现；显示；示威运动
2.	stratified ['strætifaid]	adj.	分层的；形成阶层的；分为不同等级的
3.	pragmatic [præg'mætik]	adj.	实际的；实用主义的；国事的
4.	mechanism ['mekənizəm]	n.	原理，途径；进程；机制；机械装置；技巧
5.	disparity [dis'pærəti]	n.	不同；不一致；不等
6.	provision [prəu'viʒən]	n.	规定；条款；准备
7.	efficacy ['efikəsi]	n.	功效，效力
8.	autonomy [ɔ:'tɔnəmi]	n.	自主权，自主性
9.	eligible ['elidʒəbl]	adj.	合格的，合适的；符合条件的；有资格当选的
10.	accountable for		负责，对……负责任
11.	with reference to		关于（等于 in reference to）
12.	hold accountable for		对……负责任

Exercises

I Choose the meaning of the following words used in the text.

1. manifestation
    A. a very clear sign that a particular situation or feeling exists
    B. the act of appearing or becoming clear
    C. the appearance of a ghost or a sign of its presence
    D. evidence
2. stratified

A. various

B. having several layers of earth, rock etc.

C. having different social classes

D. useful or right

3. pragmatic

    A. concerned with the study of scientific ideas

    B. solving problems in a sensible rather than fixed ideas or theories

    C. based on carefully organized methods

    D. related to the style of a piece of writing or art

4. disparity

    A. change

    B. variation

    C. equal pay, rights, or power

    D. a difference connected with unfair treatment

5. eradicate

    A. to forget

    B. to destroy or get rid of something

    C. to build

    D. to understand

6. autonomy

    A. freedom to govern a region or country without being controlled by anyone else

    B. the ability to make your own decisions without being influenced by anyone else

    C. a person who behaves like a machine, without thinking or feeling anything

    D. a machine that moves without human control

7. efficacy

    A. the quality of being able to produce the result that was intended

    B. a figure made of wood, paper, stone that looks like a person

    C. the physical or mental energy that is needed to do something

    D. an attempt to do something

8. aspiration

    A. the sound of air blowing out that happens when some consonants are pronounced

    B. someone who hopes to get a position of importance or honor

    C. a strong desire to have or achieve something

    D. a way of speaking or behaving

9. eligible

Unit 4 Educational System & Educational Law 教育制度与教育法

A. very beautiful and graceful

B. clever and simple

C. upset and unhappy

D. qualified for or allowed or worthy of being chosen

10. institutionalize

A. to make something systematize

B. cause to be admitted

C. to officially tell somebody what to do

D. to inform somebody about something

II Comprehension of the text.

Decide whether the following statements are true (T) or false (F) according to the passage.

1. The United Nations has already solved the problem of primary education for children across the globe.   (   )
2. Using legislation to promote equity in basic education is only constrained by economic conditions.   (   )
3. Levin considered education as an important vehicle of social mobility in stratified society and equal educational opportunity as a basic right of every person.   (   )
4. Iannelli and Paterson argued that education cannot be used, on its own, to eradicate social inequalities, and is relatively powerless to counter the middle-class strengths of effective networks, self-confident aspirations and sheer wealth.   (   )
5. Providing and legislating compulsory schooling means the complete eradication of educational inequalities in compulsory schooling.   (   )

III Translate the following sentences into Chinese.

1. While the United Nations is striving for universal primary education for children across the globe by 2015, educational inequality persists and has become a significant challenge for educational policy-makers, scholars, and practitioners worldwide.
2. With reference to compulsory schooling legislation, in China, law is used in policy-making as a pragmatic instrument to address specific educational problems, and as a last resort, holds governments of various levels accountable for improving education.
3. Equality of opportunity within education, as Bilton argued, needs to be ensured so that opportunities for success in school are the same for everyone with similar abilities, regardless of sex, ethnicity, and socio-economic background.

4. In the Universal Declaration of Human Rights, the UN declared that "everyone has the right to education" and that education shall be "free" and "compulsory", at least during the elementary and fundamental stages.
5. As a result, despite such problems as gender disparity, the number of children in the world enrolled in primary school increased by 6% to 688 million from 1999 to 2005, and the number of children out of school dropped from 96 million in 1999 to 72 million in 2005.

Useful phrases and expressions

职业指导 vocational guidance
死记硬背 rote learning
特殊教育 special needs education
继续教育 continuing education
专门教育 specialized education
民办教育 private school
产教融合办学体制 the mechanism for integrating vocational education with industry
一流大学和一流学科 world-class universities and academic disciplines
在线教育 online education
以学生为主体的教育 student-oriented education

We saw to it that compulsory education was provided as an overall state responsibility; and we guided and regulated the development of private schools.
坚持义务教育由国家统一实施，引导规范民办教育发展。
We took active yet prudent steps to advance comprehensive reform of the college entrance examination system and raised the gross enrollment ratio for higher education from 45.7 percent to 59.6 percent. Universities and colleges continued to enroll more students from central and western regions and rural areas.
积极稳妥推进高考综合改革，高等教育毛入学率从 45.7%提高到 59.6%，高校招生持续加大对中西部地区和农村地区倾斜力度。
The goal of universal senior secondary education was attained. Vocational education was made more adaptable, and conditions in vocational schools were steadily improved.
普及高中阶段教育目标已实现。职业教育适应性增强，职业院校办学条件持续改善。
Steps will be taken to strengthen professional ethics among teachers. A mechanism will

be established whereby our schools, families and whole society work together to advance education.

加强师德师风建设，健全学校家庭社会协同育人机制。

We will ensure that compulsory education teachers receive their pay packages in full and strengthen targeted training programs, on-the-job training, and salary guarantees for rural teachers.

全面落实义务教育教师工资待遇，加强乡村教师定向培养、在职培训与待遇保障。

We will promote general and proficient use of standard spoken and written Chinese.

提升国家通用语言文字普及程度和质量。

To develop modern vocational education, we will upgrade vocational schools, refine the mechanism for integrating vocational education with industry, and enhance the adaptability of vocational education.

发展现代职业教育，改善职业教育办学条件，完善产教融合办学体制，增强职业教育适应性。

We will promote the development of world-class universities and academic disciplines on a categorized basis, move faster to train professionals we are badly lacking in the fields of science, engineering, agriculture and medicine, and support the development of higher education in central and western regions.

分类建设一流大学和一流学科，加快培养理工农医类专业紧缺人才，支持中西部高等教育发展。

We launched a plan that enables institutions of higher learning to recruit students who excel in basic academic disciplines, as well as a plan to cultivate top talent in basic disciplines. We continued to develop world-class universities and world-class disciplines. By doing so, we have laid a solid foundation for talent development.

深入实施"强基计划"和基础学科拔尖人才培养计划，继续推进世界一流大学和一流学科建设，不断夯实发展的人才基础。

Unit 5 Educational Justice
教育公平

Text A   Educational Justice in Schools

导读：教育公平是要确保每个人不受性别、种族、出身、经济地位、居住环境等条件的影响，均享有平等的受教育的权利和义务，被提供相对平等的受教育的机会和条件。然而受教育者之间存在差异，每个人又是各不相同的，接受教育和掌握知识的水平不一致，仅仅保证教育权利和教育条件的公平，还不足以保证受教育者的公平。

What are the right normative grounds for evaluating education policy? I want to propose, briefly, four proper goals of education, and one distributive principle. The goals are as follows:

- Education should prepare children to become autonomous, self-governing individuals, capable of making good judgments about how to live their own lives, and to negotiate for themselves the complexity of modern life;
- Education should equip children with the skills and knowledge necessary for them to be effective participants in the economy, so that they can have a good range of options in the labor market, and have access to the income necessary to flourish in a market economy;
- Education should play a role in preparing children to be flourishing adults independently of their participation in the economy;
- Education should prepare children to be responsible and effective participants in political life—good citizens. It should do this both for their sake, because a flourishing life is more secure if one is capable of making use of the rights of citizenship; and for the sake of others, because a flourishing life is more secure if others are capable of abiding by the duties of good citizenship.

The distributive principle is the principle of educational equality: The simple version says that every child should have an equally good education. But what this means is obviously contested. When you compare children with similar talents, and similar levels of willingness to exert effort, it is pretty intuitive to say that educational equality is satisfied when they receive a similar level of educational resources. But consider Hattie, who is blind, and Sid, who is equally talented and hardworking, but sighted. In their case it seems intuitive that equality requires that more resources should be devoted to Hattie in particular, resources devoted to correcting fully for her disability. Consider an even more difficult case: Kenneth, who is highly talented, and Hugh, who has a serious cognitive disability. Again, it seems that Hugh should be granted more resources, but this time it is hard to see that they could correct for the disability, unless we were willing to disable Kenneth. I shall not resolve these difficulties here. The principle of educational equality has two straightforward implications. First, children with similar levels of ability and willingness to exert effort should face similar educational prospects, regardless of their social background, race, ethnicity, or sex. Second, that children with lower levels of ability should receive at least as many educational resources as those who are more able.

Since most of the ensuing discussion focuses on the principle of educational equality rather than the goals of education, I want to emphasize the importance of equality rather than improving the prospects of the least advantaged. The egalitarian theory within which my own view of educational justice is nested in fact emphasizes not equality, per se, but benefiting the least advantaged, and gives that principle priority over equality—so that when we have a choice between an equal distribution of a smaller pie and an unequal distribution of a larger pie in which all get more than under the equal distribution of the smaller pie, we choose inequality. If a tax proposal, for example, were to inhibit growth so that the worst off were even worse off, although more equally well off with others, that would be a bad thing for them, and for everyone else. But this general rule does not apply to all areas of life. The quality of someone's education has a real influence on their expected lifetime income, but its influence is dependent on the quality of her competitors' education.

Getting Sharon from only 2 up to 3 grade Cs does not do much good for her if we simultaneously get her nearest competitor Linda up from 3 to 4 grade Cs. The employer will still prefer Linda to Sharon. So merely raising the floor of achievement in education does not help the less advantaged in the pursuit of earnings in the labor market unless we simultaneously diminish the achievement gap. The size of the gap matters because of the particular connection education has to other, unequally distributed, goods. When I refer to "benefiting the least (or less) advantaged" in the context of education, then, I should be understood as being concerned with benefiting the least advantaged relative to others.

New words and expressions

1. normative ['nɔːmətiv]　　　　　　adj.　规范的，标准的
2. equip with　　　　　　　　　　　　　装配，配备，备有
3. flourish ['flʌriʃ]　　　　　　　　　vi.　繁荣，兴旺；茂盛；活跃
4. for the sake of　　　　　　　　　　　为了；为了……的利益
5. abide by　　　　　　　　　　　　　　遵守……
6. intuitive [in'tjuːitiv]　　　　　　adj.　直觉的；凭直觉获知的
7. egalitarian [iˌgæli'tɛəriən]　　　adj.　平等主义的
　　　　　　　　　　　　　　　　　　　n.　平等主义；平等主义者
8. per se　　　　　　　　　　　　　　　本身，自身
9. be worse off　　　　　　　　　　　　处境较坏，情况恶化
10. be concerned with　　　　　　　　　涉及……；担心……

Exercises

I Choose the correct letter A, B, C, or D.

1. What are the right normative grounds for evaluating education policy according to the

writer?

    A. Four proper goals of education.

    B. One distributive principle.

    C. Four goals of education and one distributive.

    D. Two distributive principles.

2. The followings are the goals of education except _____.

    A. Education should play a role in preparing children to be flourishing adults independently of their participation in the economy

    B. Education should prepare children to be responsible and effective participants in political life—good citizens

    C. Education should equip children with the skills and knowledge necessary for them to be effective participants in the economy, so that they can have a good range of options in the labour market, and have access to the income necessary to flourish in a market economy

    D. Everyone should have an equal education

3. What is the distributive principle of education?

    A. Every child should have an equally good education.

    B. Children should become autonomous, self-governing individuals, capable of making good judgments about how to live their own lives, and negotiate for themselves the complexity of modern life.

    C. Children are full of the skills and knowledge necessary for them to be effective participants in the economy.

    D. Children can have a good range of options in the labour market, and have access to the income necessary to flourish in the market economy.

4. The writer mentioned the example of _____ to show some difficulties in the principle of educational equality.

    A. considering Hattie

    B. considering Sid

    C. considering Kenneth and Hugh

    D. all of above

5. Which is not the idea of the writer?

    A. To emphasize the importance of equality rather than improving the prospects of the least advantaged.

    B. Children with similar talents, and similar levels of willingness to exert effort will get the similar quality of education.

C. The quality of someone's education has an influence which is dependent on the quality of her competitors' education on their expected lifetime income.
D. Children with lower levels of ability should receive at least as many educational resources as those who are more able.

II Vocabulary.

Fill in the blanks with the most suitable words. Change the form when necessary.

| equip | flourish | abide | egalitarian | intuitive |
| priority | exert | talented | emphasize | normative |

1. He won both games without even seeming to _____ himself.
2. The plants _____ in the warm sun.
3. The boys _____ themselves with torches and rope, and set off.
4. He seemed to have a/an _____ awareness of how I felt.
5. Manufacturers are making safety a design _____.
6. You have to _____ by the referee's decision.
7. There are some _____ issues with social service forces.
8. The _____ artist carved an interesting decoration from this piece of tree root.
9. Our government tries to establish an _____ country.
10. It should be _____ that flying is a very safe way to travel.

III Translate the following sentences into Chinese.

1. Education should prepare children to become autonomous, self-governing individuals, capable of making good judgments about how to live their own lives, and to negotiate for themselves the complexity of modern life.
2. Education should equip children with the skills and knowledge necessary for them to be effective participants in the economy, so that they can have a good range of options in the labor market, and have access to the income necessary to flourish in a market economy.
3. Education should play a role in preparing children to be flourishing adults independently of their participation in the economy.
4. Education should prepare children to be responsible and effective participants in political life—good citizens.
5. When you compare children with similar talents, and similar levels of willingness to

exert effort, it is pretty intuitive to say that educational equality is satisfied when they receive a similar level of educational resources.

Text B Efficiency and Equity of European Education and Training Policies

导读：教育与培训政策的平等是民主化的一个重要内容，是人们不受政治、经济、文化、民族、信仰、性别、地域等的限制，在法律上享有同等的受教育与受培训权利、在事实上具有同等的受教育和培训机会。而教育与培训政策的有效性是指教育与培训政策能完成活动和达到的结果的程度。二者的有效性与平等性时而互补互助，相辅相成，时而互不影响，各自发展，时而又给对方的发展造成不利影响。

Any society aims for economic prosperity coupled with equality of opportunity. Thus, it is not a surprise that European Union heads of state could agree on the so-called "Lisbon strategy" with its goal to become "the most competitive and dynamic knowledge-based economy in the world, capable of sustainable economic growth with more and better jobs and greater social cohesion". At the same time, it has been realized that education and training systems that create efficient and equitable outcomes are key to economic prosperity and social cohesion. This has been stressed by leading European economic advisors, and the European Union puts education and training at center stage in its agenda for jobs and growth. For example, the European Council concludes that "education and training are critical factors to develop the EU's long-term potential for competitiveness as well as for social cohesion". But how can an efficient and equitable education and training system be achieved in practice?

The strong upsurge of applied research in the economics of education over the past decade has produced ample evidence that the monetary and non-monetary prosperity of individuals and nations indeed hinges on education and training. Education produces substantial returns to the individual in terms of earnings and employability, significant effects on economic growth and noteworthy non-monetary benefits for the individual and for society as a whole, among others in terms of superior health, civic participation, and reduced crime. Given the effects of education on individual well-being, the distribution of education is also crucial for societal inequality.

So, efficient education and training systems can create economic growth, and equitable systems can create social cohesion. For some European politicians, education and training are, therefore, high on the policy agenda because they can boost efficiency, for others because they can boost equity. But what is the relationship between efficiency and equity? Many governments tend to think that there is a trade-off that forces them to choose between efficiency and equity in their prioritizing. But achieving more equity in the design of education systems may help to evade the need for intense re-distributive policies at later ages, which are often viewed as obstacles to the creation of growth and jobs in Europe.

In reality, the relationship between efficiency and equity in education and training systems may take different forms. In some cases, efficiency and equity may be independent from one another. In other cases, there may be trade-offs in the extent to which the two goals can be achieved. And in still other cases, there may be complementarities in the achievement of the two goals. Thus, certain policies may bring education and training systems closer to efficiency without having any impact on equity. Other policies may be highly equitable without affecting efficiency. Other policies may advance both efficiency and equity in a complementary way. And still other policies may show a trade-off by advancing either efficiency at the detriment of equity or equity at the detriment of efficiency.

The reviewed evidence shows that efficient policies need not be inequitable, and equitable policies need not be inefficient. Countries do not necessarily have to choose between efficiency and equity. There are ways to evade trade-offs between them, whereas current attempts to reach one or the other sometimes turn out to be both inefficient and inequitable.

While a universally accepted definition of equity is elusive, it seems that most people could agree to some variants close to the concept of equality of opportunity proposed by Roemer. The central idea of this concept is that inequality should be tolerated only if it is due to differences in effort, but not if it is due to circumstances which are beyond a person's control. Thus, equity would demand that a person's expected educational outcome should be a function only of her effort, but not of her circumstances, such as race, gender, or family background. The concept of efficiency is much more straightforward, representing a situation where a maximum aggregate outcome of the educational production process is obtained with given input or a given aggregate outcome with minimum input. Under this concept, an efficient situation is one which would be preferred by any individual who is ignorant of her position in society. In the calculus of applied welfare economics, equity and efficiency goals can be combined by maximizing welfare functions.

Relative to the well established and extensive literature on the economic and social impacts of education and training, many parts of the literature on efficiency and equity in education and training are not as well developed. Ultimately, profound country specific empirical assessments would be required to evaluate the specific efficiency and equity consequences of different policies. Still, the available literature has produced evidence consistent enough to warrant a general unifying perspective and many specific features for a Europe-wide assessment. At the same time, it should be borne in mind that uncertainties remain for some parts of the assessment, which will be mentioned where necessary.

1. **European Union (EU)**（欧洲联盟）: European Union is an economic and political union of 27 member states which are located primarily in Europe. The EU traces its origins from the European Coal and Steel Community (ECSC) and the European Economic Community (EEC) formed by six countries in the 1950s. In the intervening years the EU has grown in size by the accession of new member states, and in power by the addition of policy areas to its remit. The Maastricht Treaty established the European Union under its current name in 1993. The last amendment to the constitutional basis of the EU, the Treaty of Lisbon, came into force in 2009.

2. **Lisbon Strategy**（里斯本策略）: Lisbon Strategy also known as the Lisbon Agenda or Lisbon Process, was an action and development plan for the economy of the European Union between 2000 and 2010. It was set out by the European Council in Lisbon in March 2000, and by 2010 most of its goals were alleged by some as not achieved.

3. **The European Council**（欧洲理事会）: The European Council refers to the regular meetings of the heads of state or of government in the European Union. It comprises the

heads of state or government of EU member states, along with its President and the President of the Commission. The High Representative takes part in its meetings, which are chaired by its President: currently Herman Van Rompuy.

4. **Roemer**（Buddy Roemer）：Roemer is an American politician who served as the 52nd Governor of Louisiana, from 1988 to 1992. He was elected as a Democrat but switched to the Republican Party on March 11, 1991. Prior to serving as Governor, he was a member of the United States House of Representatives from 1981 to 1988.

New words and expressions

1. sustainable [sə'steinəbl]   *adj.* 可以忍受的；足可支撑的；养得起的
2. cohesion [kəu'hi:ʒən]   *n.* 凝聚；结合
3. upsurge ['ʌpsə:dʒ]   *n.* 高潮，高涨
                      vi. 涌起，高涨
4. in terms of   依据；按照；在……方面；以……措词
5. wellbeing   *n.* 幸福；福利；安乐
6. trade-off ['treidɔf]   *n.* 交换，交易；权衡；协定
7. elusive [i'lju:siv]   *adj.* 难懂的；易忘的；逃避的；难捉摸的
8. variant ['vɛəriənt]   *adj.* 不同的；多样的
9. calculus ['kælkjuləs]   *n.* 微积分学
10. aggregate ['æɡriɡət]   *adj.* 聚合的；集合的；合计的
11. couple with   与……相结合，伴随
12. ample ['æmpl]   *adj.* 丰富的；足够的；宽敞的
13. monetary ['mʌnitəri]   *adj.* 货币的；财政的
14. hinge on   以……为转移，靠……转动
15. noteworthy ['nəut,wə:ði]   *adj.* 值得注意的；显著的
16. evade [i'veid]   *vt.* 逃避；规避；逃脱
17. complementary [,kɔmpli'mentəri]   *adj.* 补足的，补充的
18. detriment ['detrimənt]   *n.* 损害；伤害
19. straightforward [,streit'fɔ:wəd]   *adj.* 简单的；坦率的；明确的；径直的
20. warrant ['wɔrənt]   *vt.* 保证；担保；批准；辩解

Unit 5 Educational Justice 教育公平

I Choose the correct letter A, B, C, or D.

1. The goal of _____ is to become the most competitive and dynamic knowledge-based economy in the world, capable of sustainable economic growth with more and better jobs and greater social cohesion.
   A. European Union   B. European Council
   C. Lisbon Strategy   D. European economic advisors

2. Education and training systems that create efficient and equitable outcomes are important for _____.
   A. economic prosperity
   B. jobs
   C. social cohesion
   D. economic prosperity and social cohesion

3. The research in the economics of education shows that the monetary and non-monetary prosperity of individuals and nations hinges on _____.
   A. education   B. training
   C. job   D. education and training

4. According to the writer, efficient education and training systems can create _____, and equitable systems can create _____.
   A. economic growth; social cohesion
   B. social cohesion; economic growth
   C. economic growth; earnings
   D. earnings and employability; social cohesion

5. Achieving more equity in the design of education systems may help to _____ the need for intense re-distributive policies at later ages.
   A. increase   B. get out of   C. admit   D. face with

6. The following sentences can show that the relationship between efficiency and equity in education and training systems may take different forms except _____.
   A. Some policies may bring education and training systems closer to efficiency without having any impact on equity
   B. Some policies may show that efficiency and equity may be dependent of each other

C. Some policies may be equitable without influencing on efficiency

D. Some policies may advance both efficiency and equity in a complementary way

7. Which statement is not true according to Roemer?
   A. Inequality should be tolerated only if it is due to differences in effort.
   B. Inequality should not be tolerated if it is due to circumstances which are beyond a person's control.
   C. Equity would demand that a person's expected educational outcome should be a function of her effort and circumstances.
   D. The concept of efficiency is much simpler.

8. What is the central idea of Roemer's concept of equality of opportunity?
   A. Inequality should be tolerated only if it is due to differences in effort, but not if it is due to circumstances which are beyond a person's control.
   B. Equity would demand that a person's expected educational outcome should be a function only of her effort, but not of her circumstances, such as race, gender, or family background.
   C. The concept of efficiency is much more straightforward, representing a situation where a maximum aggregate outcome of the educational production process is obtained with given input or a given aggregate outcome with minimum input.
   D. An efficient situation is one which would be preferred by any individual who is ignorant of her position in society.

9. What is the meaning of "elusive" in the 6th paragraph?
   A. difficult to find   B. difficult to achieve
   C. difficult to see   D. difficult to describe

10. Which is not the meaning of "warrant" in the last paragraph?
    A. guarantee   B. provide   C. assure   D. confirm

II Vocabulary.

Fill in the blanks with the most suitable words. Change the form when necessary.

| equitable | ample | evade | warrant | upsurge |
| variant | elusive | boost | assess | straightforward |

1. The meaning of the poem was somewhat _____.
2. You will have _____ opportunity to state your case later.
3. There has been an _____ in complaints about the police.

4. Gorky said, "Time is the most _____ judge."
5. There are wide regional _____ in house prices.
6. You cannot go on _____ your responsibilities forever.
7. The system itself is perfectly _____.
8. The advertising campaign is intended to _____ sales.
9. The Company shall use its best endeavors to provide accurate information but shall not _____ the accuracy thereof.
10. It is difficult to _____ the effects of the new legislation just yet.

III Comprehension of the text.

Decide whether the following statements are true (T) or false (F) according to the passage.

1. European Union heads of state could agree on the goal of the so-called "Lisbon Strategy". ( )
2. Given the effects of education on social cohesion, the distribution of education is crucial for societal inequality. ( )
3. For all the European politicians, education and training are high on the policy agenda. ( )
4. There are many accepted definitions of equity so that most people could not agree to the concept proposed by Roemer. ( )
5. In the calculus of applied welfare economics, equity and efficiency goals can be combined by maximizing welfare functions. ( )

▶▶ Useful phrases and expressions ◀◀◀◀◀

学费减免 tuition reduction or exemption
国家助学贷款 national student loans
公费教育 government-paid education
国家奖学金 national scholarship
高质量教育体系 high-quality education system
"双减"（减轻义务教育阶段学生作业负担和校外培训负担） ease the burden of excessive homework and off-campus tutoring for students undergoing compulsory education
应试教育 exam-oriented education
优师计划 targeted teacher training plan
义务教育质量评价 evaluation of compulsory education quality

为党育人、为国育才 cultivate talent for the Party and the State

We developed more equitable and higher-quality education. Education is pivotal to the enduring prosperity of a country.

促进教育公平和质量提升。百年大计，教育为本。

We will promote high-quality, well-balanced development and urban-rural integration of compulsory education. We will allocate educational resources according to the size of residential population, see that school-age children can enroll in nearby schools, and ensure that all children of rural migrant workers in cities have access to education.

推动义务教育优质均衡发展和城乡一体化，依据常住人口规模配置教育资源，保障适龄儿童就近入学，解决好进城务工人员子女就学问题。

Primary and middle school teachers in Beijing's public school system will be required to take part in rotation programs to further improve education equity and quality in the city.

北京市公办中小学教师都将参加轮岗项目，促进教育优质均衡。

We should stick to the socialist orientation in running schools, the non-profit nature of education and developing education that the people are satisfied with.

坚持社会主义办学方向，坚持教育公益性原则，办好人民满意的教育。

We has set up a financial assistance system covering all students from disadvantaged backgrounds at all levels of education

国家已经建立了覆盖各教育阶段、各级各类学校、所有家庭经济困难学生的资助政策体系。

The right to education is guaranteed. Investment in education has grown substantially; conditions and standards in schools have greatly improved; rural education has been strengthened, and major strides have been made in ensuring equal access to education. Free compulsory education is available across the country.

国民受教育权利得到保障。教育投入大幅增长，办学条件显著改善，办学水平不断提高，农村教育得到加强，教育公平迈出重大步伐。全国实行免费义务教育。

The unique advantages of MOOCs and online education have been leveraged to promote educational equity and sharing of quality educational resources so that everyone can learn whenever and wherever they want.

慕课和在线教育的独特优势得以充分利用来推动教育公平及优质教育资源共享，实现人人皆学、处处能学、时时可学。

The completion rate of nine-year compulsory education is expected to reach 95 percent by the end of 2020, the guideline said, calling for ongoing efforts to make sure children from impoverished families have access to compulsory education.

意见提出，贫困家庭义务教育阶段适龄儿童少年不失学辍学，确保2020年全国九年义务教育巩固率达到95%。

The nation and the people's future hinges on the youth's healthy growth, the Chinese Communist Youth League (CCYL) organizations should better promote the program and offer more assistance to the young generation in the new era.

让青少年健康成长，是国家和民族的未来所系。进入新时代，共青团要把希望工程这项事业办得更好，努力为青少年提供新助力、播种新希望。

China's northwestern region lags behind in development due to natural conditions, Xi said, noting that although development conditions vary from region to region, there should be no difference in equality of opportunity. To solve this problem, it is essential to develop education, especially vocational education, Xi Jinping said.

习近平强调，西北地区因自然条件限制，发展相对落后。区域之间发展条件有差异，但在机会公平上不能有差别。要解决这个问题，关键是要发展教育，特别是职业教育。

Unit 6 Educator & Educational Thoughts
教育家与教育思想

Text A   Disciples of Confucius

导读：孔子是我国古代伟大的思想家和教育家，儒家学派创始人，世界最著名的文化名人之一。孔子首次提出"有教无类"，认为世界上一切人都享有受教育的权利。他认为教师在教书育人的过程中应该"诲人不倦"，"循循善诱"，"因材施教"；认为学生应该有好的学习方法如"举一反三""温故而知新"；学习还要结合思考"学而不思则罔，思而不学则殆"；好学"三人行必有我师"；学习态度要端正。孔子的教育思想，至今仍然有重要的启发和教育意义。

Confucius's teachings were later turned into an elaborate set of rules and practices by his numerous disciples and followers who organized his teachings into the Analects. Confucius' disciples and his only grandson, Zisi, continued his philosophical school after his death. These efforts spread Confucian ideals to students who then became officials in many of the royal courts in China, thereby giving Confucianism the first wide-scale test of its dogma.

Two of Confucius's most famous later followers emphasized radically different aspects of his teachings. In the centuries after his death, Mencius and Xunzi（荀子）both composed important teachings elaborating in different ways on the fundamental ideas associated with Confucius. Mencius articulated the innate goodness in human beings as a source of the ethical intuitions that guide people towards rén, yì, and lǐ, while Xunzi underscored the realistic and materialistic aspects of Confucian thought, stressing that morality was inculcated in society through tradition and in individuals through training. In time, their writings, together with the

Analects and other core texts came to constitute the philosophical corpus of Confucianism.

This realignment in Confucian thought was parallel to the development of Legalism, which saw filial piety as self-interest and not a useful tool for a ruler to create an effective state. A disagreement between these two political philosophies came to a head in 223 BC when the Qin state conquered all of China. Li Ssu, Prime Minister of the Qin Dynasty convinced Qin Shi Huang to abandon the Confucians' recommendation of awarding fiefs akin to the Zhou Dynasty before them which he saw as counter to the Legalist idea of centralizing the state around the ruler. When the Confucian advisers pressed their point, Li Ssu had many Confucian scholars killed and their books burned—considered a huge blow to the philosophy and Chinese scholarship.

Under the succeeding Han Dynasty and Tang Dynasty, Confucian ideas gained even more widespread prominence. During the Song Dynasty, the scholar Zhu Xi (AD 1130-1200) added ideas from Daoism and Buddhism into Confucianism. In his life, Zhu Xi was largely ignored, but not long after his death his ideas became the new orthodox view of what Confucian texts actually meant. Modern historians view Zhu Xi as having created something rather different, and call his way of thinking Neo-Confucianism. Neo-Confucianism held sway in China, Korea, and Vietnam until the 19th century.

The works of Confucius were translated into European languages through the agency of Jesuit scholars stationed in China. Matteo Ricci started to report on the thoughts of Confucius, and father Prospero Intorcetta published the life and works of Confucius in Latin in 1687. It is thought that such works had considerable importance on European thinkers of the period, particularly among the Deists and other philosophical groups of the Enlightenment who were interested by the integration of the system of morality of Confucius into Western civilization.

In the modern era Confucian movements, such as New Confucianism, still exist but during the Cultural Revolution, Confucianism was frequently attacked by leading figures in the Communist Party of China. This was partially a continuation of the condemnations of Confucianism by intellectuals and activists in the early 20th Century as a cause of the ethnocentric close-mindedness and refusal of the Qing Dynasty to modernize that led to the tragedies that befell China in the 19th Century. In modern times, Asteroid 7853, "Confucius", was named after the Chinese thinker.

1. **Mencius**（孟子）: Mencius, also known by his birth name Meng Ke or Ko, was born in the State of Zou. He was a Chinese philosopher who was arguably the most famous Confucian after Confucius himself.

2. **Legalism**（法家）: Legalism is a classical Chinese philosophy that emphasizes the need for order above all other human concerns.

3. **Matteo Ricci**（利玛窦）: Matteo Ricci was an Italian Jesuit priest, and one of the founding figures of the Jesuit China Mission, as it existed in the 17th-18th centuries. His current title was Servant of God.

4. **Li Ssu**（李斯）: Li Ssu was the influential Prime Minister of the feudal state and later of the dynasty of Qin, between 246 BC and 208 BC. A famous Legalist, he was also a notable calligrapher. Li Ssu served under two rulers: Qin Shi Huang, king of Qin and later First Emperor of China—and his son, Qin Er Shi. A powerful minister, he was central to the state's policies, including those on military conquest, draconian centralization of state control, standardization of weights, measures and the written script, and persecution of Confucianism and opponents of Legalism. His methods of administration of China are seen by some as being an early form of totalitarianism.

5. **Zhu Xi**（朱熹）: Zhu Xi was a Song Dynasty (960-1279) Confucian scholar who became the leading figure of the School of Principle and the most influential rationalist Neo-Confucian in China. His contribution to Chinese philosophy included his assigning special significance to the Analects of Confucius, the Mencius, the Great Learning, and the Doctrine of the Mean, his emphasis on the investigation of things, and the synthesis of all fundamental Confucian.

6. **The Deists**（自然神论者）: The Deists are a partial list of people who have the belief in a God based on natural religion only, or belief in religious truths discovered by people through a process of reasoning, independent of any revelation through scripture or prophets. They have been selected for their influence on Deism, or for their fame in other areas.

Unit 6　Educator & Educational Thoughts　教育家与教育思想

New words and expressions

1. dogma ['dɔgmə]　　　　　　　n.　教条，教理；武断的意见
2. underscore [ˌʌndə'skɔː]　　　vt.　强调；画线于……下
3. inculcate ['inkʌlkeit]　　　　 vt.　教育；谆谆教诲；教授；反复灌输
4. analects ['ænəlekts]　　　　　n.　文选；论集
5. filial ['filjəl]　　　　　　　　adj.　孝顺的；子女的，当作子女的
6. orthodox ['ɔːθədɔks]　　　　　adj.　正统的；传统的；惯常的
7. deist ['diːist]　　　　　　　　n.　自然神论者；自然神论信仰者
8. condemnation [ˌkɔndem'neiʃən]　n.　谴责；定罪；非难的理由；征用
9. ethnocentric [ˌeθnəu'sentrik]　　adj.　种族优越感的；民族中心主义的
10. realignment [ˌriːə'lainmənt]　　n.　重新排列；重新组合；改组

Exercises

I Choose the correct letter A, B, C, or D.

1. _____ continued his philosophical school after his death.
   A. Confucius' followers
   B. Confucius' followers and his only grandson
   C. Confucius' followers and his disciples
   D. Confucius' disciples and his only grandson

2. _____ who composed important teachings elaborating in different ways on the fundamental ideas associated with Confucius' were two of Confucius' most famous later followers.
   A. Xunzi and Zisi　　　　　　B. Xunzi and Mencius
   C. Mencius and Zisi　　　　　D. Zisi and Zhu Xi

3. _____ convinced Qin Shi Huang to abandon the Confucians' recommendation of awarding fiefs akin.
   A. Li Ssu　　B. Zhu Xi　　C. Legalist　　D. Zisi

4. Which dynasty did not accept Confucian thought?
   A. Han Dynasty　　　　　　　B. Tang Dynasty
   C. Qin Dynasty　　　　　　　D. Song Dynasty

5. _____ started to report on the thoughts of Confucius, and _____ published the life and works of Confucius in Latin in 1687.
   A. Jesuit scholars; Matteo Ricci
   B. Jesuit scholars; Prospero Intorcetta
   C. Prospero Intorcetta; Matteo Ricci
   D. Matteo Ricci; Prospero Intorcetta

II Vocabulary.

Fill in the blanks with the most suitable words. Change the form when necessary.

underscore	inculcate	constitute	conquer	orthodox
dogma	filial	ethnocentric	attack	articulate

1. This is an _____, arrogant attitude.
2. The numbers _____ a trend that has occurred in previous economic downturns.
3. Her staff find her bossy and _____.
4. The _____ Thanksgiving dinner includes turkey and pumpkin pie.
5. The village had been _____ by the French air force.
6. She tries very hard to _____ traditional values into her students.
7. Now I've tried to _____ exactly what I felt to be the truth.
8. The 50 states _____ the USA.
9. Ching Ming Festival is a way that Chinese show _____ piety.
10. The Normans _____ England in 1066.

III Read the text and answer the following questions.

1. What did Xunzi stress according to Confucian thought?
2. What did Li Ssu do to abandon Confucian thought?
3. Whose thought called Neo-Confucianism was famous in China, Korea and Vietnam?
4. How was Confucian thought spread to Europe?
5. What is the main idea of this passage?

Unit 6 Educator & Educational Thoughts 教育家与教育思想

Text B Educational Thought and Teaching

导读： 教育思想是指人们对人类特有的教育活动现象的一种理解和认识，这种理解和认识常常以某种方式加以组织并表达出来，其主旨是对教育实践产生影响。教育思想具有实践性、多样性、历史性、社会性、继承性、可借鉴性、预见性和前瞻性的特征。教育思想有助于人们理智地把握教育现实，使人们依据一定的教育思想从事教育实践；有助于人们认清教育工作中的成绩和弊端，使教育工作更有起色；有助于人们合理地预测未来，勾画教育发展的蓝图。

The oriental world contains the two oldest and if they could be juxtaposed the two basic theories of education. In Indian philosophies we find strong elements of other earthly concentration and contemplation of Heaven. In the teachings of Chinese philosophies there appears an equally strong theme of preparation for life of activity on Earth. Every subsequent theory embodies in some measure man's explorations in these two directions.

The teachings emanating from India were and are a majestic illustration of a whole range of oriental philosophies which regard education as a means through which men can prepare themselves for life, or for the life of the spirit. One of the central heaven-centered conceptions of this education is dharma or duty, the capacity to uphold and support the eternal laws within and without one. Human desires, the quest for satisfaction of material needs, the thirst for fulfillment of the senses, these are the obstacles with which men must contend in their search for eternity. In extreme forms of reflection only the relinquishment of mortal wants can ensure repose and happiness and ultimately salvation. Education thus is a process of inculcating self discipline, so that the mind and the body can be freed from concern for life. To this heavenward aim, other aims are subordinated. Inward-directedness, self-introspection, and contemplation are the ends of schooling.

The teaching coming from China stressed the opposite tradition in education. At its center lies the wholehearted dedication to life and the proprieties of daily living. Men like Confucius do not reject the heritage of divine revelation and the supernatural derivation of the moral order. On the contrary they have often busied themselves with the salvaging and re-edition of sacred Chinese scriptures. But for the Chinese, Heaven is a given quantity, a heritage to be accepted piously and without question. The more immediate concern of man is life. "While you don't know about life, what can you know about death?" For Confucius and his future countless followers, the class of Chinese literati, who through his precepts became the class of officials in China, the virtuous life, decorum in mores and manners, service and responsibility toward others, were the canons of the system. Education was to be completely dedicated to these canons. It thus became a means to inculcate good precepts, and a way to pass on ancient wisdom. Teaching by example, by immersing oneself in the cultural heritage of the age became the model of good living and good pedagogy.

Both the heaven-centered and the earth-centered teachings resulted in practice in systems of formal education in which children were forced to memorize ancient writings by repetition by rote, while older students apprenticed or clustered informally around their teachers. Oriental education allowed much room for mystic or intellectualized approach to living. More practical preparation was less conspicuous or imparted on a family basis. This may be the reason why in the nineteenth and twentieth century the education of Asians was affected by the more practical Western theories, with British type of education in India, French and Dutch intellectual influences on Indonesia, former Soviet influences on China and UNESCO's fundamental education in all underdeveloped regions.

Western educational practices owe a great deal to Plato and Aristotle. The teachings of these two philosophers are best known parts of development of Greek thought and practice in education. The early Greek cosmologists were concerned with the nature of existence and with man's relationship to the universe. On the other hand, concern with the cosmos did not prevent the Greeks from developing a scientific philosophy which arose alongside with the rationalistic conception of man as the center of knowledge. The Greek philosophy recognized that the aim of education is to sensitize man both to the infinity, and to the business of social life on earth. The model to which all educational processes were destined to lead was "man beautiful and virtuous". Greek education remained for all times a model of activity of man as idealistic and thinking, but also rational and political being adjusting himself through reason to social and spiritual levels of life. Plato and Aristotle left provocative social proposals in Republic and Politics respectively, but they also pointed the way to eternal verities, the logos.

Greek thought had a significant impact upon Rome. One of the several outstanding

Roman thinkers, Quintilian concentrated on elaborating a system of education based on oratory as a means to restore the moral virtues. Quintilian emphasized both moral values and "actual practice and experience of life", a natural interest in a nation whose claim to fame lay not only in the powers of intellectual concentration but also in military prowess and administrative skill. Part of Quintilian's tragedy was that he advocated eloquence and republican virtue at the time when it could no longer serve public good, but it could only be used by careerists and sycophants around the imperial throne. His precise pedagogical devices were thus deprived of the vigorous goals, in the service of which they could have been used in an earlier age.

With Aquinas the dichotomy between earth-centered and heaven-centered education loses its overwhelming significance. Several later heaven-centered and mystic schools such as the pietists of Hermann Francke continued to flourish. Several educational theories retain a spiritual and idealistic dimension. But in the broadest sense man surrenders his curiosity and quest of the unknown to the overriding certainty that life on earth must be seriously cultivated.

1. **UNESCO (United Nations Educational, Scientific, and Cultural Organization)** （联合国教科文组织）: UNESCO is a specialized agency of the United Nations established on 16 November 1945. Its stated purpose is to contribute to peace and security by promoting international collaboration through education, science, and culture in order to further universal respect for justice, the rule of law, and the human rights along with fundamental freedoms proclaimed in the UN Charter. It is the heir of the League of Nations' International Commission on Intellectual Cooperation.

2. **Plato** （柏拉图）: Plato was a classical Greek philosopher, mathematician, student of Socrates, writer of philosophical dialogues, and founder of the Academy in Athens, the first institution of higher learning in the Western world. Along with his mentor, Socrates, and his student, Aristotle, Plato helped to lay the foundations of Western philosophy and science.

3. **Aristotle** （亚里士多德）: Aristotle was a Greek philosopher, a student of Plato and teacher of Alexander the Great. His writings cover many subjects, including physics, metaphysics, poetry, theater, music, logic, rhetoric, linguistics, politics, government, ethics, biology, and

zoology. Together with Plato and Socrates, Aristotle is one of the most important founding figures in Western philosophy. Aristotle's writings were the first to create a comprehensive system of Western philosophy, encompassing morality and aesthetics, logic and science, politics and metaphysics.

4. **Thomas Aquinas**（托马斯·阿奎纳）: Thomas Aquinas was an Italian Dominican priest of the Catholic Church, and an immensely influential philosopher and theologian in the tradition of scholasticism, known as Doctor Angelicus, Doctor Communis, or Doctor Universalis. He was the foremost classical proponent of natural theology, and the father of Thomism. His influence on Western thought is considerable, and much of modern philosophy was conceived as a reaction against, or as an agreement with his ideas, particularly in the areas of ethics, natural law and political theory.

New words and expressions

1. juxtapose [ˌdʒʌkstə'pəuz] vt. 并列；并置
2. emanate from v. 发源于；出自；放射
3. majestic [mə'dʒestik] adj. 庄严的；宏伟的
4. dharma ['dɑːmə] n. （佛教中的）达摩（指佛的教法、佛法、一切事物和现象）；（印度教的）法则
5. eternity [i'təːnəti] n. 来世，来生；不朽；永世
6. decorum [di'kɔːrəm] n. 礼仪；礼貌；端正；恪守礼仪
7. pedagogy ['pedəgɔgi] n. 教育；教育学；教授法
8. apprentice [ə'prentis] n. 学徒；生手
   vt. 使……当学徒
   vi. 当学徒
9. cluster ['klʌstə] vi. 群聚；丛生
   vt. 使聚集；聚集在某人的周围
10. conspicuous [kən'spikjuəs] adj. 显著的；显而易见的
11. infinity [in'finəti] n. 无穷；无限大
12. provocative [prəu'vɔkətiv] adj. 刺激的，挑拨的；气人的
13. eloquence ['eləkwəns] n. 口才；雄辩；雄辩术；修辞
14. sycophant ['sikəfənt] n. 谄媚者；奉承者
15. secularism ['sekjulərizəm] n. 世俗主义；现世主义；宗教与教育分离论

Unit 6   Educator & Educational Thoughts   教育家与教育思想

I Choose the correct letter A, B, C, or D.

1. What is the meaning of "juxtapose" in the first paragraph?
   A. to give some examples   B. to put things together
   C. to compare the things   D. to make things different
2. What is the meaning of "illustration" in the second paragraph?
   A. the truth or example   B. a picture
   C. an article   D. a book
3. The teachings emanating from India regard education as _____.
   A. dharma or duty
   B. a process of inculcating self discipline
   C. the life of the spirit
   D. a means through which men can prepare themselves for life, or for the life of the spirit
4. The role of education as a process of inculcating self discipline is _____.
   A. for human desires   B. for the life of the spirit
   C. for human duty   D. for the mind and the body
5. What is not Heaven for the Chinese?
   A. A given quantity.   B. An accepted heritage.
   C. A system.   D. An unquestioned heritage.
6. Teaching by example, by immersing oneself in the cultural heritage of the age became the model of_____.
   A. good living   B. good pedagogy
   C. good spirit   D. good living and good pedagogy
7. Western educational practices owe a great deal to _____.
   A. Plato and Aristotle   B. Plato and Socrates
   C. Alexander and Socrates   D. Alexander and Aristotle
8. Which of the following statements is not true according to Greek thought?
   A. The early Greek cosmologists were concerned with the nature of existence and with man's relationship to the universe.
   B. The concern with the cosmos prevented the Greeks from developing a scientific

philosophy which arose alongside with the rationalistic conception of man as the center of knowledge.

C. The Greek philosophy recognized that the aim of education is to sensitize man both to the infinity, and to the business of social life on earth.

D. Greek education remained for all times a model of activity of man as idealistic and thinking, but also rational and political being adjusting himself through reason to social and spiritual levels of life.

9. Which of the following statements is not true of Quintilian?

  A. He concentrated on elaborating a system of education based on oratory as a means to restore the moral virtues.

  B. His tragedy was that he advocated eloquence and republican virtue at the time when it could no longer serve public good, but it could only be used by careerists and sycophants around the imperial throne.

  C. He emphasized both moral values and actual practice, experience of life and a natural interest in a nation whose claim to fame lay only in the powers of intellectual concentration.

  D. His precise pedagogical devices were deprived of the vigorous goals, in the service of which they could have been used in an earlier age.

10. What is the meaning of "surrender" in the last paragraph?

  A. to stop fighting   B. to give
  C. to control   D. to give up

II Comprehension of the text.

Decide whether the following statements are true (T) or false (F) according to the passage.

1. Human desires, the quest for satisfaction of material needs, the thirst for fulfillment of the senses, these are the obstacles with which men must contend in their search for eternity.   (   )

2. Education became a means to inculcate good precepts, and a way to pass on ancient wisdom.   (   )

3. Both the heaven-centered and the earth-centered teachings resulted in practice in systems of formal education in which children were forced to memorize by writing.
                                                              (   )

4. That more practical preparation was less conspicuous or imparted on a family basis was the reason why the education of Asia was affected.   (   )

5. The teachings of Plato and Aquinas are best known parts of development of Greek

Unit 6　Educator & Educational Thoughts　教育家与教育思想

thought and practice in education.　　　　　　　　　　　　　　　　(　)

III　Translate the following sentences into Chinese.

1. Education is a process of inculcating self discipline, so that the mind and the body can be freed from concern for life.
2. Both the heaven-centered and the earth-centered teachings resulted in practice in systems of formal education in which children were forced to memorize ancient writings by repetition by rote, while older students apprenticed or clustered informally around their teachers.
3. The Greek philosophy recognized that the aim of education is to sensitize man both to the infinity, and to the business of social life on earth.
4. His precise pedagogical devices were thus deprived of the vigorous goals, in the service of which they could have been used in an earlier age.
5. In the broadest sense man surrenders his curiosity and quest of the unknown to the overriding certainty that life on earth must be seriously cultivated.

Useful phrases and expressions

墨家学派　the Mohist school
孔子学院　Confucius Institute
礼乐文化　rites and music culture
礼义廉耻　Courtesy, Justice, Integrity and Sense of Shame
道德修养　moral self-cultivation
道法自然　Tao models itself after nature
慎言敏行　diligent in duties and careful in speech
厚德载物　great virtue promotes growth
修身、齐家、治国、平天下　self-cultivation, a well-managed family, and the ability to administer the state and to bring peace to the nation
孔孟之道　Confucius-Mencius doctrines

In the Spring and Autumn Period, private schools prevailed and many scholars of different schools of thought spread their teaching in this way.
春秋时期私学盛行，许多来自不同学派的学者都以这种方式来传播教学。
It is said that over three thousand disciples followed him, among whom there were 72 sages who went on to broaden the acceptance of the philosophy set out by their master—

Confucianism.

相传孔子门下有三千多名弟子，其中的 72 位圣贤继续传播他们老师的哲学——儒家思想。

By ranking candidates for official positions in this way, the government was able to make a choice of the best people for various posts.

通过以这种方式来划分官职等级，政府能够为不同的职位挑选出最合适的人才。

In Confucianism, the golden mean or the doctrine of the mean was understood as a primary virtue.

在儒家思想中，中庸之道被视为一种基本美德。

According to Confucius, the best teaching method is to make sure instructions are suitable for the student's abilities.

孔子认为最好的教学方法是因材施教。

Confucius once said, "Do not do to others what you do not want others to do to you."

孔子说："己所不欲，勿施于人。"

Building a world-class university with Chinese characteristics would not work by blindly following others or simply copying foreign standards and models. It requires blazing a new path instead.

建设中国特色、世界一流大学不能跟在别人后面依样画葫芦，简单以国外大学作为标准和模式，它需要开辟一条新的道路。

China's higher education should make contributions to the prosperity of the country, the rejuvenation of the Chinese nation and the well-being of the people.

我国高等教育要为服务国家富强、民族复兴、人民幸福贡献力量。

Xi also stressed the important role of graduate education in boosting innovation, catering for economic and social development, as well as modernizing the system and capacity for governance in China.

习近平强调，研究生教育在提高创新能力、服务经济社会发展、推进国家治理体系和治理能力现代化方面具有重要作用。

Graduate education bears the task of boosting innovation and creation and serves as a cornerstone of China's development and social progress.

研究生教育肩负着创新创造的重要使命，是国家发展、社会进步的重要基石。

Unit 7　Educational Objectives
教育目的

Text A　Aims and Objectives of Education

导读：教育的目的是根据一定社会的政治、经济、生产、文化科学技术发展的要求和受教育者身心发展的状况确定的。它反映了一定社会对受教育者的要求，是教育工作的出发点和最终目标，也是确定教育内容、选择教育方法、检查和评价教育效果的根据。目的不明确的教育就像一条无舵的船只。

Introduction

The importance of aims and objectives of education is recognized by all the educational, professional, political, nonpolitical and religious associations, organizations and groups at various levels in their memoranda, letters and brochures. It is said that education without clear cut aims is like a rudderless ship. The following comparisons emphasize this point fully well.

Every pilot has a route-chart and set timing of landing at predetermined destination. There is a constitution or set of principles and traditions through which a country is governed. Similarly, there should be properly defined and declared principles, aims and objectives of education or the basis of which policies and programs of education have to be formulated to achieve the set goals without wasting scarce energies and resources in chasing the wild goose.

It is generally felt that our educational system has not followed the desired aims as a result that it does not produce ideal citizens in the country. It has followed rather a narrow aim of preparing individuals for livelihood, as mentioned in one of the documents received from an organization.

The main reason of failure of educational system is that it basically stands on pre-independence system. The main objective of its products was how to take degree and to earn money and to be careerists without consideration of ethical values and national spirit. It has also been pointed out that it is unreasonable to criticize educational system alone because it is based on the other subsystems accepted by us.

On the one hand, we are developing and cultivating the British given economy, judicial system and system of administration and parliament; and on the other, we are decrying and criticizing the education system which merely fulfills the needs of the British systems that we are propagating.

As pointed out in a memorandum of an association, "the main defect of the old Education policy is that it had completely ignored the Indian culture and the interest of the masses of India and has left them economically too backward and socially too fragmented to articulate their miseries…"

The aims and objectives of education, suggested in the documents, include individual as well as social aids, with emphasis of social transformation aiming at reconstructing society to make it modernized, productive, participative, and value oriented nation committed to its constitutional obligations.

Individual development

Development of an individual—physically, mentally and spiritually is well known as aim of education. Objectives related to this aim of individual development have been expressed in various ways in the memoranda:

Developing physical and mental faculties;

Acquiring the capacities of understanding, appreciation and expression through word and act is the fundamental aim of education;

Aim of education should be to make children self-confident and self-dependent, and to make them strong physically and mentally;

Education is meant to develop every child's character, personality and culture and as much knowledge as the child can assimilate not merely memorize.

The best expression of complete development of an individual and the harmonious development of personality, however, is found in the following paragraph.

The policy should be directed to the aim of enlightenment of head and heart; illumination of consciousness for all-round development of individual personality. Education should enable a human being to attain the greatest possible harmony, internal and external, spiritual and material, for the fullest possible development of human potentialities and capacities.

Social and national development

Social aim of education is equally important because an individual lives in society and has his obligations towards his nation. There is a realization that, "The present education system does not yield required results mainly because it is divorced from the real social content and social goals."

It has, therefore, been suggested that education should be able to discharge its natural functions and must correspond to its structure, goals and content in the interest of national development and social progress. It has also been suggested in this connection that students from young age should be made aware of the social responsibility cast on them.

At the same time, there are certain constitutional commitments, which are intimately related to this aim. We as the citizens of the republic are constitutionally committed to democracy, social justice, equality of opportunity, secularism and above all to a welfare state. It has, therefore, been suggested that, "Educational policy and educational program should clearly reflect these commitments."

The objectives of developing a sense of national identity, unity and patriotism are advocated by many associations. It is pointed out that the national objectives of planning and programs and development with special emphasis on popular participation and the national problems that we face in different fields should be taught at relevant stages.

Individual and social aims of education are not contrary to one another. In fact they are complementary to one another. The following view strikes a balance between individual and social aims of education.

The purpose of education should be the development of the fullest possible capacities and potentialities physical and spiritual of a "total man". It should make a man capable of earning his livelihood reasonably well to enjoy a happy and secure life while making effective contributions to the society and national effort of making India strongly advanced and prosperous.

Social transformation

Education should not merely equip an individual to adjust with society to its customs and conventions, but it should enable him to bring desirable changes in the society. It has been, therefore, suggested that, "Every educational institution from secondary school to university college should be developed to become an agency of change..."

However, it is essential that we should be quite clear about the purpose of change. It is, therefore, natural to ask the question, "Reform and change to achieve what? What type of society we aim at and what type of citizens we wish to produce?" The following ideas give an indication of the kind of changes education is expected to bring about.

Modernization

Modernization of society in terms of scientific and technological advancement is a view which seems to be quite popular. It is thought that education should enable us to move with times and attain excellence in science and technology.

Scientific and technological advances are gaining momentum and conscious efforts are made to incorporate them into the development sectors. This calls for modernization of education in order to make it in conformity with the modern times and to keep pace with the advances in the world.

Modernization, however, is not interpreted and equated with westernization. In fact, lot of emphasis is given to "Indianness" while talking about modernization. One of the suggestions explicitly points out that, our education should integrate and unite the people of India, modernize society while preserving what is authentically Indian in our cultural and spiritual heritage.

The following suggestion beautifully reconciles the twin objectives of modern technical sophistication and the ancient spirituality.

"New education policy of India should be built on the foundation of ancient spirituality and modern culture and technical sophistication. It should develop scientific temper and spirit of enquiry in the students."

Productivity

Some documents have insisted on linking education with productivity and thus making individuals as productive citizens to build a productive society. One of the suggestions, in a memorandum, for example, says, "It should bring about a social transformation, and enhance greater efficiency and productivity in all sectors: agriculture, industry and service." It is in this context that Mahatma Gandhi's system of basic education is still considered as a basically sound system and a suggestion has been made that with necessary modification elements of basic education may form part of education not only at the primary stage but at all stages in our national system of education. These elements are:

Productive activity in education;

Correlation of the curriculum with productive activity and physical and social environment;

Intimate contact between the school and the local community.

Community participation

In a democracy education without community participation is barren. This aim of education is, therefore, voiced by a number of groups and organizations. The change that is envisaged on this front is that of integrating education with community in all respects. To quote a suggestion in this regard:

The education system in all its branches and sectors should get itself involved in activities related to problems of local community life and shall thus endeavor through the desirable community participation and community involvement in the educational field to bring all education of its rightful place in community life.

Acquisition of values

Moral, cultural and spiritual values in education have been given immense importance in the Memoranda documents. One of the expressions emphatically points out that, "certain basic values as respect for others, responsibility, solidarity, creativity and integrity must be fostered in our children."

It is interesting that a number of specific values have been suggested in the documents. The values which are considered important are mentioned below:

Emphasis should be given in cultivating good qualities like cooperation, good will, forgiveness, tolerance, honesty, patience, etc. in order to encourage universal brother-hood and to prepare students to be worthy citizens of the country;

Values of optimism and secularism, and service to the poor should be stressed on the young minds.

Summing up

It is worth reproducing what a document mentions about the aims of education.

The aim of education is two-fold: development of the individual in society; and consequent development of the society. The aim of education in relation to individual may be spelt out as follows:

To produce full human personality with courage, conviction, vitality, sensitivity and intelligence so that men and women may live in harmony with the universe;

To bring out the fullest potential of child and prepare him for life and its varied situations so that he becomes a cultured and responsible citizen dedicated in the service of community.

In relation to the society, the aim of education is to create:

A sane and learning society where made of material production will be such that no section of the society remains unemployed. In the Indian context such a mode of production will be necessarily based on a decentralized economy utilizing all available manpower;

A society where the conditions of work and general environment will offer psychic satisfactions and effective motivations to its members;

A society reconciling technological and scientific advancement with general well-being and security of its members, enhancing joy of life and eliminating all forms of exploitation.

The broad objective of education should, therefore, be to look beyond the existing society and to develop men and women amenable to the advent of a sane and healthier society of tomorrow.

While summing up, it may be pointed out that various dimensions of individual and social development, social transformation, value acquisition etc. have been well identified in the memoranda documents. The following words briefly summarize the various dimensions which are considered important indeed for marching into the 21st century: We are of the opinion that Indian education should aim at producing men and women of knowledge, character and cultural values and trained skills to achieve excellence in their career and life. Let us make it clear that we wish to prepare youth to march into the 21st century on the ideals of truth and non-violence as shown to us by our great leaders.

1. **Memorandum**（备忘录）：A memorandum or memo is a document or other communication that helps the memory by recording events or observations on a topic, such as may be used in a business office. The plural form is either memoranda or memorandums.

2. **Ethical Value**（伦理价值）：In ethics, value is a property of objects, including physical objects as well as abstract objects (e. g. actions), representing their degree of importance. Ethic value denotes something's degree of importance, with the aim of determining what action or life is best to do or live, or at least attempting to describe the value of different

actions. It may be described as treating actions themselves as abstract objects, putting value to them. It deals with right conduct and good life, in the sense that a highly, or at least relatively highly, valuable action may be regarded as ethically "good" (adjective sense), and an action of low, or at least relatively low, value may be regarded as "bad".

3. **Judicial System**（司法制度）: Judicial system is the system of courts that interprets and applies the law in the name of the state. It also provides a mechanism for the resolution of disputes. Under the doctrine of the separation of powers, it generally does not make law (that is, in a plenary fashion, which is the responsibility of the legislature) or enforce law (which is the responsibility of the executive), but rather interprets law and applies it to the facts of each case.

4. **Social Transformation**（社会转变）: One definition of social transformation is the process by which an individual alters the socially ascribed social status of their parents into a socially achieved status for themselves. However, another definition refers to large scale social change as in cultural reforms or transformations. The first occurs with the individual, the second with the social system.

5. **Modernization**（现代化）: In the social sciences, modernization refers to a model of an evolutionary transition from a "pre-modern" or "traditional" to a "modern" society. The teleology of modernization is described in social evolutionism theories, existing as a template that has been generally followed by societies that have achieved modernity.

New words and expressions

1.	objective [əb'dʒektiv]	adj.	客观的；目标的；宾格的
		n.	目的；目标
2.	association [ə,səusi'eiʃən]	n.	协会，联盟，社团；联合；联想
3.	rudderless ['rʌdəlis]	adj.	无舵的；无指导者的
4.	chase [tʃeis]	vt.	追逐；追捕；试图赢得
		vi.	追逐；追赶；奔跑
5.	propagate ['prɔpəgeit]	vt.	传播；传送；繁殖；宣传
		vi.	繁殖；增殖
6.	fragment ['frægmənt]	n.	碎片；片段或不完整部分
		vt.	使成碎片
		vi.	破碎或裂开

7. assimilate [ə'simileit]	vt.	吸收；使同化；把……比作；使相似	
	vi.	吸收；同化	
8. enlightenment [in'laitənmənt]	n.	启迪；启蒙运动；教化	
9. external [ik'stə:nəl]	adj.	外部的；表面的；[药] 外用的；外国的；外面的	
10. discharge [dis'tʃɑ:dʒ]	vt.	解雇；卸下；放出；免除	
	vi.	排放；卸货；流出	
	n.	排放；卸货；解雇	
11. intimately ['intimitli]	adv.	熟悉地；亲切地；私下地	
12. patriotism ['pætriətizəm]	n.	爱国主义；爱国心，爱国精神	
13. relevant ['reləvənt]	adj.	有关的；中肯的；有重大作用的	
14. prosperous ['prɔspərəs]	adj.	繁荣的；兴旺的	
15. convention [kən'venʃən]	n.	大会；[法] 惯例；[计] 约定；[法] 协定；习俗	
16. desirable [di'zaiərəbl]	adj.	令人满意的；值得要的	
	n.	合意的人或事物	
17. essential [i'senʃəl]	adj.	基本的；必要的；本质的	
	n.	本质；要素；要点；必需品	
18. indication [ˌindi'keiʃən]	n.	指示，指出；迹象；象征	
19. incorporate [in'kɔ:pəreit]	vt.	包含，吸收；体现；把……合并	
	vi.	合并；混合；组成公司	
	adj.	合并的；一体化的；组成公司的	
20. equate [i'kweit]	vt.	使相等；视为平等；	
	vi.	等同	
21. heritage ['heritidʒ]	n.	遗产；传统；继承物；继承权	
22. sophistication [səˌfisti'keiʃən]	n.	复杂；诡辩；老于世故；有教养	
23. barren ['bærən]	adj.	贫瘠的；不生育的；无益的；沉闷无趣的；空洞的	
	n.	荒地	
24. envisage [in'vizidʒ]	vt.	正视，面对；想象	
25. acquisition [ˌækwi'ziʃən]	n.	获得物，获得	
26. sane [sein]	adj.	健全的；理智的；[临床] 神志正常的	
27. decentralized [ˌdi:'sentrəlaizd]	adj.	分散的；分散化，分散式；分散管	

			理的；去中心化
28. reconcile ['rekənsail]		vt.	使一致；使和解；调停，调解；使顺从
29. amenable [ə'mi:nəbl]		adj.	有责任的，应服从的；有义务的；经得起检验的
30. dimension [di'menʃən]		n.	［数］维；尺寸；次元；容积
		vt.	标出尺寸
		adj.	规格的

I Vocabulary.

Match the word in Column A to the correct definition in Column B.

Column A
1. objective   2. relevant
3. convention   4. reconcile
5. in a close manner

Column B
A. having a bearing on or connection with the subject at issue
B. be attained
C. way of approaching sb. /sth.
D. something regarded as a normative example
E. bring into consonance or accord

II Comprehension of the text.

Decide whether the following statements are true (T) or false (F) according to the passage.

1. Our educational system has followed the desired aims and it produces ideal citizens in the country.
2. The aims and objectives of education, suggested in the documents, include individual

as well as social aids.

3. Individual and social aims of education are contrary to one another and are complementary to one another.
4. Education should not merely equip an individual to adjust with society to its customs and conventions, but it should enable him to bring desirable changes in the society.
5. Modernization is actually interpreted and equated with westernization.

III Try to fill in the spaces with the suitable words.

1. The main reason for failure of educational system is that it basically stands on _____.
2. Acquiring the capacities of understanding, appreciation and _____ is the fundamental aim of education.
3. The present education system does not yield required results mainly because it is divorced from the real _____.
4. Values of _____, and service to the poor should be stressed on the young minds.
5. The aim of education is two-fold: development of _____ and consequent development of _____.

Text B Education, Basics of Education and Educational Objectives

导读：教育是培养新生一代准备从事社会生活的整个过程，也是人类社会生产经验得以继承发扬的关键环节。20世纪50年代，布卢姆等人提出将教学活动所要实现的整体目标分为三大领域——认知领域、情感领域和动作技能领域。他们的教育目标分类强调指导教学过程和对结果进行评价，其实是一种教学目标分类。

Definition of education

Education can be defined as a continuous process that aims at bringing about desirable changes in the behaviour of learners on a relatively permanent basis and which are evident by way of acquisition of knowledge, proficiency of skills and development of values.

History of taxonomy of educational objectives

For a long time, organised educational system is facing difficulties with student evaluation. A group of educational psychologists took up the challenge of infusing transparency in teaching and evaluation. Thus, at the convention of American Psychological Association in 1948, a group of teachers decided to adapt the model of taxonomy used in biology for educational practices. They described this classification Taxonomy of Educational Objectives.

Their findings were published in the book—*Taxonomy of Educational Objectives: The Classification of Educational Goals, Handbook* 1: *Cognitive Domain* in the year 1956. This group of psychologists identified that most of educational objectives can be grouped under three headings—cognitive, affective and psychomotor. The cognitive domain, according to this book includes such educational objectives as dealing with recall or recognition of knowledge and development of intellectual abilities and skills. The educational objectives in affective domain are concerned with "changes in the interest, attitudes and values, and the development of appreciations and adequate adjustments". The educational objectives belonging to psychomotor domain refer to "the manipulative or motor skill area".

Further, this book explained the various levels of cognitive domain. The hierarchy of objectives in affective domain was explained in *Taxonomy of Educational Objectives: The Classification of Educational Goals, Handbook* 2: *Affective Domain* that was published in the year 1964.

This group did not explore the hierarchy of educational objectives in psychomotor domain. Many others attempted to develop this hierarchy and in the year 1972, Elizabeth Simpson presented the levels of objectives in psychomotor domain. The taxonomy marked an important milestone in the field of higher education. Since learners in higher education are adults, and seek reasons and purpose for their learning, educational objectives and their hierarchy provide a useful benchmark.

Aims and objectives

Definition of aim

Aim can be defined as a broad statement of educational activity, e. g. , to understand disease. It describes what one intends to achieve at the end of an educational activity.

Definition of objective

Objective is a precise point in the direction of aim, e. g. identifying uncommon symptoms. It can be defined as a statement of intent in an educational context. Other terms that are synonymous with educational objectives are—teaching objectives, learning objectives, intended learning objectives, enabling objectives, instructional objectives, curriculum objectives, terminal objectives, operational objectives, performance objectives, outcomes, competencies, etc. Of these, the terms performance objectives and competencies refer more specifically to objectives in psychomotor domain.

Educational objective can be defined as a statement of intent in an educational context, which is demonstrable and measurable on predetermined parameters. Thus, educational objective is a statement that clarifies the complete range of activity and expected performance outcomes.

Functions of objectives

Purpose for teaching

- Direction to teaching
- Teaching made easy
- Structure for teaching

The sequencing of objectives not only makes it easy to teach, but also provides a comprehensive structure to teaching.

- Layers of educational objectives—core, intermediate, peripheral

Educational objectives determine learning contents. Because educational objectives determine what has to be learnt, it becomes necessary to know how much has to be taught/learnt. This classification of learning is made under three headings—must know, desirable to know and nice to know. This classification is equally applicable to each of the three domains of learning. The "must know" segment consists of educational objectives that represent the core competences of the discipline. The learner must acquire the knowledge, skill and attitude listed in this category, if he/she has to be certified as competent/successful. These comprise of 70% of the total statements of educational objectives in the discipline. The other category is "desirable to know", which constitutes 20% of educational objectives. This includes statements, which are not core competences, but something beyond it. These objectives complement the core competences and may become core objectives in higher levels of learning. "Nice to know" consists of objectives that are of "general knowledge" interest. The significance of must know category is to ensure that the student passing out with a health sciences degree must have the basic and necessary competences to practice and provide health services competently and comprehensively. The purpose of including desirable and nice to know components is to differentiate the exceptional learner from the average ones for awarding grades in certifying exams.

• Levels of educational objectives—institutional, departmental and specific learning

Educational objectives can also be classified at three different levels. The statements in this classification are more in the form of goals than objectives, as explained earlier to differentiate goal/aim and objectives.

The most broad and general form of goals are said to be institutional or course goals. These list the competences that a graduate has to acquire at the end of the course of study. These are mainly drawn from the national health policy and the strengths of the health sciences discipline for which the course is being prepared. While listing these goals, not only the current health needs, but also the future needs of the community have to be kept in mind, so that the course does not become obsolete and lose its relevance to society.

Departmental goals refer to the statements made for the subject/department in the context of the course. For example, anatomy is taught for various health science disciplines like medicine/dentistry, nursing, physiotherapy, etc. But the teaching of anatomy in each of these disciplines is determined by the course goals. There are situations, where goals of two or more departments within a course may overlap or complement each other. For example, the departments of Community Medicine and Paediatrics may share the goal for immunisation. Or the departments of Community Medicine and OBG may share the goals for Family Planning. Speaking of the homeopathic course, the departments of Community Medicine and Homeopathic Philosophy may share the goals of prevention of epidemics. The statements, which express these shared goals, are known as interdepartmental goals. These are at the same level as departmental goals.

Specific learning goals are the same as instructional objectives. These are the specific statements, which are written for each departmental goal. These explain the precise and specific performance that is expected of the learner in the department at the end of a specified educational activity.

SLOs or Educational Objectives as they are more conventionally known are explained in three different domains—cognitive, affective and psychomotor. The significance of knowing domains of learning is the possibility to plan the educational activity in an accountable manner. Such a planned educational activity provides space to think, understand and justify teaching/learning. In the absence of planning, the entire exercise may become vague, opinion based and dogmatic. As the saying goes, "If you fail to plan, you plan to fail."

Domains of education

Educational activity is broadly classified into three domains—cognitive, affective or psychomotor, depending on the type of intended learning objectives—whether it is acquisition of knowledge, development of attitude or proficiency of skill.

- Cognitive domain is about learning the behaviours that involve thinking, understanding or explaining. It ranges from simple recalling of facts to implementation and justification of ideas and concepts.
- Affective domain includes the learning behaviour that involves demonstration of feelings/values towards facts or concepts. It ranges from receptivity for people or events to automated empathy for them.
- Psychomotor domain includes all the skill-based performances like eye-hand/foot coordination.

Characteristics of educational objectives

Relevant—It is already noted that while stating educational objectives we have to keep in mind the national health needs. Any effort made towards realising such health needs adds relevance. It can therefore be said that relevance of educational objectives depends on the extent to which these statements conform to the national health needs. Relevance of educational objectives is a three tier process—first determine course goals, second the departmental ones and finally the specific learning goals. Thus, educational objectives that are written can be said to be relevant.

Valid—It is the degree to which the statement conforms to the domain to which it belongs.

Clear—The words must be precise and sentences clear. The idea is that message has to reach "clear and correct". There should be no room for confusion, misinterpretation or vagueness. The major ingredient of any educational objectives statement is an active verb. The entire statement revolves around explanation for the verb, which must be clear and unambiguous.

Feasible—The statement has to tell what is possible to do, both in terms of human capacity and resources/infrastructure available.

Observable—The very definition of learning is change in learner behaviour. Thus, to know whether learning has taken place, it is necessary to observe the changes that have taken place. Therefore, educational objectives have to be stated in terms that are observable.

Measurable—Measurability does not mean that learning has always to be quantitative. But to know whether learning has taken place, one has to measure the extent of change. Learning a skill could be qualitative, but the time taken to perform the skill before and after a learning session could be used as a benchmark to measure qualitative change.

Elements of educational objectives

Act—What the learner will be able "to do" at the end of a learning session. This could be in any of the three domains. Depending on the domain, the appropriate verb has to be identified to state the act.

Content—It is the performance that learner is expected to demonstrate.

Condition—The conditions under which the performance is done. It includes the enabling and restraining factors. It also denotes the range of manoeuvrability.

Act, Content and Condition together constitute the Task.

Criterion—This is the degree of freedom allowed for performance.

1. **American Psychological Association**（美国心理学协会）：The American Psychological Association (abbreviated APA) is the largest scientific and professional organization of psychologists in the United States. It is the world's largest association of psychologists with around 150,000 members including scientists, educators, clinicians, consultants and students. The APA has an annual budget of around $115m.

2. **Elizabeth Simpson**（伊丽莎白·辛普森）：Elizabeth Inchbald (née Simpson)（1753-1821）was an English novelist, actress, and dramatist.

3. **OBG**（牛津商业集团）：Oxford Business Group

4. **SLO**（学生学习成果）：Student Learning Outcome

New words and expressions

1. proficiency [prəu'fiʃənsi]   n.   精通，熟练
2. taxonomy ['tæk'sɔnəmi]   n.   分类学；分类法
3. psychologist [psai'kɔlədʒist]   n.   心理学家，心理学者
4. transparency [træns'pærənsi]   n.   透明，透明度；幻灯片；有图案的玻璃
5. cognitive ['kɔgnitiv]   adj.   认知的，认识的
6. psychomotor [,psaikə'məutə]   adj.   精神运动的
7. domain [dəu'mein]   n.   领域；域名；产业；地产
8. adequate ['ædikwit]   adj.   充足的；适当的；胜任的
9. hierarchy ['haiə,rɑːki]   n.   层级；等级制度
10. milestone ['mailstəun]   n.   里程碑，划时代的事件
11. symptom ['simptəm]   n.   [临床]症状；征兆
12. synonymous [si'nɔniməs]   adj.   同义的；同义词的；同义突变的
13. parameter [pə'ræmitə]   n.   参数；系数；参量
14. peripheral [pə'rifərəl]   adj.   外围的；次要的
15. segment ['segmənt]   vi.   分割
    n.   段；部分
    vt.   分割
16. competence ['kɔmpitəns]   n.   能力，胜任；权限；作证能力；足以过舒适生活的收入
17. obsolete ['ɔbsəliːt]   adj.   废弃的；老式的
    n.   废词；陈腐的人
    vt.   淘汰；废弃
18. anatomy [ə'nætəmi]   n.   解剖；解剖学；剖析；骨骼
19. physiotherapy [,fiziəu'θerəpi]   n.   物理疗法
20. overlap [,əuvə'læp]   n.   重叠；重复
    vi.   部分重叠；部分的同时发生
    vt.   与……重叠；与……同时发生
21. immunization [,imjuːnai'zeiʃən]   n.   免疫
22. homeopathic [,həumiə'pæθik]   adj.   顺势疗法的；同种疗法的
23. vague [veig]   adj.   模糊的；含糊的；不明确的；暧昧的
24. empathy ['empəθi]   n.   神入；移情作用

Unit 7   Educational Objectives   教育目的

25. tier [tiə]	n.	层，排；行，列；等级
	vt.	使层叠
	vi.	成递升排列
26. misinterpretation ['misin,tə:pri'teiʃən]	n.	误解；误释
27. unambiguous [,ʌnæm'bigjuəs]	adj.	不含糊的；清楚的；明白的
28. quantitative ['kwɔntitətiv]	adj.	定量的；量的，数量的
29. benchmark ['bentʃmɑ:k]	n.	基准；标准检查程序
	vt.	用基准问题测试（计算机系统等）
30. manoeuvrability [mə,nu:vrə'biləti]	n.	机动性；可移动；操纵的灵敏性

I Vocabulary.

Match the word in Column A to the correct definition in Column B.

Column A
1. proficiency   2. cognitive
3. adequate   4. synonymous
5. vague

Column B
A. of or being or relating to or involving cognition
B. the quality of having great facility and competence
C. not clearly understood or expressed
D. enough to meet a purpose
E. (of words) meaning the same or nearly the same

II Comprehension of the text.

Decide whether the following statements are true (T) or false (F) according to the passage.

1. This group explored the hierarchy of educational objectives in psychomotor domain in

the year 1972. ( )
2. Educational objectives determine learning contents. ( )
3. The "must know" segment comprises of 60% of the total statements of educational objectives. ( )
4. Specific learning goals are different from instructional objectives. ( )
5. Any effort made towards realising such health needs adds relevance. It can therefore be said that relevance of educational objectives depends on the extent to which these statements conform to the national health needs. ( )

III Try to fill in the spaces with the suitable words.

1. This group of psychologists identified that most of educational objectives can be grouped under three headings—cognitive, _____.
2. Educational objective can be defined as a statement of intent in an educational context, which is _____ on predetermined parameters.
3. _____ not only makes it easy to teach, but also provides a comprehensive structure to teaching.
4. Educational objectives can also be classified at three different levels. The most broad and general form of goals are said to be _____.
5. SLOs or _____ as they are more conventionally known are explained in three different domains—cognitive, affective and psychomotor.

Useful phrases and expressions

人民满意的教育 education that meets the people's expectations
担当民族复兴大任的时代新人 new generations of talent with strong moral character
扎根中国，融通中外 China-rooted and globally connected
发展中国特色世界先进水平的优质教育 develop world-class education with Chinese characteristics
推动各级教育高水平高质量普及 promote equal access to quality education at all levels
实现基本公共教育服务均等化 achieve universal and equal access to basic public education services
构建服务全民的终身学习体系 build lifelong learning systems for all
加快信息化时代教育变革 accelerate ICT-based education reform
开创教育对外开放新格局 open up education to the outside world
推进教育治理体系和治理能力现代化 modernize the education governance system and

capacity

Education is of critical importance to the future of our country and our Party.
教育是国之大计、党之大计。

Education is essential to meeting people's growing desire for a better life.
教育是满足人民日益增长的美好生活需要。

Education is the cornerstone of national rejuvenation and social progress, and it is a benevolent project that will benefit generations to come. It plays a decisive role in improving the nation's character, promoting the comprehensive development of individuals, enhancing China's creativity and innovative capacity, and realizing the rejuvenation of the Chinese nation.
教育是民族振兴、社会进步的重要基石，是功在当代、利在千秋的德政工程，对提高人民综合素质、促进人的全面发展、增强中华民族创新创造活力、实现中华民族伟大复兴具有决定性意义。

Xi Jinping has emphasized on several occasions the importance of moral education in nurturing new generations of socialist builders who are morally, intellectually, physically, and aesthetically developed with a love for labor.
习近平总书记多次强调要坚持把立德树人作为根本任务，培养德智体美劳全面发展的社会主义建设者和接班人。

What kind of people we should cultivate, how, and for whom—these are the fundamental issues that education must address.
培养什么人、怎样培养人、为谁培养人是教育的根本问题。

When the virtuous are numerous in the state, order will be stable; when the virtuous are few, order will be unstable.
国有贤良之士众，则国家之治厚；贤良之士寡，则国家之治薄。

The People's Republic of China is a socialist country led by the Communist Party of China, which determines that the fundamental task of our education must be nurturing new builders of socialism, or talent who support the leadership of the CPC and the country's socialist system and devote their lives to China's socialist cause.
我国是中国共产党领导的社会主义国家，这就决定了我们的教育必须把培养社会主义建设者作为根本任务，培养一代又一代拥护中国共产党和我国社会主义制度、立志为中国特色社会主义奋斗终身的有用人才。

In 2018, General Secretary Xi emphasized at the meeting with teachers and students of Peking University, "Cultivating the people needed for social development is, to be specific, to train those required for social development, knowledge accumulation, cultural inheritance, national survival, and system functioning."

2018年，习近平总书记在北京大学师生座谈会上强调："培养社会发展所需要的人，说具体了，就是培养社会发展、知识积累、文化传承、国家存续、制度运行所要求的人。"

General Secretary Xi Jinping has unequivocally stated that our education should follow the guidance of Marxism and serve the people, the CPC governance of China, socialism with Chinese characteristics, reform and opening up, and socialist modernization.

习近平总书记鲜明地提出，教育要坚持以马克思主义为指导，坚持为人民服务，为中国共产党治国理政服务，为巩固和发展中国特色社会主义制度服务，为改革开放和社会主义现代化建设服务。

Xi Jinping has emphasized that education in China should train a new generation of capable young people who are well-prepared participants of the socialist cause instead of bystanders or, worse still, opponents and gravediggers.

习近平总书记强调，我国教育要培养的是社会主义建设者和接班人，而不是旁观者，更不是反对派和掘墓人。

Unit 8　Teacher & Student
教师与学生

Text A　The Teacher, the Student and the Classroom

导读：教师是学生在知识海洋中追随的灯塔，帮助学生明确目标，在学生遇到困难时及时地答疑解惑；而学生个人才是学习的主体，他们持有一把独一无二的钥匙，只有通过自身努力才能开启知识宝库和未来成就的大门。教师为学生铺路，学生沿着这条道路驶向目的地。然而，事情并不是这么简单。在学生成长的过程中，他们会遇到许许多多不确定因素诱使他们偏离原先的道路。因此，教师应该不断鼓励学生抵制诱惑，认清方向，奋发向前。

The talk mainly focuses on the job of a teacher in the classroom majoring on the relationship of the two. In the talk the presenter will loosely emphasize the fact that the teacher is the light which the students, living either in total darkness in some instances or in twilight, need to follow if they want to be enlightened. More so, that the student is the sole holder of the key to personal glory and success in school. The teacher paves the way and the student (already containing the fuel got from socio-economical backgrounds) moves along to the set direction. However, it has to be stated that the primary school student has many things that attract him/her off the road. Therefore, the teacher should be close enough to perpetually encourage the student to ignore the attractions and continue on his/her journey.

The road is not easy. We would acknowledge that what attract children are small colorful details hardly noticeable to the adult eyes. Thus the onus is on the teachers to find a way to discover and then channel these attractions to the purpose of learning. The more we find how these minor details such as cartoons, games, jokes, songs, trivial chats etc. can be incorporated in our lessons with attached significance (teaching objective), the more we make the road more attractive to the student. Without this, there is nothing a student will look forward to in school.

Who then is a Good Teacher?

From the above discussion, we could state that a good teacher is an educator or facilitator who leads the learner into the untrodden paths of knowledge. In doing so, the teacher (who in this case is a leader) needs to fulfill certain conditions in relation to whom he/she is leading. The best analog for this situation is to compare a teacher to an army commander in the battlefield:

- Never leave anyone behind—a teacher must be ready to let all the students follow the lesson without any left behind. To concentrate on the fast learners on the expense of the slow coachers is unbecoming of a teacher. One must learn to strike a balance between the slow and the fast in a way that they are not boring to the fast or incomprehensible to the slow;
- Curry the weak/wounded—different lessons have different difficulties thus the teacher must be cautious of those fast or otherwise who might have special problems with the topic. It is absurd to think that clever students would always follow the teacher without problems and also that slow students would always be a step behind. To curry the weak or wounded in this case is to create equilibrium in the flow of knowledge with a concentration on these with difficulty;
- Encourage the discouraged—for one reason or the other, students tend to have their favorite subjects. If yours is not the one a particular student likes, try to find the missing link. A student might be discouraged by the absence of challenges or the level and type of difficulty. (e. g. A science-oriented student might find arts to be very way out of their track and thus might do badly and consequently be discouraged.) The teacher must, therefore, encourage the student and direct them to perceive the subject in question with a different attitude;
- Motivate the lazy—some students might find a particular subject too easy to their ability. In the long run, they tend to be lazy (or spend little time in their work, do their tasks rapidly and carefree) and eventually fall behind or start performing badly. The teacher must use other means possible to motivate them to use the

required amount of concentration in the subject;

- Give hope to the hopeless—some students seem not to absorb the knowledge in particular subjects. They can't get it right. After a couple of tries, they lose all hope and convince themselves that they can't learn that particular subject. Teachers should remember that psychology plays an equal amount of contribution towards anybody's performance and success. From this point of view, the teacher must find all viable means to give hope to the student. One way is to let the student work out simple tasks first (those his/her peers would scorn) and gradually increase the difficulty;

- Criticize less and praise often—some teachers seem to take criticizing and teasing as a hobby. Criticism, a more especially negative one, saps the criticized of all the self-confidence. The student would eventually fear or shudder when responding to even a known question. The contrary is also true, when you praise one for the effort they put in giving a wrong answer, they will confidently and zealously respond next time with greater chances of getting it right;

- Never shout but calmly chasten—a shout sends fear to the body but a calm whisper delivers wisdom to the heart. There are many ways of teaching a child but constant shouting is not one of them. The more one shouts, the more the recipient builds a wall of protection around oneself. This wall would be in form of cold shoulder, deaf ear, ignorance, etc. at the end the teacher might call the student stubborn not knowing that teachers create stubborn students (Stubborn children are not necessarily stubborn students);

- Let everyone be your favorite—it is human nature to have favorites within a given group. However, in a classroom situation, favoritism should only be tolerated in extra-curricular activities. In most cases, good students tend to win favor in the teacher's eyes. In extreme cases, those who are low achievers fall on the sidetrack and are left in darkness even where other activities are concerned. The teacher must treat all students equitably, giving total concern to the deserving;

- Never label—some teachers are in a habit of openly classifying, sub-classifying and categorizing the students. Whilst this should be done in the teacher's report book, the task goes even in the classes such that the students know, and tend to live with it, how the teacher thinks of them. Like in a marathon race, some are slow starters but that does not mean they will remain at the tail. The difference is in the instance where their trainer constantly tells them that they are slow, and if they assimilate it they might take it that any effort to win the race might be a sheer waste of energy. From the teaching experience we can concur that some slow starters sometimes finish first.

The school is the battlefield. The enemy is illiteracy. Everyone needs to have a good start for them to survive in the race for life. If students don't have a good foundation, they are unlikely going to survive by the time they reach middle school. Thus we as teachers must be very careful with how and what we teach. We risk putting the future of the country in jeopardy. It is said, "Lack of education leads to elimination."

A good teacher is known by his/her ability to teach those who are slow or can't learn to learn and be able to apply the learned items in problem solving in their exams or real life. If you teach the able to do what they are able to without difficulties, it is hard to draw a line whether you are a good teacher or not. "A good tradesman is known by the product not by the tool." In fact, one who has the worst tool but up-to-date product is the master of them all.

Primary School Students

Building a foundation is the heaviest task, for it will determine how long a building will last. In education sense, primary school is the construction of the academic world foundation of the children. A carefree constructer (teacher) will cause the children to fall in times of rain and storm. All children (unless gifted) have the ability to benefit equally from the teacher. Thus, a strict yet captivating mode of instruction has to be used as teachers go about their teaching business. At this level, teachers must never consider students as grown-ups who know what they want from school. They should bear in mind that some children are just forced to come to school and thus the last person they would like to meet is a bully for a teacher. Others don't have a slightest clue of what is going on at this stage of life. Yet still others think school is a trick by parents to stop children from playing. Some take school as a drop in centre the community has devised to take care of children while parents are at work. To the rich children school could be an instrument poor people use to gain something, thus they see no reason to be there. The duty is for the teacher to construct a basic foundation on which all these contradicting thoughts are brought to book.

A primary school student is a child. Let's face it: The prime aim of children is "play". To be a teacher of this type of person, one must be very understanding and tolerant. In teacher training programs, there is an emphasis on teachers lowering themselves to the level of their students. It is common knowledge that we learn best when the information comes from a familiar source or one we can easily identify with.

To the primary school student:

Unit 8   Teacher & Student   教师与学生

- Play is the reason they exist—primary school age is a very delicate time for adventure and discovery. They want to explore and learn latest activities and tricks seen on TV, read in books and talk about among peers. All these collectively make up child play. A classroom deprived of these would be to the child a nightmare. What all children would be looking forward to is break time. But if the teacher integrates these in his/her lessons, classroom would be a better place.
- Provoking/irritating others is a sport—students like making others for fun. If the teachers fall for this trap then the students would do everything to make the teacher angry. This requires a teacher to be at the same level with the students, to be able to take charge and enhance learning.
- Disobedience is a standard—there are many reasons which may lead a child to be disobedient. A forceful teacher is one of them. A teacher who wants something to be done in a given way at a given time, without considering the students creative ability is inviting disobedience. To give room for personal creativity allows children to respect yours.
- Being directed is an offence—most children just like adults, don't like to be told what to do. Everyone wants to be seen as being able to think independently. A teacher should lead by example. The tendency of directing is: One shows the way without having to tread.
- Mischief is fun—getting in trouble is one way of being noticed so many children enjoy that. However, a teacher must encourage being noticed through hard work and other worth activities.
- Jokes are entertainment—if a teacher should encourage entertainment then the class will be interesting. An ever-serious teacher is hard to follow because no one would like to be in that state for hours.
- Being lazy is a "virtue"—in management psychology we learn that humans have an innate tendency of not wanting to do work. Therefore, instead of punishing them for their attitude, we must find ways to motivate them. The best ways to curb laziness are, therefore, through reward and motivation.
- Nothing is good enough—for most children at this age (school going age) they don't know what they want in life. They are at the breaking age of discovery and are still discovering themselves. What interests them today might not be tomorrow. What they need most is moderation. Accept them as they are while carefully giving the viable advice.

- Being underestimated is fatal—it is hard without proper assessment to determine what the children are capable of. However, to take thing for granted and make it general that they don't know ABC will be making a grave mistake. This might affect the child's perception of self. If the perception is duly negative, then the child will lose self-confidence and esteem.

We mentioned earlier that the student is the sole holder of the key to success. The question arises: How can someone who doesn't know what life is all about hold the key? The answer to the question lies in the understanding that one can never force a donkey to drink water. In the classroom situation, the teacher should win, through tricks if necessary, the confidence and interest of the students. Children, due to lack of understanding of consequences, are very good at giving deaf ears. They can even decide to "turn off" their minds from the teacher. This could be evident when they are tired or the teacher is "killing" them with boredom and the bell goes, one can see them jump and cheer while, as though planned, dashing to the door.

We should understand that while the teacher holds the key to imparting knowledge, the learner holds the key to receiving the knowledge. The teacher cannot learn on behalf of the student, thus he can never claim the key. Some teachers think they can beat, force or shout lessons into the students. The more they do it, the harder it is for the students to understand. They build numerous rules and rigorous regulations, standards and values for their classes which have little to do with teaching and learning. They use corporal punishments for academic flouting. In doing so, the relationship between the teacher and the students change to "cat and mouse". When the teacher goes away, all the students sigh.

The Classroom

If teachers are commanders and the students are soldiers, then the classroom is the battlefront. (Remember we are shooting down illiteracy not personality.) Unlike where the enemy is external, the teacher like a doctor must see the symptoms and use them to cure the infected person. The teacher must carefully scrutinize each case and find ways to help the victim. He should, however, also bear in mind that each case is unique and must be treated unequally.

Thus the classroom is a treatment area and every teacher must:
- Avoid taking in personal complaints—there is nothing sickening than a teacher who always has a personal problem and seeks sympathy from the students. In the long run the students may consider their teacher as their big baby they need to protect rather than someone they look up to for help.

- Avoid releasing frustrations on the students—we all have our sets of frustrations, but to release these to our innocent children will cause not only a bad relationship but also uncalled for tension between the teacher and the students. This causes a blockage in learning.

- Avoid bringing in home issues—social problems, especially adult related, are not to be taken into the classroom (this we know). Most teachers, however, forget that the teacher's uniform shields them from portraying any social related problems (just as it is unbecoming of the doctor to show that he can too get sick). Though not perfect, a teacher can be well received and respected if they are blemish free.
- Avoid ignoring "simple" behavioral outbursts—the key to controlling a class lies in the way the teacher checks nonsensical behavioral attitudes. In language teaching, these attitudes include those that deal with student's verbal behavior, participation, response etc.
- Never release their anger to the students—there is no room for anger in the classroom. Consider a classroom as a dispensary; it would be absurd for a doctor to be angry at the patients. The students come to school to seek help in their world of knowledge. If they do any unbecoming thing, it is digging a pit to bury another pit if the teacher rages with anger to correct a child.
- Never tease lazy students—negative teasing which sends the child into self pity and sups confidence should be discouraged at all times. Some children don't know things not because they are dull but due to many other factors. A teacher should aim at correcting the child rather than play him or her for a fool. There are honest mistakes which must be taken seriously.
- Tell students that they will definitely fail—even to a nonstarter child, plain straightforward negative talk will send them back into their hole. However, they will be satisfied that at least people understand their situation and that even though they don't do anything about it is still okay.

However, as teachers we should expect students to come in the class with all of the above. The onus again is on the teachers not to castigate the children but to help them get over their many problems including age.

A good teacher always has good results and contributes positively to the general growth of the children and the nation as a whole. The classroom is a place for the dissemination of information and a treatment area for problems. Whether in or outside the four walls a teacher is still a teacher and must as though impelled, curry the classroom tendencies wherever they go. A student is a learner whether within or without the classroom and they address teachers as teachers even in the supermarket. This serves to mean that our classroom is not limited to the four walls but in the abstract sense to the world of teaching and learning. The students are the people that make the profession worthwhile. Without them, all that is called teaching would be useless. Thus to help them learn is the teacher's main objective and to do so with courtesy and dedication.

Verbal Behavior（言语行为）：Verbal behavior is a methodology that is based upon behavioral principles, but combines the functionality and generalization of Floortime.

New words and expressions

1. perpetually [pə'petʃuəli]   adv.   永恒地，持久地
2. onus ['əunəs]   n.   责任，义务；负担
3. channel ['tʃænəl]   vt.   引导，开导；形成河道
    n.   通道；频道；海峡
4. trivial ['triviəl]   adj.   不重要的，琐碎的；琐细的
5. incorporate [in'kɔːpəreit]   vt.   包含，吸收；体现；把……合并
    vi.   合并；混合；组成公司
    adj.   合并的；一体化的；组成公司的
6. analog ['ænəlɔg]   n.   [自]模拟；类似物
    adj.   [自]模拟的；有长短针的
7. equilibrium [ˌiːkwi'libriəm]   n.   均衡；平静；保持平衡的能力
8. viable ['vaiəbl]   adj.   可行的；能养活的；能生育的
9. sap [sæp]   n.   [植]树液；精力，元气；活力；坑道
    vt.   使衰竭，使伤元气；挖掘以破坏基础

Unit 8 Teacher & Student 教师与学生

10. shudder ['ʃʌdə]	n.	发抖；战栗；震动
	vi.	发抖；战栗
11. zealously ['zeləsli]	adv.	热心地，积极地
12. chasten ['tʃeisən]	vt.	惩罚；磨炼；抑制
13. whilst [hwailst]	conj.	同时；时时，有时；当……的时候
14. assimilate [ə'simileit]	vt.	吸收；使同化；把……比作；使相似
	vi.	吸收；同化
15. illiteracy [i'litərəsi]	n.	文盲；无知
16. jeopardy ['dʒepədi]	n.	危险；（被告处于被判罪或受处罚的）危险境地
17. captivating ['kæptiveitiŋ]	adj.	迷人的；有魅力的
	v.	使……着迷（captivate 的 ing 形式）
18. provoke [prəu'vəuk]	vt.	驱使；激怒；煽动；惹起
19. bizarre [bi'zɑ:]	adj.	奇异的（指态度，容貌，款式等）
20. curb [kə:b]	n.	抑制；路边；勒马绳
	vt.	控制；勒住
21. moderation [ˌmɔdə'reiʃən]	n.	适度；节制；温和；缓和
22. rigorous ['rigərəs]	adj.	严格的，严厉的；严密的；严酷的
23. corporal ['kɔ:pərəl]	adj.	肉体的，身体的
	n.	下士
24. scrutinize ['skru:tinaiz]	vi.	细阅；作详细检查
	vt.	详细检查；细看
	n.	仔细或彻底检查
25. unbecoming [ˌʌnbi'kʌmiŋ]	adj.	不适当的，不相称的；不合身的，不得体的
26. blemish ['blemiʃ]	n.	瑕疵；污点；缺点
	vt.	玷污；损害；弄脏
27. nonsensical [nɔn'sensikəl]	adj.	无意义的；荒谬的
28. dispensary [dis'pensəri]	n.	药房；（学校、兵营或工厂的）诊疗所；防治站
29. castigate ['kæstigeit]	vt.	严惩；苛评；矫正；修订
30. courtesy ['kə:tisi]	n.	礼貌；好意；恩惠
	adj.	殷勤的；被承认的；出于礼节的

I Vocabulary.

Fill in the blanks with the most suitable words. Change the form when necessary.

| onus | trivial | shudder | zealously | illiteracy |
| captivating | provoke | blemish | nonsensical | courtesy |

1. The main task of our government is eliminating poverty, disease and _____.
2. It's very annoying and the most _____ business situation I have ever been involved in.
3. I still _____ when I think of that moment.
4. Who could look away from Suzanne Somers' sad but _____ efforts to turn back time?
5. The _____ is on the Government to create the necessary conditions for credible and inclusive elections.
6. Those measures sought to _____ a court challenge of the U. S. Supreme Court's 1973 Roe v.
7. Nevertheless, women of all ages still appreciate this _____.
8. A lawyer should represent a client _____ within the bounds of the law.
9. The extra security precautions are not _____ and affect most communication technology on the market.
10. That is no doubt my fault, and a great _____ in me.

II Comprehension of the text.

Decide whether the following statements are true (T) or false (F) according to the passage.

1. What attract children are small colorful details which are also noticeable to the adult eye.   (   )
2. A teacher must be ready to let most of the students follow the lesson and can leave some students behind.   (   )
3. The school is the battlefield. The enemy is illiteracy. If students don't have a good foundation, they are still likely going to survive by the time they reach middle school.
                                                                                                                                                                (   )
4. Instead of punishing them for their attitude, we must find ways to motivate students.

The best ways to curb laziness are, therefore, through reward and motivation.　　(　　)
5. We should understand that while the teacher holds the key to imparting knowledge, the learner holds the key to receiving the knowledge.　　(　　)

III Try to fill in the spaces with the suitable words.

1. _____ is the sole holder of the key to personal glory and success in school.
2. The teacher should be close enough to perpetually _____ the student to ignore the attractions and continue on his/her journey.
3. From the above discussion, we could state that a good teacher is an educator or _____ who leads the learner into the untrodden paths of knowledge.
4. A student might be discouraged by _____ of challenges or the level and type of difficulty.
5. _____ is the heaviest task, for it will determine how long a building will last.

Text B　Teacher-Student Attachment and Teachers' Attitudes towards Work

导读：无论是在课内还是在课外，教师都被认为是学生学习的榜样。罗丝曾经对教育者在正式或非正式场合所起到的榜样作用进行调查研究，并强调了榜样对群体的某些态度、观点和生活方式的影响；罗丝发现学生通常把教师视为与其父母同等重要的榜样。凯尔认为："不论一个教师教的是哪门学科，他都在孩子的教育过程中起到榜样的作用。教师应该为人正直，不赌博，不酗酒，不做荒淫的勾当，不与不道德的人为伍。"

Introduction

Teachers are expected to be positive role models for their students, both inside and outside the classroom. The role of educators as role models in formal and informal education has been examined. The role models can expose groups to specific attitudes, lifestyles and outlooks. Children often see teachers as important role models on a par with parents. Teachers, regardless of subject area, have a moral role to play in education. It is the teachers' duty to be socially acceptable by keeping themselves morally upright, refraining from gambling, abhorring drunkenness and other excesses, and avoiding immoral relations.

Teachers' actions could actually have some lasting negative effects on students. Unfortunately, on top of that, it is reported that researchers often tend to overlook teachers as a potential source of problems in the classroom. Compared to the large body of literature that focuses on positive teacher communication behaviors, fewer studies have been done on negative teacher communication behaviors. Concurrently, educational reform tends to focus only on curricula, neglecting the importance of effective teacher-student interaction. Teacher support can be conceptualized similarly to social support in schools, which is strongly related to a student's psychological well-being (acceptance, care, encouragement and approval from others) and may improve students' self-esteem and self-evaluation. On the other hand, it was asserted that lack of teacher support would hinder students from developing a positive self-concept.

Despite all these compelling reasons to study teachers' behavior, researching negative teacher-student interactions is often considered a taboo, which can make study in this area difficult. Besides, it is ironic to study a teacher's mistakes or faulty education when their primary aim is to be educational agents. Unfortunately, studying the characteristics of effective teachers will not give us all the elements necessary to understand teachers' misbehavior. However, it might give us a better understanding and provide a discussion frame for such problems in order to improve teacher training programs. In this paper, we examine the relationship of teacher-student attachment to teachers' attitude towards work.

Teacher-student attachment

Ainsworth and her colleagues were the first to provide empirical evidence for Bowlby's attachment theory. Using the strange situation procedure, Ainsworth and Bell classified infants into one of three categories: (1) secure, in which infants use the mother as a secure base for exploration and seek contact with her after separation; (2) anxious-ambivalent (later called "resistant"), in which infants are unable to use the mother as a secure base and are often angry and push her away upon reunion; (3) anxious-avoidant, in which infants fail to use the mother as a secure base for exploration and avoid the mother upon reunion or approach her only indirectly. More recent work presented a fourth category (disorganized-disoriented), in which infants have no predictable or effective pattern of eliciting care-giving behaviors when stressed. Each of these attachment classifications, across the lifespan, falls on a continuum of emotional regulation for managing affect, events, and relationships. This conceptualization places the anxious-avoidant style, with its overly organized strategies for controlling and minimizing affect, at one end of the continuum, and the relatively uncontrolled, poorly managed affect of anxious-resistant styles at the opposite end. Secure attachment, falling along the midpoint of the emotional continuum, reflects a balance of the two extremes of emotional regulation. Those with disorganized-disoriented attachment classifications may present a range of behaviors involving under-controlled emotional reactions such as impulsive verbal or physical aggression or over-controlled responses in which emotions are difficult to express and behavior may reflect withdrawal and difficulty handling conflict. Thus, their emotional reactions are unpredictable and typically maladaptive.

It is suggested that attachment is a special emotional relationship that involves an exchange of comfort, care, and pleasure. Previous research has found that adults differ according to their own attachment style in their ability to act as a secure base for children in their care. Secure adults are typically better at realistically evaluating their own relationship histories and responding sensitively and appropriately to a child's attachment needs than adults with an insecure attachment history. Some researchers define positive teacher-student relationships as "warm, close and communicative" and such relationships are linked to behavioral competence and better school adjustment. Teacher and student attachment has been identified as a significant influence on students' overall school and behavioral adjustment. Moreover, interaction with other people (students, other teachers, and staff) is actually a major part of most teachers' school days. Therefore, it is important to study the naturalness and quality of teacher-student relationships, as it influences the quality of their relationships. According to researchers, the qualities that lead to effective teacher-student relationships are positive affection, warm attitude, tact in teaching, teacher immediacy and teacher power, teacher assertiveness and responsiveness, and low differential treatment. Lack of any of these traits may negatively influence teacher-student interaction.

Teachers with a dismissing (avoidant) attachment style may have difficulty recognizing their own lack of warmth, trust and sensitivity in their relationships with their students. These teachers may have unrealistic expectations for their students' maturity and independence, as they themselves may have learned to be overly self-reliant and distant in their own interpersonal relationships. Teachers with a dismissing status may generally respond to students by distancing themselves, demonstrating a lack of warmth and understanding. The teacher with a preoccupied (resistant) style may be intermittently attuned to students' needs and easily become involved in dealing with specific observable behaviors without addressing underlying problems. Researcher furthermore reported that teachers, regardless of their attachment status, may perceive the anxious-avoidant student as passively aggressive, angry, withdrawn, and uncooperative and the anxious-resistant students as overly dependent and reactive, demanding of attention, and prone to impulsivity and acting-out behavior. The disorganized student may be viewed as aggressive, reactive, unpredictable, and difficult to manage. Because of their own relationship needs, teachers may be more accepting of students with one attachment style than students with another one. Teachers with preoccupied status, because of their own dependency needs, may be more supportive of the anxious-resistant student and rejecting of anxious-avoidant and disorganized students, bolstering the negative internal working model of relationships for these children. Teachers with a dismissing attachment style (with the need to maintain an emotional distance from others) would be expected to show less acceptance of anxious-resistant and disorganized students (who need too much help or supervision), but also fail to support avoidant children (who are reluctant to ask for assistance). Both dismissing and preoccupied teachers would be expected to work best with children secure in attachment style. The secure teacher, on the other hand, may recognize in the anxious-avoidant students' withdrawal and aloofness, the anxious-resistant students' dependency and the disorganized students' acting out behavior, the need to foster positive supportive interaction, trust, and relatedness in their relationship.

As reported, the organizational climate in schools, teachers' ideologies, and their level of burnout (outcome of stress) could harm teacher-student relationships. Affected teacher-student relationships can in turn cause teacher-conflict-inducing attitudes (lack of teacher emotional support, teacher misbehavior or hostility). It is reported that the quality of teacher-student relationships can influence students' educational and psychosomatic outcomes. Concurrently, high incidences of educational, psychological and somatic complaints are seen in students whose teachers they characterize as more hostile in their attitude towards them. Teachers who have lower morale due to school climate conditions and who are more likely to burn out tend to adopt conflict-inducing attitudes towards students, which will in turn lead to educational and psychosomatic complaints in students.

Teacher-student relationships are one of the factors that influence teachers' stress, and the stresses developed by teachers are reflected in their behavior towards students. Teachers have different perceptions and experienced different stress levels with regard to specific students in classroom (behaviorally challenging students and typical students). These perceptions and stress levels are linked to their classroom behaviors and may bias a teacher's behavior towards those students. In addition, teachers' behavior towards challenging students involved greater amounts of negative and neutral behaviors compared to the control students. Briefly, if teachers' stress levels increase, this will decrease their positive behavior towards the students, and the teacher will avoid contact or ignore the students. The more stress induced by the students, the less engaged the teacher will be with the students, which affects the teacher-student relationship.

Teachers' attitudes towards work

The word "attitude" is defined within the framework of social psychology as a subjective or mental preparation for action. It defines outward and visible postures and human beliefs. Attitudes determine what each individual will see, hear, think and do. They are rooted in experience and do not become automatic, routine conduct. Furthermore, "attitude" means the individual's prevailing tendency to respond favorably or unfavorably to an object (person or group of people, institutions or events). Attitudes can be positive (values) or negative (prejudices). There are three components of attitudes: affective, cognitive and behavioral. The affective component is a feeling or an emotion one has about an object or situation. The cognitive component is the beliefs or ideas one has about an object or situation, whereas the behavioral component of attitude reflects how one intends to act or behave towards someone or something. In most situations, the three components appear concomitantly to shape teachers' classroom postures, through direct and indirect interaction between society, school and teachers. Moreover, teachers' styles and attitudes are strong context outcomes rooted in experience. They do not become automatic routine behaviors, in the sense that they are developed through very slow interactions (action and reaction), and become well-established constructs for each individual only after some time. In that sense, attitudes can be modified only by each individual, when they become aware, through elements and evidence, that new postures would be better to deal with the surrounding world.

Attitudes towards work mean perceptions that affect how employees perform in their positions. In the mid-1970s, it was found that many educational researchers have supported the idea that teachers' attitudes and expectations can be self-fulfilling prophecies. It was also proposed that once teachers develop a particular attitude or belief, they may begin to treat students differently in ways that help bring about the outcomes that they expect. On the other hand, attitude and behavior are defined comprehensively as individuals' general evaluations about themselves, others, other objects, events and problems. Briefly, attitudes do predict people's behavior. In order to understand teachers' attitudes and understand how attitude reflects teachers' behavior, we could examine many components of attitude in context of organizational behavior. In this study, we would like to focus on four components of attitude used to assess teachers' attitude towards work: Job satisfaction, commitment, communication, and alienation.

In the organizational behavior field, job satisfaction is the most important and frequently studied attitude. It reflects the extent to which people like their jobs. As expected, teachers' working conditions, assessed by their level of job satisfaction, affect teacher-student interaction. Hence, higher levels of job satisfaction improve teachers' morale, which students perceive positively.

"Commitment" is a term used to distinguish those who are "caring", "dedicated", and who "take the job seriously" from those who "put their own interests first". Commitment is an important work attitude, because committed individuals are expected to be willing to work harder to achieve their goal and remain employed. Nonetheless, teachers do not all have the same level of commitment to their job. For some teachers, commitment is a major part of their lives, and they afford it extensive consideration and high priority. Others may perceive it differently, seeing teaching as just a job. Meanwhile, a reflexive account of research over a 20-year period with 54 primary school teachers indicated that the word "commitment" appeared in almost every interview. In a different context, the moral purposes of teachers are to use words such as "courage", "integrity", "honesty", "care" and "fairness". It is easy to see how these words may be associated with commitment. The more obvious signs of commitment are enthusiasm for the job and for the people with whom one works. Individuals' commitment levels affect their performance at work. However, findings on commitment outcomes, particularly turnover, absenteeism, tardiness, and work performance, are mixed, weak, or inconsistent.

Communication manifests itself in attitudes as accuracy and openness of information exchange. Effective communication is the heart of creating and maintaining an effective school. Communication that occurs within schools is crucial in shaping teachers' social reality. School excellence is directly related to what teachers think and do. Teachers' attitudes and behavior strongly rely on their perceptions about their schools.

The fourth component of attitude is alienation, meaning the extent to which staff members feel disappointed with their careers and professional development. On the whole, the concept of positive student-teacher interaction is multi-dimensional, as it involves organization, workload (difficulty), expected fairness of grading, instructor knowledge, and perceiving learning.

Teaching has been identified as a stressful profession. High stress among teachers has many negative consequences, including higher than average levels of anxiety and depression and a desire to quit the profession and to use drugs. Indeed, teachers' relationships with their students affect their stress levels significantly. Teachers with depersonalization (an "alteration" in the perception or experience of the self so that one feels "detached" from one's mental processes or body) will behave immorally and fail to give information to their students. These teachers tend to deny opinions and ideas from students as well as fail to interact or communicate with their students. Several studies show that teacher stress predicted negative teacher and student relationships. Significant correlations were found among teacher stress and negative relationships between teacher and student. Teacher stress arises from being unable to discipline pupils in the way they would prefer.

Teacher commitment has been found to be a critical predictor of teachers' work performance, absenteeism, retention, burnout and turnover. Teachers remained committed to their beliefs throughout their professional life. Although their levels of engagement with particular practices were modified through various life events and activities, their commitment to their ideological positions did not diminish. However, some teachers' commitment might vary over time, because different people have different levels, and some can plateau earlier or later than others. Commitment was moderated through a range of factors; some of which were sustaining and some diminishing. Teachers were less likely to engage in particular activities or behave in particular ways at one point in time, depending on various work and life contextual factors such as school contexts, and relationships with students and colleagues. These seemed to be the major work and life factors that diminished commitment.

The relationship between job satisfaction and stress coping skills of primary school teachers has been studied extensively, which shows a statistically significant difference in job satisfaction between male and female primary school teachers. However, in case of stress coping skills, they found no statistically significant difference. Some studies also show a significant and positive correlation between job satisfaction and stress coping skills, which are self-reliance, pro-active attitude, adaptability and flexibility, and total stress coping skills. In brief, the ability to cope with stress can increase teachers' job satisfaction.

Notes

Role Model（行为榜样）：The term role model generally means any "person who serves as an example, whose behavior is emulated by others". The term first appeared in Robert K. Merton's socialization research of medical students. Merton hypothesized that individuals compare themselves with reference groups of people who occupy the social role to which the individual aspires.

New words and expressions

1. abhor [əb'hɔː]	vt.	痛恨，憎恶
2. excesses	n.	过分荒淫的行为；剩余额（excess 的复数）
3. assert [ə'səːt]	vt.	断言；主张；声称；维护，坚持
4. hinder ['hində]	vi.	成为阻碍
	vt.	阻碍；打扰
	adj.	后面的
5. compelling [kəm'peliŋ]	adj.	引人注目的；强制的；激发兴趣的
6. ambivalent [æm'bivələnt]	adj.	矛盾的；好恶相克的
7. elicit [i'lisit]	vt.	抽出，引出；引起
8. avoidant [ə'vɔidənt]	adj.	回避反应的
9. overly ['əuvəli]	adv.	过度地；极度地
10. resistant [ri'zistənt]	adj.	抵抗的，反抗的；顽固的
	n.	抵抗者
11. withdrawal [wið'drɔːəl]	n.	撤退，收回；提款；取消；退股
12. maladaptive [ˌmælə'dæptiv]	adj.	适应不良的；不适应的；不利于适应的
13. assertiveness [ə'səːtivnis]	n.	魄力，自信
14. responsiveness [ri'spɔnsivnis]	n.	响应能力；有同情心
15. bolster ['bəulstə]	n.	长枕；支持
	vt.	支持；支撑
16. aloofness [ə'luːfnis]	n.	冷漠；高傲；超然离群

Unit 8　Teacher & Student　教师与学生

17. ideology [ˌaidi'ɔlədʒi]　　　　　n.　意识形态；思想意识；观念学
18. hostility [hɔ'stiləti]　　　　　n.　敌意；战争行动
19. psychosomatic ['psaikəusəu'mætik] adj.　身心的；身心失调的；身心治疗的
　　　　　　　　　　　　　　　n.　身心上有病的人
20. concurrently [kən'kʌrəntli]　　adv.　兼；同时发生地
21. hence [hens]　　　　　　　　adv.　因此；今后
22. morale [mɔ'rɑːl]　　　　　　n.　士气，斗志
23. dedicated ['dedikeitid]　　　　adj.　专用的；专注的；献身的
24. reflexive [ri'fleksiv]　　　　　adj.　反身的；[物]反射的
25. inconsistent [ˌinkən'sistənt]　　adj.　不一致的；前后矛盾的
26. manifest ['mænifest]　　　　　vt.　证明，表明；显示
　　　　　　　　　　　　　　　vi.　显示，出现
　　　　　　　　　　　　　　　adj.　明显的
27. alienation [ˌeiljə'neiʃən]　　　n.　疏远；转让；精神错乱；[哲]异化；
　　　　　　　　　　　　　　　　　[戏]离间效果
28. depersonalization [diːˌpəːsənəlai'zeiʃə]
　　　　　　　　　　　　　　　n.　[心理]人格解体，人性之丧失
29. absenteeism [ˌæbsən'tiːizəm]　n.　旷工；旷课；有计划的怠工；经常无故缺席
30. retention [ri'tenʃən]　　　　　n.　保留；扣留，滞留；记忆力；闭尿

I　Vocabulary.

Fill in the blanks with the most suitable words. Change the form when necessary.

abhor	assert	hinder	compelling	maladaptive
assertiveness	hostility	concurrently	morale	manifest

1. Even now, I still believe the logic is _____.
2. Opposition to the war, he still thinks, explains much of the _____ to him.

3. They _____ all forms of racial discrimination.
4. "The suggestion that I've done anything to warrant criminal investigation, it is _____ nonsense," said Muthaura.
5. _____, a serious diplomatic effort is needed to address the major anomaly of the Afghan war.
6. China's growing military reach and _____ are fuelling neighbors' uncertainty about its strategic intentions.
7. Schizophrenia—a group of disorders manifested in delusions, disturbances in language and thought, mood shifts, and _____ behaviors.
8. Its statesmen used to _____ that Germany had no independent foreign policy, only a European policy.
9. Low pay in recent years has led to low _____.
10. Officials say Williams' death could _____ the work of non-government groups in the country.

II Comprehension of the text.

Decide whether the following statements are true (T) or false (F) according to the passage.

1. Teachers are expected to be positive role models for their students only inside the classroom.   (   )
2. Ainsworth and Bell classified infants into one of three categories: anxious-avoidant, in which infants are unable to use the mother as a secure base and are often angry and push her away upon reunion.   (   )
3. Secure adults are typically better at realistically evaluating their own relationship histories and responding sensitively and appropriately to a child's attachment needs than adults with an insecure attachment history.   (   )
4. Teachers with preoccupied status, because of their own dependency needs, may be more supportive of the anxious-resistant student and rejecting of anxious-avoidant and disorganized students, bolstering the negative internal working model of relationships for these children.   (   )
5. The word "attitude" is defined within the framework of social psychology as a subjective or mental preparation for action.   (   )

III Try to fill in the space with the suitable words.

1. Despite all these compelling reasons to study teachers' behavior, researching _____ is often considered a taboo, which can make study in this area difficult.

2. Bowlby (1988) suggests that _____ is a special emotional relationship that involves an exchange of comfort, care, and pleasure.
3. Teachers with a dismissing status may generally respond to students by distancing themselves, demonstrating a lack of _____.
4. Teacher-student relationships are one of the factors that influence teachers' stress, and the stresses developed by teachers are reflected in _____.
5. There are three components of attitudes: affective, _____ and behavioral.

Useful phrases and expressions

大先生 master teachers
塑造生命 shape lives
道德情操 moral conduct
栋梁之材 pillars of the nation
传播真理 disseminate the truth
学识渊博 be well-grounded in knowledge
塑造新人 prepare the young for the future
教书育人 impart knowledge and cultivate moral character
德才兼备 with moral integrity, and professional competence
加强师德师风建设 enhance professional ethics and integrity of Chinese teachers

It would be a blessing to have met a good teacher in your life; it would be the glory of a school to be lined with great teachers; it would be the beacon of our nation to have generations of excellent teachers.

一个人遇到好老师是人生的幸运，一个学校拥有好老师是学校的光荣，一个民族源源不断涌现出一批又一批好老师则是民族的希望。

Xi Jinping has pointed out, "The prosperity of our country, rejuvenation of our nation, and development of education are contingent on nurturing a well-structured, high-quality professional body of teachers characterized by nobility, vitality, and expertise. And we need quantity too."

习近平总书记强调："国家繁荣、民族振兴、教育发展，需要我们大力培养造就一支师德高尚、业务精湛、结构合理、充满活力的高素质专业化教师队伍，需要涌现一大批好老师。"

Teachers are hailed by Xi Jinping as builders of the nation's "Dream Team". Accordingly, good teachers are measured against four criteria: they should have ideals and beliefs, moral integrity, knowledge, and compassion.

广大教师是打造中华民族"梦之队"的筑梦人,要努力成为"有理想信念、有道德情操、有扎实学识、有仁爱之心"的好老师。

To make teaching a great career choice, fostering public respect for the teaching profession and teachers is of major importance.

要在全社会营造尊师重教的良好氛围,让教师成为令人羡慕的职业。

In the past, we believed that teachers should have a bucket of water before they can give students a bowl of water. This is not enough today, as they should have a pond of water before they can give students a bowl of water.

过去讲,要给学生一碗水,教师要有一桶水,现在看,这个要求已经不够了,应该是要有一潭水。

Apart from their knowledge and ability, teachers also influence their students through personal conduct and the values they hold toward the country, the people, the public, and the private.

老师对学生的影响,离不开老师的学识和能力,更离不开老师为人处世、于国于民、于公于私所持的价值观。

Xi Jinping emphasized at the National Education Conference that teachers should guide students in character building, encourage learning and creative thinking, and act as their examples for devotion to the nation.

习近平总书记在全国教育大会上强调,广大教师要做学生锤炼品格的引路人、学习知识的引路人、创新思维的引路人、奉献祖国的引路人。

Since the 18th CPC National Congress, Xi Jinping has advised teachers and students to "know great virtues, maintain public virtues, and practice personal virtues."

党的十八大以来,习近平总书记对广大师生明确提出"明大德、守公德、严私德"的要求。

A country will be full of hope and have a great tomorrow only when its younger generations have ideals, ability, and a strong sense of responsibility.

青年一代有理想、有本领、有担当,国家就有前途,民族就有希望。

Teachers and students are firm believers, active communicators, and model practitioners of core socialist values.

广大师生要做社会主义核心价值观的坚定信仰者、积极传播者和模范践行者。

Unit 9 School & Family
学校与家庭

Text A   School and Family Cooperation Models for Reducing Social Problems

导读：社会排斥是拉脱维亚七到十五岁的学生可能遇到的成长问题之一。本文中的研究对象是寄宿学校的学生，寄宿学校的学生与综合学校的学生在团体关系方面是很不一样的。因为寄宿学校的学生通常来自不甚富裕和不利环境的家庭，有些学生缺少父母的照顾，有些学生无家可归，有些学生达到上学年龄却没能上学，有些学生由于父母在外工作而被其他亲朋监护，也有些学生存在许多类似上述的问题……

Pupils' (7-15 years old) social exclusion is one of contemporary problems in Latvia. The chosen target group for research is pupils living and studying in the boarding school. The membership of pupils in the boarding school highly differs from comprehensive schools in Latvia, because they usually are pupils from low-income and disadvantageous families, as well as children without parental care, those who have wandered for a long time, have not acquired education according to their age, children being left under relatives' supervision because their parents have left for working abroad and also children with many similar problems. A large part of these pupils have not only limited possibilities to adopt themselves to the social life, to have exciting spare time, to contact with equals in age, to identify and develop their skills, abilities and interests, but also lack socially meaningful experience regarding the conventionalities and a moral, ethic model for imitation of these norms.

The micro-society, life conditions in families where pupils live, unfortunately, do not develop conventionalities, but encourage anti-social behavior.

Admittedly, pupils in boarding schools have fair intellect, they are physically fit, with sufficient potential of energy being impossible to put into practice within the pedagogical context that could help them socialize and express themselves. Education is regarded as a value in the family, however, the socially-psychological characteristics also affect the learning process, because we can often notice explicit Attention Deficit Syndrome lowering their working capacity. In order to facilitate the reduction of pupils' social exclusion in the boarding school and their incorporation into the social life, as well as to prevent critical situations, these pupils and their parents need special support, because the pupil's identity development begins in the family, but improves at school.

Along with the country's economic situation, the parents' socio-economic situation has sharply worsened. Therefore, as a result of such changes, many families have experienced stressful situations. Consequently, parents often are full of their own problems forgetting about the child's needs, interests and peculiarities of development. Parents often do not immerse into their child as an individual, do not perceive their child as a value, because in their own childhood, they had felt themselves unplumbed, troublesome, cared, teachable, pushed. Support for these children and their parents can be ensured by a complex of different educational measures and team work. One of the measures is promotion of cooperation between the school and the family, because the priority of boarding school pupils is their family, family members' opinion which is taken into account. But this cooperation must be insistent and permanent as only in this case positive results can be expected.

The research was carried on within the framework of Doctoral Thesis Holistic approach during process of socialization of social risk group pupils.

The report contains the analysis of the issue within two levels: *the theoretical level*, where the legislation of the Republic of Latvia related to social issues, children rights and parental duties as well as different models of school and family cooperation had been analyzed. Consequently, there was proposed a triangular model referring to direct cooperation between the school, NGO (non-governmental organization) and family; *the empirical level*, where the approbation of the proposed cooperation model (SCHOOL—NGO—FAMILY) was developed by interviewing the parents of the pupils. By the content-analysis, there were analyzed the implementation of the cooperation model by the mediation of NGO "Liepna Boarding School and Pupils Support Families Union" in order to reduce social problems within the boarding school.

Analysis of cooperation between the school and the family and proposed solutions

Each person is an individual system, which functions in interaction by surrounding environment, creates correlated and interacted system and aggregate of structures. It is ecosystem approach and these conditions also refer to persons from social risk groups. In general, this thesis is basis for integrative and inclusive pedagogy. In accordance with scientific cognitions of U. Bronfenbrenner, microsystem is an aggregate of activities, roles and intermediate human relations, which is being experienced by the person with its characteristic physical and psychical features at some particular sphere of life by creating interaction with other persons. Accordingly, the child, his/her family and school are three microsystems.

In child's upbringing, the family has an important role. However, the function of upbringing is also performed by the school and it means that for child's development the cooperation between school and family is important. It should be well-thought-out and organized, because every family has different resources, skills, desires and needs. One approach of cooperation does not fit to everyone. Pupils, their parents and teachers usually have different desires, aims, opinions, values; it sometimes leads to disappointment and misunderstandings between school and pupils' families. If these differences are not being recognized and solved, there is developing lack of communication; consequently, there is impossible successful cooperation between school and family. This expression is often seen in boarding schools, where the parents of the pupils has different word outlook, because the majority of these families practice antisocial life-style. It is complicated to persuade and stimulate the parents to live more qualitatively; it creates necessity to include the parents:

- In active involvement into making decisions regarding school;
- In active school's activities as volunteers and members of parents' committee;
- Leisure activities with their children;
- Regular communication with school personnel regarding child's school and general progress;

- Participation in opportunities of adults' education, offered by the school.

Families' involvement in school's activities can be one of the means by creating cooperative, tolerant community. Nowadays, when schools become more and more open to the society, communication between parents and teachers is becoming not only more intensive but also more complicated. Teachers tend to recognize that work out of classroom in this case, it is the activity in the community and communication with parents is related emotional and intellectual efforts. As a result of communication between school and family, pupils' achievements, behavior, attitude towards studies and school are improving. The cooperation depends on families' education, family and society members, who are working together for consummation of united aims.

The features of cooperation between the school and the family in Latvia had changed by historical course of time. A. Baldins and A. Razeva mention that the older generation teaching children has grown and developed their identities in other socio-economic and political relations to a great extent being typical to the conditions of a primitive society. The grounds for these relations were social and economic safety and absolutization of the country's interests. Government ensured a single educational system for all children where the school became a partial performer of the family's functions. This experience regarding the school is familiar to parents, but the contemporary school realizes only its educational functions making the family realize its responsibility and importance of the upbringing function.

In its turn, the boarding school is an educational institution carrying out not only pupils' educating but also upbringing function. Pupils spend a majority of their life in the boarding school; as a result, the school mainly takes responsibility for pupil's development as individuality, but parents' responsibility stays apart.

Basing on the Children's Rights Protection Law passed by Saeima of the Republic of Latvia prescribing children's rights to clean environment for life (Article 46); basic provisions for the protection of children from negative influences in social surroundings (Article 47); children's protection from smoking and the influence of alcoholic beverages (Article 48); children's protection from the use of narcotic, toxic and other intoxicating substances (Article 49); protection from negative influence of games, films and mass media (Article 50); restrictions for children's involvement into events (Article 501); safety requirements in children's supervisory services (Article 503); children's protection from unlawful activities (Article 51); a child—a victim of violence or other unlawful activity (Article 52); quite often the children at high risk are being sent to a boarding school and thus being isolated from their families. As a result, parents' rights to bring up their children are limited. The connection between the child and his family is broken, also the obligations of parents prescribed in the Article 24 of the Children's Rights Protection Law of the Republic of Latvia determining: "to take care of the child and his property and represent him within his private and property relations"; "to prepare the child for an independent life in the society, as much as possible respecting his/her individuality, taking into consideration his/her abilities and inclinations"; "to safe-guard the child's rights and interests protected by the law"; as well as "upon failure to discharge parental obligations, or for the malicious usage of parental authority, physical punishing of a child, as well as cruel behavior against him/her, parents shall be held accountable as determined by the law" etc.

A part of parents' obligations is performed by the boarding school, and exactly by the school support measures. It is possible to maintain and improve the existent relations between the child, parents and teachers, but positive moral concepts being acquired at school are not always supported by the families of the social risk group, because in most cases parents have transferred their own negative experience regarding school to their children. The majority of parents are unemployed at the moment due to the economic crisis and they are followers of the anti-social environment, quite often these parents, when bringing their children to grade 1, give them for school's care and upbringing for over nine years. However, the positive result of child's upbringing can be reached only in case school efforts are being supported by the family. Otherwise, a child acquires different skills and habits; but consequently the positive influence in school often vanishes because of the lack of support in the family.

It creates the necessity to develop cooperation between the school and the family corresponding to school's intentions and motivating parents to arrive at school in order to see their child's growth. Frequently, the class teacher is the person informing parents about their children's interests, abilities, competences, needs, problems, friends, state of health. Usually it is quite difficult to involve parents into organization of the educational process, because there is a psychological barrier between the school and parents that is not easy to hurdle. The school visit mainly is connected to their child's bad behavior and insufficient success, the research shows that parents usually do not want to visit school and help its work due to the following reasons:

- They are not sure that their help is truly necessary;
- They are afraid to be mistaken;
- There is a lack of information regarding the form of the required support;
- Low self-esteem, busyness;

- Illness;
- Alcoholism, drug addiction;
- They are undereducated and low-income people often with the inferiority complex.

As V. Senko notes, the time of negative experience accumulating for pupils in junior grades is noticeably shorter than for youngsters; therefore, the departure from the norm is not yet established. Their psyche is characterized by its flexibility and this feature facilitates the reformatory process. By the time when the child starts to attend school, a break of the dynamic stereotype happens and it goes quite easily, because the negative acquirements and habits have not become permanent. Therefore, the initiative of the pedagogical cooperation between the school and the family should be taken by the school without waiting for parents' interest. But families having pedagogical neglect require special attention and approach, because it is necessary to practise both the educating and the reformatory or reeducating function at the same time. It requires energy to improve educational conditions in families, help parents change their attitude towards their children and achieve a single influence of the school and the family upon the child.

As part of its effort to build the capacity of schools, the Network facilitates linkages among schools and between schools and other key institutional players that can support schools. The support for schools includes education departments at the district and state level, as well as universities and organizations, communities, and national school reform movements.

Indication of effective cooperation between school and family is unity in accomplishing purposes. Cooperation process requires uninterrupted planning of works, their drafting and evaluation. Schools have to undertake the leading role in organizing of the cooperation by providing environment and culture, helping families to perform their role of partnership.

Present situation in Latvian education, deep economic crisis and the life reality shows that the school's support team often does not work in a body, because due to the economic crisis and structural modifications of the Latvian education system, there is a lack of funding for wages of qualified employees—organizers of interest-related education, out-of-class activities, psychologists, social pedagogues etc. wherewith the school has no opportunities to perform cooperation organizer's functions, as well as there is lack of funding for organizing of extracurricular activities and promotion of collaboration.

Unit 9   School & Family   学校与家庭

As the economic situation in the country is becoming worse, the social crisis has also deepened, because at the moment a great part of families where children attend boarding school faces some difficulties increasing social exclusion and problems related to it. As a result, the support is necessary for both—the pupils and their families. It creates circumstances and necessity for searching of new ways of collaboration.

1. **Social Exclusion**（社会排斥）: Social exclusion is a concept used in many parts of the world to characterise contemporary forms of social disadvantage. Dr. Lynn Todman, director of the Institute on Social Exclusion at the Adler School of Professional Psychology, suggests that social exclusion refers to processes in which individuals and entire communities of people are systematically blocked from rights, opportunities and resources (e. g. housing, employment, healthcare, civic engagement, democratic participation and due process) that are normally available to members of society and which are key to social integration.

2. **Latvia**（拉脱维亚）: Latvia, officially the Republic of Latvia, is a country in the Baltic region of Northern Europe. It is bordered to the north by Estonia (border length 343 km), to the south by Lithuania (588 km), to the east by the Russian Federation (276 km), and to the southeast by Belarus (141 km). Across the Baltic Sea to the west lies Sweden. The territory of Latvia covers 64,589 km^2 (24,938 sq mi) and it has a temperate seasonal climate.

3. **NGO (non-governmental organization)**（民间组织，非政府组织）: A non-governmental organization (NGO) is a legally constituted organization created by natural or legal persons that operates independently from any government. The term is usually used by governments to refer to entities that have no government status.

New words and expressions

1. contemporary [kən'tempərəri]   n.   同时代的人；同时期的东西
                                    adj. 当代的；同时代的；属于同一时期的
2. comprehensive [ˌkɔmpri'hensiv]   adj. 综合的；广泛的；有理解力的
                                    n.   综合学校；专业综合测验

3. parental [pə'rentl] adj. 父母亲的，父母的；亲代的，亲本的
4. supervision [ˌsjuːpə'viʒən] n. 监督，管理
5. ethic ['eθik] n. 伦理；道德规范
   adj. 伦理的；道德的（等于 ethical）
   n. 伦理；道德规范
6. admittedly [əd'mitidli] adv. 公认地；无可否认地；明白地
7. boarding ['bɔːdiŋ] adj. 供膳的
8. incorporation [inˌkɔːpə'reiʃən] n. 公司；合并，编入；团体组织
9. priority [prai'ɔrəti] n. 优先；优先权；[数] 优先次序；优先考虑的事
10. triangular [trai'æŋgjulə] adj. 三角的，[数] 三角形的；三人间的
11. implementation [ˌimplimen'teiʃən] n. 履行；实现；[计] 安装启用
12. mediation [ˌmiːdi'eiʃən] n. 调解；仲裁；调停
13. in accordance with 依照；与……一致
14. aggregate ['ægrigət] vi. 集合；聚集；合计
    vt. 集合；聚集；合计
    n. 合计；集合体；总计
    adj. 聚合的；集合的；合计的
15. intermediate [ˌintə'miːdjət] vi. 起媒介作用
    adj. 中间的，中级的
    n. [化学] 中间物；媒介
16. necessity [ni'sesəti] n. 需要；必然性；必需品
17. intellectual [ˌintə'lektjuəl] adj. 智力的；聪明的；理智的
18. consummation [ˌkɔnsə'meiʃən] n. 圆满成功；完成；成就；达到极点
19. provision [prəu'viʒən] n. 规定；条款；准备；[经] 供应品
    vt. 供给……食物及必需品
20. beverage ['bevəridʒ] n. 饮料
21. intoxicating [in'tɔksikeitiŋ] adj. 醉人的；令人陶醉的；使兴奋的
22. supervisory ['sjuːpəˌvaizəri] adj. 监督的
23. prescribe [pris'kraib] vi. 规定；开药方
    vt. 规定；开处方
24. inclination [ˌinkli'neiʃən] n. 倾向，爱好；斜坡
25. correspond [ˌkɔri'spɔnd] vi. 符合，一致；相应；通信

Unit 9 School & Family 学校与家庭

26. accumulate [əˈkjuːmjuleit] vi. 累积；积聚
    vt. 积攒
27. reformatory [riˈfɔːmətəri] adj. 改革的；感化的；革新的
    n. 少年管教所
28. stereotype [ˈsteriəutaip] vt. 使用铅版；套用老套，使一成不变
    n. 陈腔滥调，老套；铅版
29. wherewith [hwɛəˈwiθ] adv. 用什么
    pron. 用以……的东西
30. collaboration [kə,læbəˈreiʃən] n. 合作；勾结；通敌

I Vocabulary.

Fill in the blanks with the most suitable words. Change the form when necessary.

| contemporary | comprehensive | parental | supervision | ethic |
| admittedly | priority | necessity | intellectual | prescribe |

1. To pursue this vision, my administration conducted a _____ review of America's development programs.
2. "We cannot continue with costs that are out of control because reform is a _____ that cannot wait," he said.
3. "The International Monetary Fund should strengthen its _____ of capital flows between countries," he said.
4. I'm not prepared to _____ a drug to my patients that I wouldn't take myself.
5. The artist Michelangelo often stirred up the opposition of the _____ artists of his day.
6. The _____ is protecting the police and the public from their attacks.
7. The difference in _____ attitudes between first-borns and subsequent children is large and significant.
8. Optimism is an _____ choice.

9. Negativity gets on people's nerves and calls your work _____ into question.
10. _____, Mr. Yoon is no ordinary banker but a former engineer who designed the satellite communications network used in the US space shuttle program.

II Comprehension of the text.

Decide whether the following statements are true (T) or false (F) according to the passage.

1. The membership of pupils in the boarding school is the same with that of comprehensive schools in Latvia. (   )
2. Each person is an individual system, which functions in interaction by surrounding environment, creates correlated and interacted system and aggregate of structures. (   )
3. Families' involvement in school's activities can be one of the mean by creating cooperative, tolerant community. (   )
4. As a result of communication between school and family, pupils' achievements, behavior, attitude towards studies and school are improving. (   )
5. As the economic situation in the country is becoming worse, the social crisis has also deepened. (   )

III Try to fill in the spaces with the suitable words.

1. In order to facilitate the reduction of pupils' social exclusion in the boarding school and their incorporation into the social life, as well as to prevent critical situations, these pupils and their parents need special support, because the pupil's identity development begins in the _____, but improves at school.
2. In child's upbringing the family has important role, however, the function of upbringing is also performed by the school and it means that for child's development the _____ is important.
3. Pupils, their parents and teachers usually have different desires, aims, opinions, values; it sometimes leads to _____ between school and pupils' families.
4. The positive result of child's upbringing can be reached only in case school efforts are being supported by _____.
5. The support for schools includes education departments at _____ level, as well as universities and organizations, communities, and national school reform movements.

Text B The Effects of Family, School, and Classroom Ecologies on Changes in Children's Social Competence and Emotional and Behavioral Problems in First Grade

导读：课堂是学生学习知识的场所，是学生与老师、学生与学生之间互动的平台；学校比课堂的空间更大，在学校里学生不单单是学习知识，还在学习做人，学校是社会的一个小小缩影，为学生从容走入社会做好准备；良好的家庭教育环境是促进未成年人健康成长的重要一环，父母是孩子的启蒙教师，父母的言行举止和教育方法，对孩子的成长有着重大影响。

Classroom-level influences on children's in-school behaviors

Although children's classroom ecologies can be characterized according to multiple perspectives and social and structural features, we consider the social atmosphere among classmates, as rated by the children themselves, to be particularly salient for children's social, emotional, and behavioral development in first grade. Growing evidence indicates that aggregate levels of peer behaviors within classroom groupings, including aggressive or victimizing behaviors, contribute to children's adjustment in school, even after family-and school-level factors are accounted for. For instance, in an evaluation of a first-grade classroom intervention directed at reducing children's aggressive behaviors, it was found that placement in first-grade classrooms with higher aggregate levels of physically aggressive peers (as rated by teachers) contributed to boys' (but not girls') behavioral problems in middle school, independent of family economic disadvantage and school disadvantage. Illustrating the connection between individual and peer group behavior, peers reinforce episodes of school-based peer victimization by watching or by physically or verbally joining the aggressors. Evidence also indicates that children's experiences of peer victimization in schools and classrooms are reciprocally linked to their social, emotional, and behavioral problems, such that children who show these problems are more likely to be victimized, which, in turn, can further elevate their level of problems. Clearly, aggressive and victimizing peer behaviors are not limited to dyads but rather function at the group level, and being in a classroom surrounded by a hostile group of peers who manipulate or harm other children may contribute to individual risks for developmental problems.

On the other hand, concentrated exposure to positive peer affiliations can reduce risks for social, emotional, or behavioral problems. Evidence shows that being competent in the social, emotional, or behavioral domain or having friends who can provide support and protection reduces children's risk of being victimized and increases their likelihood of receiving prosocial acts from peers. The importance of positive peer affiliations was highlighted in their follow-up study of aggressive, second-grade boys who were targeted for an intervention program to improve social and problem-solving skills. Boys who associated with non-deviant peers showed lower risks for conduct disorder 4 years later than did program boys who associated with deviant peers. Having a stable group of well-adjusted, prosocial peers in the classroom increases children's exposure to more positive social learning experiences, which may, in turn, enhance their developmental outcomes. Although some research has shown that positive peer relationships and classroom environments can attenuate the negative effects of family-or school-level adversities on children's development, few studies have examined the ways that both positive and negative features of children's classrooms (particularly aggregate experiences of peer prosocial acts and victimization) shape children's behaviors in school in concert with markers of their family and school ecologies.

Family-level influences on children's in-school behaviors

Although family ecology is multidimensional and can affect children's development through many avenues, we focus specifically on indicators of family disruptiveness (household moves) and socioeconomic status (SES; mothers' education level) that can directly affect children's experiences in school. Evidence also suggests that these indicators may be linked. Research has documented that family disruptions, such as multiple household moves, contribute to social, emotional, and behavioral problems in children. Children who experienced high levels of family disruptions, including multiple household moves, in their early years were at higher risk for behavioral problems in preschool and for emotional problems in first grade than were children who experienced few disruptions. Although household moves may index changes in family SES (e.g. employment, income status), structure (e.g. divorce), or even opportunities, accumulating evidence indicates that the transitions necessitated by household moves represent an independent source of stress for children. Yet evidence on the mechanisms by which household moves affect school-age children's development is limited.

Shifts in household residences introduce disruptions into children's lives that can compromise the maintenance and accessibility of their social networks, particularly when parents' social and institutional ties are displaced. When children in a classroom have few bonds to one another outside the classroom or school environment because of residential instability, the supportive nature of the classroom climate may be threatened. On the other hand, the relation between household moves and children's behaviors may be attenuated in the presence of more constructive environmental experiences, such as classroom climates characterized by positive or supportive peer interactions.

Parental education has been positively linked to social competence and negatively related to emotional and behavioral problems in young children and may mediate the effects of household income on children's competent behaviors. Parental education indexes the human capital available to scaffold children's socialization and is less prone than household income to short-term financial fluctuations that can mask its effects, including seasonal unemployment or welfare spells. On the other hand, evidence suggests that poorly educated parents are more socially isolated, are less connected to the school system, and generate fewer social learning opportunities for their children outside of the school environment. If parents show limited engagement in their children's social experiences (e.g., rarely invite children's classmates over to play), their children may have few opportunities to develop interpersonal skills and may lack protective friendships with peers.

Evidence also indicates that low parental education can increase children's exposure to environmental stressors, including family and neighborhood poverty, family disruptions, and other adverse social conditions. When low parental education is coupled with other environmental stressors, such as high aggregate levels of poverty in schools and peer aggressiveness in classrooms, children's risks for developmental problems may be amplified. However, few studies have examined how mothers' education level and household moves influence children's in-school behaviors in the context of school-and classroom-related stressors.

School-level influences on children's in-school behaviors

Characteristics of children's school ecology are also varied and can operate on children's development through many avenues. We focus specifically on how school disadvantage (the proportion of poor students in the school) effects changes in children's in-school behaviors. Exposure to high aggregate levels of poverty (at the neighborhood and school levels) has been shown to adversely affect children's development. For instance, high levels of school disadvantage (the proportion of children eligible for free lunch) in first grade increased children's risk for behavioral problems in middle school, independent of family economic disadvantage and classroom levels of physical aggressiveness. Schools that concentrate on children who are vulnerable to social, emotional, or behavioral problems together may reduce their exposure to competent peers and positive peer interactions. For instance, a study showed that residing in poorer communities (which is, in turn, reflected in the economic characteristics of neighborhood-based schools) heightened adolescents' likelihood of associating with deviant peers, which, in turn, increased their risk for conduct problems. There is also evidence to suggest that episodes of peer victimization in classrooms are more common in disadvantaged schools than in more advantaged schools.

Associations between school disadvantage and poor developmental outcomes may also be altered by positive attributes of other salient environments, such as the prosocial or helping environment of children's classrooms. In the context of classrooms with high concentrations of prosocial, competent peer interactions, the negative influence of school disadvantage on children's development may be weakened. Yet surprisingly, few studies have explored how first-grade children's social, emotional, and behavioral trajectories are affected by the intersection of school disadvantage and the social environment of children's classrooms in the context of family-level risks.

The current study

In sum, the current study examined the independent and interactive contributions of classroom (concentrations of peer prosocial behaviors and victimization), family (household moves, mothers' education), and school (proportion of students receiving income assistance) factors to changes in children's in-school behaviors, as rated by their teachers during first grade. We expected (a) that increases in social competence across first grade would be predicted by higher levels of mothers' education and classroom prosocial behaviors, fewer household moves, and lower levels of school disadvantage and classroom victimization; (b) that increases in emotional and behavioral problems would be predicted by lower levels of mothers' education and classroom prosocial behaviors, multiple household moves, and higher levels of school disadvantage and classroom victimization; and (c) that the classroom-level variables would moderate the effects of the family-and school-level factors on changes in children's in-school behaviors. Specifically, the classroom concentration of prosocial behaviors was expected to buffer the effects of multiple household moves, low levels of mothers' education, and school disadvantage on changes in children's behaviors. The classroom concentration of victimization was expected to augment the effects of multiple household moves, low levels of mothers' education, and school disadvantage.

1. **Peer Group**（同辈群体；同龄群体）：A peer group is a social group consisting of people. Peer groups are an informal primary group of people who share a similar or equal status and who are usually of roughly the same age, tended to travel around and interact within the social aggregate. Members of a particular peer group often have similar interests and backgrounds, bonded by the premise of sameness. However, some peer groups are very diverse, crossing social divides such as socioeconomic status, level of education, race, creed, culture, or religion.

2. **Victimization**（欺负；牺牲；欺骗）：Victimization is the process of being victimized. According to Wiktionary, to victimize is to (1) make someone a victim or sacrifice, (2) punish someone unjustly, or (3) swindle or defraud someone.

3. **Socioeconomic Status (SES)**（社会经济地位）：Socioeconomic status is an economic and sociological combined total measure of a person's work experience and of an individual's or family's economic and social position relative to others, based on income, education, and occupation. When analyzing a family's SES, the household income, earners' education, and occupation are examined, as well as combined income, versus with an individual, when their own attributes are assessed.

4. **Socialization**（社会化）：Socialization is a term used by sociologists, social psychologists, anthropologists, politicians and educationalists to refer to the process of inheriting norms, customs and ideologies. It may provide the individual with the skills and habits necessary

for participating within their own society; a society develops a culture through a plurality of shared norms, customs, values, traditions, social roles, symbols and languages. Socialization is thus "the means by which social and cultural continuity are attained".

5. **Prosocial Behavior**（亲社会行为，利他行为）: Prosocial behavior is caring about the welfare and rights of others, feeling concern and empathy for them, and acting in ways that benefit others. Evidence suggests that prosociality is central to the well-being of social groups across a range of scales.

New words and expressions

1. salient ['seiliənt]	adj.	显著的；突出的；跳跃的
	n.	凸角；突出部分
2. peer [piə]	n.	贵族；同等的人；同龄人
3. aggressive [ə'gresiv]	adj.	侵略性的；好斗的；有进取心的；有闯劲的
4. reinforce [ˌriːin'fɔːs]	vt.	加强，加固；强化；补充
	vi.	求援；得到增援；给予更多的支持
5. episode ['episəud]	n.	插曲；一段情节；插话；有趣的事件
6. victimization [ˌviktimai'zeiʃən]	n.	欺负；牺牲；欺骗
7. reciprocally [ri'siprəkli]	adv.	相互地；相反地；互惠地
8. elevate ['eliveit]	vt.	提升；举起；振奋情绪等；提升……的职位
9. dyad ['daiæd]	n.	双；[生物]二分体；一对；[化学]二价元素
	adj.	双的
10. manipulate [mə'nipjuleit]	vt.	操作；操纵；巧妙地处理；篡改
11. affiliation [əˌfili'eiʃən]	n.	加入；联盟；友好关系；从属关系
12. prosocial [prəu'səuʃəl]	adj.	亲社会的；忠实于既定社会道德准则的
13. adversity [əd'vəːsəti]	n.	逆境；不幸；灾祸；灾难
14. disruptiveness [dis'rʌptivnis]	n.	破裂性
15. maintenance ['meintənəns]	n.	维护，维修；保持；生活费用
16. residential [ˌrezi'denʃəl]	adj.	住宅的；与居住有关的

17. index ['indeks]		n.	指标；指数；索引；指针
		vi.	做索引
		vt.	指出；编入索引中
18. prone [prəun]		adj.	俯卧的；有……倾向的，易于……的
19. stressor ['stresə]		n.	紧张性刺激；光彩
20. trajectory [trə'dʒektəri]		n.	[物] 轨道，轨线；[航][军] 弹道

I Vocabulary.

Match the word in Column A to the correct definition in Column B.

Column A
1. peer   2. aggressive
3. reinforce   4. elevate
5. manipulate

Column B
A. give a promotion to or assign to a higher position
B. characteristic of an enemy or one eager to fight
C. influence or control shrewdly or deviously
D. a person who is of equal standing with another in a group
E. make stronger

II Comprehension of the text.

Decide whether the following statements are true (T) or false (F) according to the passage.

1. Aggressive and victimizing peer behaviors are limited to dyads and can not function at the group level.
2. Concentrated exposure to positive peer affiliations can reduce risks for social, emotional, or behavioral problems.
3. Shifts in household residences introduce disruptions into children's lives that can

compromise the maintenance and accessibility of their social networks, particularly when parents' social and institutional ties are displaced.

4. Evidence suggests that poorly educated parents are more socially isolated but are better connected to the school system, and generate more social learning opportunities for their children outside of the school environment.

5. Yet surprisingly, few studies have explored how first-grade children's social, emotional, and behavioral trajectories are affected by the intersection of school disadvantage and the social environment of children's classrooms in the context of family-level risks.

III Try to fill in the spaces with the suitable words.

1. Peers reinforce episodes of school-based _____ by watching or by physically or verbally joining the aggressors.

2. Evidence shows that being competent in the social, emotional, or behavioral domain or having friends who can provide support and protection reduces children's risk of being victimized and _____ their likelihood of receiving prosocial acts from peers.

3. Having a stable group of well-adjusted, prosocial peers in the classroom increases children's exposure to more positive social learning experiences, which may, in turn, enhance their _____.

4. Schools that concentrate children who are vulnerable to social, emotional, or behavioral problems together may _____ their exposure to competent peers and positive peer interactions.

5. The classroom concentration of _____ was expected to buffer the effects of multiple household moves, low levels of mothers' education, and school disadvantage on changes in children's behaviors.

▶▶ Useful phrases and expressions ◀◀◀◀◀

家风 family bonds
家教 family education
学区房 school-nearby house
五好家庭 Five-Virtues Family
低收入家庭 low-income household/ family
尊师重教 respect teachers and value education

言传身教 teach sb with their own words and deeds
全国教育大会 the National Education Conference
家长教师联谊会 Parent-Teacher Association (PTA)
扣好人生的第一粒扣子 fasten the first button in life correctly

All schools must make moral education their fundamental task and integrate it into all aspects of education management. We must make sure that building strong moral character sits at the root of personnel training. The outcome of moral education should be taken as the fundamental criterion for appraising all schoolwork.

各级各类教育要坚持把立德树人作为学校办学的根本，把立德树人作为人员培训的核心。要把立德树人的成效作为检验学校一切工作的根本标准。

World-class Chinese universities must have distinctive Chinese characteristics. We will not be successful if we simply follow others and copy what they are doing.

办好中国的世界一流大学，必须有中国特色。没有特色，跟在他人后面亦步亦趋，依样画葫芦，是不可能办成功的。

Xi Jinping pointed out at the National Education Conference that families, schools, government, and society should all do their share and perform their responsibilities in education.

习近平总书记在全国教育大会上指出，办好教育事业，家庭、学校、政府、社会都有责任。

We need to improve the network where schools, families, and society work together for a common goal. Families and society are encouraged to collaborate with schools to consolidate educational outcomes by creating a positive family and social ethos. The three actors working together will create a strong synergy.

要完善学校、家庭、社会三结合的教育网络，引导广大家庭和社会各方面主动配合学校教育，以良好的家庭氛围和社会风气巩固学校教育成果，形成家庭、社会与学校同向同行、携手育人的强大合力。

No matter how times change or how life changes, family values, family education, and family bonds must be emphasized.

不论时代发生多大变化，不论生活格局发生多大变化，都要重视家庭建设，注重家庭、注重家教、注重家风。

Parents should teach their children with their own words and deeds, giving them both knowledge and virtue and practicing what they teach. They should help their children "fasten the first button in life correctly" and take the first step on the ladder of life correctly.

广大家庭要重言传、重身教，教知识、育品德，身体力行、耳濡目染，帮助孩子扣好人生的第一粒扣子，迈好人生的第一个台阶。

As the cells of society, families serve as the first schools.

家庭是社会的基本细胞，是人生的第一所学校。

Among the many aspects of family education, the most important is character-building. Parents should pass on good moral values to their children, cultivating in them integrity and compassion, and preparing them to serve the country and the people.

家庭教育涉及很多方面，但最重要的是品德教育，是如何做人的教育。作为父母和家长，应该把美好的道德观念从小就传递给孩子，培养他们做人的气节和骨气，长大后成为对国家和人民有用的人。

Parents should teach their children to appreciate the true, the good, and the beautiful, and to avoid the false, the evil, and the ugly.

家长要善于从点滴小事中教会孩子欣赏真善美、远离假丑恶。

Parents should respect the educational arrangements of schools and the creative efforts of teachers. They should cooperate with schools to ensure that their children receive a good education. Also, parents should pay close attention to psychological and behavioral changes in their children, and guide them in the right developmental paths.

家长要尊重学校教育安排，尊敬老师创造发挥，配合学校搞好孩子的学习教育，同时要注意观察孩子的思想动态和行为变化，随时做好教育引导工作。

Unit 10 Moral Education
道德教育

Text A Education as a Moral Enterprise

导读：道德教育，我们应该怎样看待它所扮演的角色？毫无疑问，在学生的成长过程中，道德教育有利于培养学生的良好品德，帮助其对有争议的良知问题做出理性的判断。

We trust it is uncontroversial to say that schooling is unavoidably a moral enterprise. Indeed, schools teach morality in a number of ways, both implicit and explicit.

Schools have a moral ethos embodied in rules, rewards and punishments, dress codes, honor codes, student government, relationships, styles of teaching, extracurricular emphases, art, and in the kinds of respect accorded students and teachers. Schools convey to children what is expected of them, what is normal, what is right and wrong. It is often claimed that values are caught rather than taught; through their ethos, schools socialize children into patterns of moral behavior.

Textbooks and courses often address moral questions and take moral positions. Literature inevitably explores moral issues, and writers take positions on those issues—as do publishers who decide which literature goes in the anthologies. In teaching history we initiate students into particular cultural traditions and identities. Although economics courses and texts typically avoid overt moral language and claim to be "value free", their accounts of human nature, decision making, and the economic world have moral implications, as we have seen.

The overall shape of the curriculum is morally loaded by virtue of what it requires, what it makes available as electives, and what it ignores. For example, for more than a century (but especially since A Nation at Risk and the reform reports of the 1980s), there has been a powerful movement to make schooling and the curriculum serve economic purposes. Religion and art, by contrast, have been largely ignored (and are not even elective possibilities in many schools). As a result, schooling encourages a rather more materialistic and less spiritual culture—a matter of some moral significance.

Educators have devised a variety of approaches to values and morality embodied in self-esteem, community service, civic education, sex education, drug education, Holocaust education, multicultural education, values clarification, and character education programs—to name but a few. We might consider two of the most influential of these approaches briefly.

For the past several decades values clarification programs have been widely used in public schools. In this approach, teachers help students "clarify" their values by having them reflect on moral dilemmas and think through the consequences of the options open to them, choosing that action that maximizes their deepest values. It is unjustifiable for a teacher to "impose" his or her values on students; this would be an act of oppression that denies the individuality and autonomy of students. Values are ultimately personal; indeed, the implicit message is that there are no right or wrong values. Needless to say, this is a deeply controversial approach—and is now widely rejected.

The character education movement of the last decade has been a response, in part, to the perceived relativism of values clarification.

Finally, we note what is conspicuous by its absence: Although all universities offer courses in ethics, usually in departments of philosophy or religious studies, very few public schools have such courses. Unlike either values clarification or character education programs, the major purpose of ethics courses is usually to provide students with intellectual resources drawn from a variety of traditions and schools of thought that might orient them in the world and help them think through difficult moral problems. As important as we all agree morality to be, it is striking that schools do not consider ethics courses an option worth offering.

Socialization, we suggested, is the uncritical initiation of students into a tradition, a way of thinking and acting. Education, by contrast, requires critical distance from tradition, exposure to alternatives, informed and reflective deliberation about how to think and live.

Not all, but much character education might better be called character training or socialization, for the point is not so much to teach virtue and values by way of critical reflection on contending points of view, but to structure the moral ethos of schooling to nurturing the development of those moral habits and virtues that we agree to be good and important, that are part of our moral consensus. This is not a criticism of character education. Children must be morally trained. But there are limitations to character education as a general theory of moral education: it was not designed to address critical thinking about those "ideologically charged" debates that divide us. Character education does appeal, as the Manifesto makes clear, to a heritage of stories, literature, art, and biography to inform and deepen students' understanding of, and appreciation for, moral virtue. Often such literature will reveal the moral ambiguities of life, and discussion of it will encourage critical reflection on what is right and wrong. But if the literature is chosen to nurture the development of the right virtues and values, it may not be well suited to nurture an appreciation of moral ambiguity or informed and critical thinking about contending values and ways of thinking and living (Of course, character education programs often nurture the virtues of tolerance, respect, and civility that play major roles in enabling educational discussion of controversial issues.)

One of the supposed virtues of the values clarification movement, by contrast, was its use of moral dilemmas and divisive issues; moreover, in asking students to consider the consequences of their actions, it required them to think critically about them. But the values clarification movement never required students to develop an educated understanding of moral frameworks of thought that could inform their thinking and provide them with critical distance on their personal desires and moral intuitions; it left them to their own inner resources.

Let us put it this way. Character education is an essential aspect of moral education, but a fully adequate theory of moral education must also address those morally divisive ("ideologically charged") issues that are sufficiently important so that students must be educated about them. Of course, one of these issues is the nature of morality itself; after all, moral education, it was not designed to address critical thinking about those "ideologically charged" debates that divide us. If students are to be morally educated—and educated about morality—they must have some understanding of the moral frameworks civilization provides for making sense of the moral dimension of life. After all, morality is not intellectually free-floating, a matter of arbitrary choices and merely personal values. Morality is bound up with our place in a community or tradition, our understanding of nature and human nature, our convictions about the afterlife, our experiences of the sacred, our assumptions about what the mind can know, and our understanding of what makes life meaningful. We make sense of what we ought to do, of what kind of a person we should be, in light of all of these aspects of life—at least if we are reflective.

For any society (or school) to exist, its members (students, teachers, and administrators) must share a number of moral virtues: They must be honest, responsible, and respectful of one another's well-being. We agree about this. Public schools have a vital role to play in nurturing these consensus virtues and values, as the character education movement rightly emphasizes; indeed, a major purpose of schooling is to help develop good persons.

If we are to live together peacefully in a pluralistic society, we must also nurture those civic virtues and values that are part of our constitutional tradition: We must acknowledge responsibility for protecting one another's rights; we must debate our differences in a civil manner; we must keep informed. A major purpose of schooling is to nurture good citizenship.

What shape moral education should take depends on the maturity of students. We might think of a K-12 continuum in which character education begins immediately with the socialization of children into those consensus values and virtues that sustain our communities. As children grow older and more mature they should gradually be initiated into a liberal education in which they are taught to think in informed and reflective ways about important, but controversial, moral issues.

Character education and liberal education cannot be isolated in single courses but should be integrated into the curriculum as a whole. We also believe, however, that the curriculum should include room for a moral capstone course that high school seniors might take, in which they learn about the most important moral frameworks of thought—secular and religious, historical and contemporary—and how such frameworks might shape their thinking about the most urgent moral controversies they face.

K-12 (pronounced "k twelve", "k through twelve", or "k to twelve" 基础教育的年龄段): is a designation for the sum of primary and secondary education. It is used in the United States, Canada, Australia, and New Zealand where K-12 is also commonly used. The expression is a shortening of Kindergarten (K) for 4-6-year-olds through twelfth grade (12) for 16-19-year-olds, the first and last grades of free education in these countries.

Unit 10　Moral Education　道德教育

New words and expressions

1. ethos ['i:θɔs]　　　　　　　n.　　民族精神，道德风貌，气质
2. anthology [æn'θɔlədʒi]　　n.　　选集，文选
3. initiate...into...　　　　　　　　传授某人奥秘
4. holocaust ['hɔləkɔ:st]　　　n.　　大屠杀，浩劫
5. conspicuous [kən'spikjuəs]　adj.　明显的，显而易见的
6. orient ['ɔ:riənt]　　　　　　v.　　使……适应，朝……方位
7. arbitrary ['ɑ:bitrəri]　　　　adj.　任意的，专制的
8. pluralistic [pluərə'listik]　　adj.　多元论的
9. capstone ['kæpstəun]　　　n.　　顶层石，顶点
10. secular ['sekjulə]　　　　　adj.　世俗的，非宗教的

I　Vocabulary.

Fill in the blanks with the most suitable words. Change the form when necessary.

conspicuous　　ethos　　anthology　　arbitrary　　capstone

1. This _____ reveals a prejudice in favor of lyric poets.
2. I guess we're not used to your _____ standards, and you'd better change your plan.
3. Lincoln is a _____ example of a poor boy's success, whose experiences have encouraged and inspired numerous young people.
4. The day could not be far distant when naturalism would dominate the _____ of American literature.
5. He stood at the _____ of his political career.

II　Comprehension of the text.

Decide whether the following statements are true (T) or false (F) according to the passage.

1. It is often claimed that values are taught rather than caught; through their ethos, schools socialize children into patterns of moral behavior.　　　　　　　(　　)

2. For the past several decades values clarification programs have been widely used in private schools. （　）
3. The major purpose of schooling is to develop good persons and nurture good citizenship. （　）
4. Character education and liberal education should be integrated into the curriculum for a moral capstone course in which school seniors learn about the most important moral frameworks of thought. （　）
5. Moral education was supposed to address critical thinking about those "ideologically charged" debates that divide us and whose moral character we should hold onto. （　）

III Discussion.

1. Does your school provide moral education for you? Is it effective?
2. What do you think are the major purposes of schooling? Try to name some.
3. One of the supposed virtues of the values clarification movement, by contrast, was its use of moral dilemmas and divisive issues. Do you think this method can be adopted here in China? Can it really work?

Text B Moral Education of Youth in the Information Age

导读：在中国，人们意识到学校教育的主要目的是教会学生做人，因此道德教育越来越被视为教育的重要部分。传统的道德教育无外乎正确道德观和价值观的反复灌输。而在信息时代，这样的教育方式，需要借助一定的信息技术，才能达到我们期望的效果。

(1) _____

Moral education in the Information Age is becoming an increasingly complex project because of the greater diversity of values that are present in our communities institutions, and life situations. When combined with the rapid pace of change that is characteristic of the Information Age, the variety of values that circulate in the communities and institutions challenge the general and uniformed applicability of moral principles that we have unquestionably accepted as truth. The emergence of values that are akin to the market and the keen competition that it generates, for example, has challenged the authority of certain time—honored values and practices, if not rendered them obsolete. Few moral principles can be exempted from the close scrutiny of moral educators who are urgently exploring ways to sustain the vitality and relevance of their work in the schools and beyond. Without beliefs and principles that are sound and lasting, moral education will have no intellectual and ethical footing. It will drift aimlessly in the sea of irrelevance.

The anxiety of moral educators has to be understood in today's context of cultural diversity and social change. The conception of cultural diversity is no longer confined within the boundaries of a country, for the Internet has quietly but effectively disseminated immense volumes of ideas, images and artifacts of culture among citizens of any nations that have access to it. Moreover, interaction among people on the internet presents a kind of social change that challenges our ability to think morally in a real yet imaginary relationship. The absence of physical contacts in the "cyber world" often distorts our views on moral obligation toward others: If we do not even have eye-contact in making the transaction, how can we be obligated toward one another? Thus immoral acts such as the non-delivery of goods purchased, thefts of intellectual properties, intrusion into others "privacy, and even the deprivation of others" right to operate their computers normally, are buried behind a curtain of anonymity in the "cyber world".

Cultural diversity and social change in the Information Age warrant a new kind of understanding of the foundations of moral education. Diversity and change afford an opportunity for us to reflect on the aims of moral education and explore ways to facilitate the attainment of goals. If diversity of values has to be understood in specific cultural and social contexts, and change has become a constant factor in our lives, then it may be tempting to take no moral stance in our judgments and actions and submit ourselves to the command of moral relativism. When this happens, moral education loses it vitality, for it is no longer a principled exercise of our hearts and minds. For moral education in schools, upholding certain defensible moral principles is a particularly important undertaking because it will determine whether moral education can continue to serve its educational purposes.

(2) _____

Fortunately for moral educators in schools, these moral principles can always be found in their schools' missions. While the continual interpretation and refinement of these principles can sustain their endeavors to a certain extent, lofty ideals that defy common wisdom may not be fully accepted by the students and their parents. For this reason, it should be the labor of moral educators to identify and uphold simple and enduring principles that can be readily embraced by all parties concerned. One of these principles is "respect for oneself and respect for others". "Respect" is a maxim in moral education that has been upheld by Chinese and western educators alike. As an essential element in any healthy social relations, "respect" refers not only to a desirable position toward others but also toward oneself. It affirms a person's worth, dignity, and rights. Because other persons have just as much worth, dignity, and rights as I, then it is reasonable for me to respect others as I should respect myself. As a guiding principle, "do not do to others what you do not want done to yourself" can be a simple but very useful constraint on one's desires and actions. More positively, "respect for others" provides an essential reference for one's attitude and conduct toward others, especially toward those persons that you do not know, or has no relations with. "Respect" magnifies the worth of a person. At the same time, it affords an axiological lens through which the worth and needs of "others" can be clearly recognized.

The students' capability of handling their relations with others can be enhanced if moral education is based on respect for others. From a social perspective, people's moral conduct is manifested in their relations with others; and moral education can only be effectively conducted with the "I-other" relationship as its epistemological and axiological basis. If our students can consider the dignity, rights, and welfare of others before they act, then it is much less likely that their actions would be harmful to others or to the common good. Moreover, if moral education call help the students to cultivate a thorough understanding of the "I-other" relationship and help them to nurture positive feelings toward others, then other important qualities such as compassion and empathy can be further developed. A desirable state in moral development is reached when altruism becomes an integral part of their character.

Given the aforementioned observation, the function of moral education is to help students handle their relations with others properly. Moral educators should guide students to appreciate the existence of others, care about their needs, understand their predicaments, empathize with their plight, and respect their rights and values. With this, the students will be able to gradually transcend their own self-interests and to give appropriate attention to matters of public interests. Their participation in the advancement of the common good will be a matter of course.

(3) _____

Many scholars and practitioners in education have assumed that the school is the only suitable sites for moral education. Indeed, as the social institution that is charged with the responsibility of teaching our children the basic literacy and social skills, the school seems to be the natural site for their moral education as well. However, today's formal schooling has lagged behind the developmental needs of the Information Age. This is especially true in terms of its requirements for human development. The examination-oriented pedagogy that is so prevalent in Chinese schools leaves little time and intellectual space for students to develop their social awareness and skills. Operating under the tyranny of an "audit culture" where "value-addedness" and academic achievement are the main concerns, our schools are consumed by the imperatives of performativity. The only emphasis of today's schooling is the demonstrable and measurable outcomes of education. Exploration of the inherent values of education is in large part being neglected by our schools; and, if such values are needed for ornamental purposes, the schools pay lip service to them and to moral education which embodies and expresses them.

Actually, the most natural site for moral education is the family. The family is considered to be the unit that consists of the most significant "others" in the lives of children and youths—their parents. The parents' influence on the moral development of their children is strong and lifelong. It is in the family where parental devotion to the well-being of the child can be considered a given, and where adult-child ratio in the educative process is definitely more favorable than that of the school. The home environment, moreover, affords a context in which intimate thoughts and feelings can be shared readily between parents and child without the social pressure and pretense that are often found in more formal social settings. Thus the family provides a more accommodating setting for moral education which warrants the exchange of ideas and inculcation of values that are personally derived. Among educators, the common concern about the family as a site of moral education is whether parents can truly understand the developmental needs of their children, and whether they are ready to engage their offspring in a knowledgeable and sensible way. Indeed, the needs of children for parental guidance and support differ from one stage of moral development to another. The manners of engagement, whether they are restrictive or supportive, in fact reflect the psychological basis on which moral education is conducted at home.

Other sites that can serve as platforms for moral education are the educational activities that are conducted outside the framework of the formal system of schooling. Rich in diversity, these activities afford a broad educational avenue through which the interests of growing children and adolescents can be served. Out-of-school programs which constitute what is known as "non-formal education" include a large variety of organized social and cultural activities that are organized by institutions and agencies such as youth palaces, cultural stations and museums, and by children and youth groups such as the Boys Scouts and Young Pioneers. In ways that are less rigid but more informal than classroom instruction, these out-of-school programs can be equally effective in inculcating desirable values and attitudes in the students. Their efficacy, however, remains to be tapped by moral educators.

Another possible site for moral education is the neighborhood. Compared to the schools and non-formal education programs, the neighborhood is much less structured. Compared to the family, it is more public; but for the social development of children and youths. It's potentiality for children's exploration and understanding of the "I-other" relations should not be underestimated. The neighborhood is where children and youths spend most of their time besides their homes and schools. Unlike homes and schools, which are highly controlled sites, neighborhoods are much less restrictive on behaviors. Thus whether neighborhoods are sites of opportunities for exploration and discovery or danger zones for indulgence and debauchery depends very much on the kind of activities that children and youths participate in. This in turn depends on the kind of peers that they choose to keep. Research has shown that risk-taking activities are more prevalent among youths in poorer neighborhoods than in densely populated urban areas. Research has also shown that youths, because they "inhabit a transitional middle-ground somewhere between childhood and adulthood", are excluded from many physical and social space in the community. For the purpose of moral education, the neighborhood can be a site where "respect for others" can be understood and practiced. If appropriate activities can be arranged, children and youths can practice neighborliness through participation in community service and observe first-hand the effects of their own contribution to the well-being of others.

(4) _____

A site for moral education that is unique to the Information Age is the "cyber world" that embodies numerous networks which serve to facilitate instant communication among users of information technologies. For moral educators, the emergence of the "cyber world" can be unsettling because of all the "demons" that lurk within a world that we cannot see. There can be little protection of the young minds if the corrupting effects are not readily discernible from their behavior. This kind of disorientation brought on by the presence of the "cyber world" poses the most serious challenge to moral education, regardless of its sites of application. This is because the "multidirectional networks" are transforming the structure of our economic and social institutions and our established system of beliefs and values would have to be able to maintain its validity and relevance in order to survive. The challenges to the established system will be multidimensional, intense and swift, because the global onslaught of axiological persuasions is projected through so many powerful lenses of informational technologies. Our world is now connected in global networks of the information and images that travel throughout the world instantly. Without a clear and strong epistemological and axiological anchor, moral education will drift in the sea of contentious ideas and values.

If we accept that moral education is an enterprise that should undergo constant review and revival, then the waves of new information that are generated from the multidirectional networks should not be feared; that is, if we can derive wisdom and insights from them. As a matter of fact, it is in this newly found wisdom that we can identify the impetus to the constant revival of moral education. New information and ideas challenge us to reflect on our own values; and if we can develop new notions of justice, rights, fairness, equity and harmony that we can uphold, and then we can confidently use them to guide our children and youths through the stages of their development with renewed interest and relevance. Moral educators should embrace the current phenomena of uncertainty and attempt to negotiate new notions of morality and education so that they do not fall too far behind the developmental needs of our children and youths. In fact, educators in other areas are attempting to do just that. The efforts of language educators to derive new meanings of literacy from the internet, for example, should serve as a useful reference for moral educators if they indeed wish to reestablish their bearings and resituate notions of morality in the realities of the "cyber world".

New words and expressions

1. render ['rendə] v. 提供，表现，使成为
2. anonymity [ænə'nimətɪ] n. 匿名，笔者不明
3. warrant ['wɔːrənt] v. 担保，给……正当理由
4. axiological [æksɪə'lɔdʒɪkəl] adj. 价值论的
5. epistemological [ɪpɪstəmə'lɔdʒɪkəl] adj. 认识论的
6. predicament [prɪ'dɪkəmənt] n. 困境
7. plight [plaɪt] n. 困境，苦境
8. lip service 说的好听的话，空口的应酬话
9. inculcation [ˌɪnkʌl'keɪʃn] n. 教授，谆谆教导
10. debauchery [dɪ'bɔːtʃərɪ] n. 放荡，沉湎酒色
11. discernible [dɪ'səːnəbəl] adj. 可辨别的

Exercises

I Read the following subheadings and put them in the blank in this text appropriately.

a. The "cyber world" as a site of moral education
b. Respect as a guiding principle for moral education
c. Sites of moral education
d. Whither is the moral education drifting?

II Comprehension of the text.

Decide whether the following statements are true (T) or false (F) according to the passage.

1. The conception of cultural diversity is limited in a nation, for people immigrate and emigrate more often than before. (   )
2. Lofty ideas defy common wisdom should not be fully acknowledged by students, so educators labor to uphold some simple principles. (   )
3. Home and neighborhood are two ideal places for children to cultivate and nurture moralities. (   )
4. Due to measures taken by the government and serious policies devoted to the protection of young minds when they are online, we totally don't have to worry about "demons", which lurk in a virtual world. (   )
5. We need to develop new notions of justice, rights, fairness, equity and harmony that we can uphold, and then we can confidently use them to guide our children and youths through the stages of their development with renewed interest and relevance, because they need various help during different steps. (   )

III Discussion.

1. How do your parents help you to cultivate your morality in different developmental stages?
2. Why do you think it is very important for us to focus on "cyber world" morality?
3. How can we make full advantage of the Internet to let it serve to the morality purpose?

Unit 10　Moral Education　道德教育

Useful phrases and expressions

全面发展　all-round development
立德树人　foster virtue through education
素质教育　quality-oriented education
高等教育　higher education
品德养成　moral character development
个性发展　personality development
教育体制　education system
知识面　the scope of knowledge
终身学习　lifelong learning
家庭教育　family education

Moral Education is a subject that helps the teachers in helping the students in learning the value and virtues that would make them a good human being in a longer run.

德育是一门帮助教师向学生传授价值及美德的学科，目的是让学生在未来更长的时间内成为一个品德高尚的人。

The values that rule coexistence, solidarity, honesty, equality, responsibility, freedom, love, respect towards life, difference and human rights, cooperation and peace and justice must be promoted in the everyday life of the educational institution and in the curricula areas.

教育机构应该在日常学习生活和课程领域之中，弘扬共存、团结、诚实、平等、责任、自由，以及爱的价值观，展示对生命、差异和人权的尊重，宣传合作、和平与正义精神。

The most basic aim of education is to foster virtue.

育人的根本在于育德。

The education department has actively built platforms for both practical and moral education, and implemented numerous projects to promote the physical and mental well-being of young people and support their all-around development.

教育部门积极搭建实践教育和道德教育平台，实施多项促进青少年身心健康、支持青少年全面发展的项目。

Since values or moral education in schools has gained much attention from educators, practitioners, policymakers and especially political leaders, a new tide of the school-based values education movement has been proposed and undertaken in response to the disappointing moral situation in society.

由于学校的价值观或道德教育得到了教育家、实践者、政策制定者，特别是政治领导人的广泛关注，一系列新的校本位道德教育运动应运而生，以此来应对社会上令人失望的道德现状。

In the post-epidemic era, schools should strengthen moral education, guide students to return to the real world from the virtual online world, and increase their interest in learning.

在后疫情时代，学校应加强道德教育，引导学生从虚拟的网络世界回归现实世界，提高学习兴趣。

In Singapore, elements of national education are incorporated into the curriculums for primary, secondary and higher education via subjects like Social Studies and Character and Citizenship Education.

在新加坡，国民教育的要素被纳入小学、中学和高等教育课程之中，包括社会研究、性格以及公民教育等科目。

Japan has made "moral education" an official subject in primary and junior high schools since April 2018 and April 2019 respectively, thereby promoting national education.

自 2018 年 4 月和 2019 年 4 月起，日本分别将"道德教育"确定为小学和初中的正式科目，由此促进国民教育的发展。

Universities should strengthen moral education for students and deal with any violations of school discipline and rules in a serious manner so as to maintain a healthy and safe learning and living environment on campus.

高校应该加强对学生的道德教育，严肃处理任何违反校纪校规的行为，以维护一个健康、安全的校园学习和生活环境。

We should promote high-quality, balanced development and urban-rural integration of compulsory education, intensify efforts to develop vocational education, and continue to explore new ground in higher education.

推进义务教育优质均衡发展和城乡一体化，大力发展职业教育，推进高等教育创新。

Unit 11　Extra-curricular Activities
课外活动

Text A　Extra-curricular Activity and the Transition from Higher Education to Work

导读：根据对英国毕业生的一份大规模调查研究显示，课外活动对毕业生从学校走向工作岗位这一过程的转变有着重大的影响。可以总结出两种情况：一种是频繁的课外活动使毕业生在转变期的表现比平均水平好；另一种是比平均水平差。为什么会这样是一个值得研究的课题。

Extra-curricular activity is important because of its potential to reinforce and market the outcomes of the education system. Any particular involvement in a certain type of extra-curricular activity may influence a graduate's transition process to the labor market, for instance, by speeding up or slowing down access to employment. Therefore, it is essential that students and graduates understand the impact of extra-curricular activity and appraise the role it may play in their strategies for transition from higher education to employment.

Analyzing the effects of extra-curricular activity is also important to guidance services. As was stressed in a recent international report, most guidance activities in higher education concentrate on course choices and on psychological counseling to deal with students' emotional and study problems. However, as educational institutions are faced with increasing competition for students and resources, the labor market outcome of graduates is becoming a key marketing argument. Therefore, as a contribution to develop knowledge on the process of transition from higher education to the labor market, analyzing the effects of extra-curricular activities is crucial to guidance services and to their host institutions.

Research attention to date has been focused on the influence of extra-curricular activity on college choice decision making, personality and social behavior and alumni generosity. Factors affecting participation in extra-curricular activities have also been studied. In contrast, little attention has been paid to the influence of extra-curricular activities on the outcome of the education-to-work transition process. Former researches have found that, in the United States, participation in varsity sports may have positive effects on earnings, although these effects may vary according to graduates' ethnic background. But researchers have generally ignored the role of other types of extra-curricular activities as well as the effects of these activities on non-salary conditions of labor market entry. Therefore, this research should be of interest to readers involved in higher education, especially students, guidance researchers and practitioners, and educational administrators interested in rethinking the place of extra-curricular activities in higher education.

The following presents a survey of graduates in UK.

Interpretative framework

Economic theory, especially statistical discrimination theory, posits that employers pay particular attention to the non-market activities of job applicants. On the one hand, some employers value the non-market activities of job applicants. These employers consider that having been involved in non-market activities is an indicator of an applicant's responsibility, citizenship and maturity which they think will be of advantage to the firm. On the other hand, other employers consider that non-market activities have a negative effect. The main concern of this second type of employer amounts to excluding high turnover rate ("*high-quit-rate*") candidates, because turnover is costly to firms. Since the turnover propensity of an applicant cannot be observed directly, these employers divide applicants into two groups: a high-attrition-rate group and a low-attrition-rate group. These employers negatively associate worker turnover with non-market activities. Two reasons may explain this perspective. First, involvement in family life or in leisure or social activities may indicate low professional commitment resulting in low productivity and eventually firing. Second, family and social life can expand or become more important to such an extent that the employee resigns from the firm. In both cases, extra-professional life would appear to be a source of turnover. Consequently, applicants considered as belonging to the high-attrition-rate group are faced with stricter employment criteria, lower wages and fewer interviews, and may therefore be excluded altogether from the recruitment process, even when they are as qualified as other candidates. The statistical discrimination theory is not but one of the multiple ways to explain restricted access to employment. A lot of alternative approaches have been developed, especially by labor economists, which take into account such diverse determinants as employers' preferences, job-searchers' strategies, the behavior of labor market intermediaries, economic structures or labor market public policies. But statistical discrimination is of particular interest because it provides a framework to interpret extra-curricular activities. Within this framework, students' leisure and social activities can be interpreted as non-market activities, which employers consider positively or negatively. In that respect, the statistical discrimination approach helps us to better understand the relationships that might be observed between extra-curricular activity and labor market entry.

Method

The survey was designed within the Research Laboratory in Theoretical and Applied Economics (Beta) at Louis Pasteur University of Strasbourg (France). Associations, offices, and networks of alumni from higher education were contacted in the UK and were requested to invite their members to respond a questionnaire on the survey website.

The questionnaire had three parts. Part one focused on personal details and education, part two on the respondents' extra-curricular non-market activities while students, and part three on their experiences during the transition process from higher education to the labor market. The transitional period was defined as the three years immediately following graduation.

One hundred nineteen individuals responded to the questionnaire. These respondents constitute the sample of the survey. This is clearly a small sample. The effects of extra-curricular activity were investigated by means of regression analysis. Five explanatory variables were taken into account: the involvement in extra-curricular activities, the type of activity, and the time spent in the activity, the intensity of the involvement and the context of practice. In addition, the degree levels and subjects were included as independent variables in the estimates too, in order to clearly make the difference between their own effects and those of the five extra-curricular factors mentioned above. Three degree levels (bachelor, master and doctorate) and four degree subjects were distinguished. Given that different variables can yield similar effects because of inter-correlations between variables, inter-correlations were checked. No case of strong inter-correlation among the independent variables could be observed. The effects of these potential factors were investigated on five categories of dependent variables: job security, occupational status, access to large firms, wages and unemployment. For each outcome variable, several alternative specifications were used in order to avoid missing any significant effect. It was also checked that these outcome variables were uncorrelated. Linear regression analysis (ordinary least squares) was used when the dependent variables were quantitative while logistic regression analysis was used when they were qualitative. A two-step estimation procedure was adopted. The first step consisted in estimating the effects of involvement within the whole sample. The second step consisted in estimating the effects of all other factors put together within the group of respondents with extra-curricular experience.

Results and comments

Extra-curricular experience has a twofold influence on the outcome of the transitional process. On the one hand, having been involved in extra-curricular activity creates an advantage in terms of occupational status. As compared with graduates who were involved in extra-curricular activities, those who did not participate were almost three times more likely to begin their careers as office employees rather than as managers. On the other hand, graduates without extra-curricular experience had been unemployed for a significantly shorter period of time before getting their first jobs. These findings show that involvement in extra-curricular activities makes a difference. Further investigations demonstrate that within the group of the graduates who decided to be involved, the nature of the extra-curricular experience matters.

Job security

Within the group of graduates with extra-curricular experience, 93.75 per cent obtained an open-ended employment contract before the end of the transitional period (78.12 per cent right from the first job on). The most important factor favoring job security is participation in cultural activities.

As compared with other respondents, those who participated in cultural and spiritual activities were more likely to get open-ended contracts. Conversely, three characteristics were strongly linked with job insecurity. The first one has to do with the depth of the involvement. Graduates who engaged in an activity for a long period of time or at leadership level had fewer chances of getting open-ended contracts. Additionally, participation in the social sector led to fixed-term rather than open-ended contracts. Finally, the graduates who had practiced with their families or as clients were less likely to be employed under open-ended contracts within the transitional period.

Occupational status

Of the respondents with extra-curricular experience, 71.87 per cent reached a managerial position within the transitional period (59.37 per cent right from the first contract on). The access to a managerial position mainly depends on the depth and length of the involvement in activities as well as of the context of practice. A leadership experience gives more chances of reaching managerial positions. However, the whole extra-curricular experience should be kept in reasonable limits: The longer the experience, the fewer the chances of reaching managerial positions. Practice with family or with friends is also significantly correlated with becoming a manager. The types of activity play a role too.

Although no type of extra-curricular activity gives particular chances of becoming a manager, it seems that participation in student associations or in cultural activities are especially inadequate and tend to shift the graduates towards lower supervisory or office employee positions, at least for the first jobs.

Access to large firms

Of the respondents with extra-curricular experience, 51.56 per cent were employed in large firms during the transitional period (42.18 per cent right from the first job on).

Participation in sports was the less efficient extra-curricular activity as regards beginning one's career in a large firm. In comparison with participation in sports, involvement in student associations, in the social sector or in cultural activities gave better chances of joining a large firm right from the first job on. Graduates with an experience in citizenship activities also began their careers in larger firms. And at the end of the transitional period, graduates who had been participating in student associations or in citizenship activities were working in larger firms than those who participated in sports. Only the type of activity seems to matter. No other extra-curricular factor seems to have an influence on the access to large firms.

Wages

Wages are influenced by the context of practice and by the type of activity. Two observations may be made. The first one is that, as compared with practice within associations, practice with family seems to be more closely linked with better wages at the end of the transitional period. The second observation is that the graduates who participated in student associations or in the social sector had lower first-job wages than those who participated in sports.

Unemployment

Fifty percent of the respondent graduates with an extra-curricular experience have been unemployed at some time within the transition period (46.87 per cent before the first job). The risk and length of unemployment depend on the four extra-curricular factors. On one hand, two characteristics lower the risk and length of unemployment. First, the graduates who had been leaders in their extra-curricular activities had a lower risk of experiencing unemployment before the first job. Second, as regards the length of unemployment, the graduates who had practiced their activity with their family were unemployed during a significantly shorter period of time than others both before and after the first job. On the other hand, some other characteristics increase the risk and length of unemployment. First, participation in cultural activities and long-term involvement increase the risk of experiencing unemployment before the first job. Second, practice with friend or as a client lengthens the spells of unemployment.

Extra-curricular profiles

It thus can be seen that within the group of graduates with an extra-curricular experience, the nature of the extra-curricular activity makes a difference to entry into the workforce. Although most extra-curricular factors have a twofold influence, three clear-cut profiles could finally be distinguished.

Profile 1 comprises "Leaders and Citizens". The graduates who engaged at leadership level had better access to managerial positions and the lowest risk of unemployment before the first job. Those who participated in citizenship activities had access to large firms right from the first job on, and all along the transition period. Their spells in unemployment also seem to have been shorter.

Profile 2 represents the "Sports persons". This profile corresponds to the most frequent extra-curricular behavior, which consists in practicing sports as simple participant within associations. Profile 2 appears to be generally associated with average transition outcomes.

Profile 3 comprises "Activists and Clients". This profile features long-term participation and practice as a client. It could be observed that the graduates who practiced for a long period or as clients had fewer chances of getting open-ended contracts or managerial positions, and were at more risk of unemployment. According to the interpretative framework, this means that most employers considered long-term extra-curricular involvement and practice as a client as predictors of low professional commitment, low productivity, and high risk of turnover either by firing or by quitting.

These results emphasize the strategic potential of extra-curricular activity for students and graduates wishing improved transition to the labor market. Of course, extra-curricular activity is not only a matter of career development. It surely has much to do with personal development. But insofar as employers take account of the non-market involvement of job applicants, neither students nor education and guidance institutions should ignore the professional dimension of extra-curricular activity. Thus, for instance, it might be suggested to graduates to highlight in their resumes their "Profile 1" features. Awareness of the strategic potential of extra-curricular experience should also encourage guidance institutions to survey employers' extra-curricular preferences at the local level in order to assist graduates in building university-to-work transition strategies including effective extra-curricular participation. Furthermore, reconsidering the position and recognition of extra-curricular activities within higher education and their links with regular curricula might be of advantage to educational institutions facing competition in the higher education market. However, these results also raise the question of the way employers derive turnover and resignation probabilities from the nature of any extra-curricular activity. Why should employers unanimously appreciate involvement in citizenship activities but have diverging perspectives regarding participation in the social sector or in cultural and spiritual activities? A better understanding of employers' rationale and preferences regarding extra-curricular experience surely calls for further investigation.

OECD（经济合作与发展组织）: The Organization for Economic Co-operation and Development is an international economic organisation of 34 countries founded in 1961 to stimulate economic progress and world trade. It is a forum of countries committed to democracy and the market economy, providing a platform to compare policy experiences, seek answers to common problems, identify good practices, and co-ordinate domestic and international policies of its members.

New words and expressions

1. alumni [ə'lʌmnai] n. （男）校友；（男）毕业生
2. propensity [prəu'pensiti] n. 倾向；习性
3. criteria [krai'tiəriə] n. （criterion 的复数）（批评、判断的）标准，准则，尺度
4. regression [ri'greʃən] n. 回归
5. quantitative ['kwɔntitətiv] adj. 数量（上）的；量化的；定量性的
6. twofold ['tu:fəuld] adj. 两倍的，双重的
7. supervisory [,sju:pə'vaizəri] adj. 管理的，监督的
8. correspond [,kɔ:ri'spɔnd] v. 相符合，相一致
9. insofar [,insəu'fɑ:] 在这个范围；到这种程度
10. derive [di'raiv] v. 得到；（从……中）获得
11. estimate ['estimeit] n. 估计，估价

Exercises

I Vocabulary.

Fill in the blanks with the most suitable words. Change the form when necessary.

| propensity | insofar | derive | correspond | estimate |

1. Your account of events does not _____ with hers.
2. _____ as I can see, the representatives are all satisfied with the arrangement.
3. I can give you a rough _____ of the amount of wood you will need.
4. She _____ great pleasure from painting.
5. He has a _____ to exaggerate.

II Comprehension of the text.

Decide whether the following statements are true (T) or false (F) according to the passage.

1. Much attention has been paid to the influence of extra-curricular activities on the outcome of the education-to-work transition process.

2. Some employers consider that having been involved in non-market activities is an indicator of an applicant's responsibility, citizenship and maturity which they think will be of advantage to the firm.
3. Graduates who engaged in an activity for a long period of time or at leadership level had more chances of getting open-ended contracts.
4. The graduates who engaged at leadership level had better access to managerial positions and the lowest risk of unemployment before the first job.

III Translate the following sentences into Chinese.

1. Therefore, it is essential that students and graduates understand the impact of extra-curricular activity and appraise the role it may play in their strategies for transition from higher education to employment.
2. Consequently, applicants considered as belonging to the high-attrition-rate group are faced with stricter employment criteria, lower wages and fewer interviews, and may therefore be excluded altogether from the recruitment process, even when they are as qualified as other candidates.
3. Five explanatory variables were taken into account: the involvement in extra-curricular activities, the type of activity, and the time spent in the activity, the intensity of the involvement and the context of practice.
4. However, the whole extra-curricular experience should be kept in reasonable limits: The longer the experience, the fewer the chances of reaching managerial positions.
5. Furthermore, reconsidering the position and recognition of extra-curricular activities within higher education and their links with regular curricula might be of advantage to educational institutions facing competition in the higher education market.

Text B Extra-curricular Physical Activity and Socioeconomic Status in Italian Adolescents

导读：体育活动和健康状况之间的关系已经被人们深入研究过，而体育活动和社会经济状况之间的关系较少被涉及。本文以对意大利几个地区高中生展开问卷调查的形式，来探讨青少年的体育活动和他们家庭的社会经济地位之间的关系。调查结果证实了青少年课外体育活动和其家庭的社会经济地位之间的关系，并对教育管理者及政治家们如何弥补贫富家庭子女的隔阂提供了帮助。

The relationship between physical activity and health status has been described extensively in several studies. Active lifestyles are often associated with better health status and quality of life, however, the relationship between socio-economic status (SES) and physical activity has been investigated less. In regards to this subject, the definition for SES seems to be extremely variable. Some researchers evaluate SES according to residence in low, middle or high income geographical areas; some consider employment exclusively; while others distinguish between the different socio-economic levels based on family income, for example, low (up to $26,200), middle (between $26,200 and $50,000) and high (>$50,000). Anyway, most of the studies on socio-economic determinants influencing physical activity choices consider education as a discriminating factor.

In Italy there isn't an individual SES classification available, territorial data (ISTAT data) is based on personal economic consumption rather than income and education. Another possible classification of personal income comes from the Italian financial acts and the different levels of income tax rates. However, this data is not easily inferable from statistical sampling including adolescents. The aim here was to investigate the relationship between adolescents' extra-curricular physical activity and the SES of their families.

The survey was carried out by submitting an anonymous questionnaire in junior high school students who were randomly selected in regions in Italy, during the school year 2002-2003. Sample size calculations (alpha=0.05; beta=0.20) suggested to sample 2,502 students. We obtained informed consent for interviewing minors in our research from their parents. Students absent during the first submission were given the questionnaire in the days following. 2,411 students (96.4% of the eligible individuals) agreed to participate in the research. The research was conducted according to the Declaration of Helsinki.

The questionnaire, already validated in a pilot study, contained information about the following areas:

-scholastic physical activity;

-extra-curricular physical activity;

-physical activity attitudes;

-lifestyle habits;

-parents' physical activity, education and work activity;

-students'socio-demographic data.

As far as it concerns physical activity of the adolescents, the questionnaire investigated whether or not extra-curricular physical activity is conducted, which type of physical activity is chosen by, how many hours per week are devoted to this activity. Concerning attitudes toward physical activity, it was asked if physical activity is considered useful in preventing obesity, in socializing, and in character-building. Moreover, we collected information on the following lifestyle habits, as dichotomous variables (yes/no): cigarette smoking, coffee and alcohol drinking. The following data from students' parents were collected: weekly physical activity, described as intense (more than two times per week), regular (two times per week), scarce (once per week) and absent; educational levels, indicating the level reached: Degree, Senior High school, Junior High school, Primary school; regarding work activities, we used a classification cited in another research: Managers/ Professionals, Office workers/Skilled workers, Non-skilled workers, Unemployed, Pensioners. In this classification housewives were considered equivalent to non-skilled workers.

Certain information about family income was impossible to obtain from the students. Therefore, SES was estimated considering parents' educational levels and work activities. The families' socio-economic levels were classified as: Very high, High, Middle, Middle-Low and Low.

Data from the questionnaires was collected in a suitable relational database and analyzed with SPSS statistical package.

Chi-square (χ^2) and chi-square for trend test for qualitative variables and student t-test for quantitative variables were applied to test the differences between the groups, considering $p<0.05$ as statistically significant.

Furthermore, multiple logistic regression analysis was performed, using two different models. The first verified the influence on the variable "extra-curricular physical activity" of the following covariates: age group (reference group: 10-12 years), sex (reference group: males), educational level of both parents (reference group: primary school), father's job (reference group: unemployed), parents' physical activity (reference group: no physical activity), student's opinions about sport as a means of socialization, character-building and prevention of obesity (reference group: negative responses).

The second regression analysis model evaluated the influence of the same covariates used in the first model (with the exception of the father's job) and that of socio-economic level (reference group: low socio-economic level) on the variable "extra-curricular physical activity". Analysis was performed using the Hosmer and

Lemeshow method.

Participants were 1,121 males (46.5%) and 1290 females (53.5%), aged between 11 and 17 years (median age 12 years). 33.7% of the students attended the first class, 38.5% the second and 27.8% the third one, 86.4% of them participated in school-based physical activity for two hours per week and 13.6% for three hours per week or more.

The types of school-based physical activity undertaken were as follows: 71.1% did gymnastics; 81.7% volleyball; 37.8% basketball; 10.7% football; 36.8% handball; 22.3% long jump; 21.6% high jump and 48.8% running.

71.1% of students declared to participate in extra-curricular physical activity with the following breakdown: 20.2% for one-two hours per week, 23.8% for three-four hours per week, while 56% stated they did five hours or more per week.

Concerning extra-curricular sports, 30.1% of the students played football, 19.7% did dancing/aerobics/gymnastics, 14.5% swam, 14.2% played volleyball, 5.8% played basket ball, 5.4% did fitness/body-building, 3.9% did martial arts, and 1.8% cycled.

370 students (15.3%) state to take nutritional supplementation before or after physical activity. 68.2% of students practicing extra-curricular physical activity stated that they paid a monthly fee.

Concerning attitudes toward physical activity, 79.9% of participants considered constant physical activity useful in preventing obesity, 5.6% did not and 14.5% were unsure. 82.7% of students considered physical activity important in socializing, 5.9% did not and 11.6% remained unsure. 56.1% of responders considered physical activity important in character-building, 15.8% did not and 19.1% did not know.

As for unhealthy lifestyles, 37.8% stated that they were smokers or had started smoking, 43.8% drank coffee and 43.4% drank alcohol, especially beer, wine, alcoholic lemon drinks and vodka.

With regards to parental physical activity levels, fathers were significantly more active than mothers (χ^2=15.41; p=0.001,5). However, there were not significant differences between parental education (χ^2=4.113; p=0.249).

The main parental work activities were: Office workers/ skilled workers (36.5%) and Non-skilled workers (34.3%) for fathers and housewives (59.3%) and office workers (28.3%) for mothers. According to our SES classification adolescents' families were categorized in the following way: very high 16.8%, high 14.5%, middle 37.2%, middle-low 30.1% and low 1.4%.

In relation to the SES of the students' family, the variables parents' educational levels and work activities were considered. The educational level attained by the father seems to considerably influence the student's physical activity. Students with fathers who graduated with a Degree practice extra-curricular physical activity more frequently (χ^2=64.764; p<0.000,1) and more intensively (χ^2=21.091; p<0.000,1) than those with fathers characterized by lower educational attainment.

86.3% of students with fathers graduated with a degree considered constant physical activity helpful in preventing obesity, compared to 85.2%, 80.7% and 69.4%, of students respectively, with fathers holding a diploma, a secondary-school leaving certificate or a primary school leaving certificate (χ^2=35.421; p<0.000,1). 86.7% of students with fathers graduated with a Degree considered constant physical activity helpful in socializing, versus 84.5%, 88% and 75.5% respectively, of students with fathers holding a diploma, a secondary school-leaving certificate, a primary school/leaving certificate (χ^2=11.155; p=0.084).

Mother's educational level also seemed to considerably influence the determinants of the student's physical activity and the total number of extra-curricular weekly physical activity hours. Students with mothers graduated with a Degree were more likely to practice extracurricular physical activity (χ^2=55.512; p<0.000,1) and undertook physical activity, for more than three hours per week (χ^2=19.65; p<0.000,1), than those whose mothers have a lower educational level.

86.4% of students with mothers graduated with a Degree and 86.5% of those whose mothers have a diploma considered physical activity important in socializing, compared to 84.6% and 78.1%, respectively, of students whose mothers have a secondary-school leaving or a primary school-leaving certificate (χ^2=12.817; p=0.046).

83.5% of students with graduated mothers considered constant physical activity useful in preventing obesity, compared to 85.3%, 80.4% and 77%, respectively, of students with mothers holding a diploma, a secondary school leaving certificate, a primary school-leaving certificate (χ^2=15.11; p=0.019).

Furthermore, extra-curricular physical activity is related to the parents' work activity. Students whose fathers are Managers/Professional or Office-workers/Skilled workers showed a significantly higher level of extra-curricular physical activity than students with fathers who were non-skilled workers, Unemployed or Retired from work (χ^2=39.029; p<0.000,1).

The mother's work activity also considerably influences the students' extra-curricular physical activity (χ^2=64.319; p<0.000,1). Adolescents with mothers who are Non-skilled workers/Housewives or Unemployed undertake less extra-curricular physical activity than those with mothers who were Managers/Professionals or Office workers/Skilled workers.

Weekly hours of extra-curricular physical activity show a similar trend: percentages of students practice physical activity for three hours per week or more. Frequency of extra-curricular physical activity performed during the week appears to be related to the work activity level of both parents, with a statistically significant difference for fathers (χ^2=8.229; p=0.048) and even more so for the mothers (χ^2=28.321; p<0.000,1).

Several studies show evidence of a relationship between socio-economic level and health status. As demonstrated by some studies, higher family income is associated with lower alcohol and cigarette consumption and a lower level of sedentary behavior. In Anglo-Saxon countries slums represent an obstacle to the practice of physical activity for several reasons ranging from absence of pavements, public parks and gardens to excessive traffic.

The likelihood of undertaking adequate physical activity is low for subjects who have a low family income and for not skilled Workers or Unemployed.

Studies on the relationship between physical activity and parents' educational level show that higher educational levels are determinant factors for children's physical activity. In particular, it is showed that demographic variables are good predictors of children's physical activity, and ethnic and SES differences are potential correlates of physical activity among adolescents. In a previous research, in 1,357 students in Central Italy, we found a strong relationship between weekly physical activity of adolescents, their BMI levels (overweight and obesity) and parents' educational levels and nutritional status, with a higher participation in physical activity shown above all in children with highly educated parents.

Our results confirm the relationship between family socio-economic, parents' educational levels and physical activity of adolescents.

Moreover the classification of socio-economic index used in this survey, derived by the combination of the parents' work activities (Very High, High, Middle, Middle-Low and Low), appears to be comparable to the distribution of family income levels.

Given these results, which are in agreement with other international surveys conducted in USA, South Africa, and Canada, we can say that family SES plays a key role in determining extra-curricular physical activity of students: the highest educational levels and the most remunerative work activities are directly related to the sporting practices of adolescents. Children with parents characterized by higher educational levels are encouraged more than others to practice constant and demanding extra-curricular sport. It is, demonstrated that among minority and low-SES adolescents (high school population) in USA, the prevalence rate of vigorous exercise tends to decrease with age or when this kind of population is not required to participate in school physical education. It is found that South African children belonging to the highest SES quartile were highly physically active, watched less television and had greater lean tissue than children in lower quartiles. In Canada, among adolescents aged 12-20 years, individuals from low income families had a 30% higher probability of being inactive than those from high income families. Families with high SES consider physical activity useful both in preventing chronic and degenerative diseases and for socialization, and essential for the correct physical and psychological development of adolescents.

SES is therefore clearly related to parents' educational levels, and parents' low educational levels and low remunerative work activities can negatively influence the participation of children in extra-curricular physical activity.

In addition, it must be considered the inadequate knowledge about benefits of physical activity, related to low socio-economic and cultural levels.

As far as concerns internal validity, we sampled randomly the participants, and used a validated questionnaire. Misclassification bias could arise if incorrect information on both exposure (SES status) and outcome. The accuracy of self-reported physical activity of adolescents should have been avoided, given the reliability of the tool we used, which had been validated before. Moreover, we collected detailed information on potential confounding factors and took it into account in the analysis of possible effects.

As far as external validity, a potential selection bias could have been avoided, even if a cross-sectional type of research design is used. Finally, the precision of the estimates is comparable with that had been designed for.

Nevertheless, to our knowledge this is the first attempt in Italy to evaluate the relationship between SES, based either on a family income index or parents' educational status, and adolescents' extra-curricular physical activity.

Here, parents' physical activity is a good predictor of adolescents' extra-curriculum physical activity, accordingly to previous researches. In a recent review on correlates of physical activity of children and adolescents, it is demonstrated that for children, among other factors, parental overweight status, physical activity preferences, intention to be active and program/facility access were statistically associated to physical activity. For adolescents, variables consistently associated with physical activity were perceived activity competence, intentions, but also sports conducted at community level, parent support, sibling physical activity, direct help from parents and opportunities to exercise. In that sense, social, cultural and economic deprivation has an effect on extra-curricular physical activity participation. A strong help in this task could derive from school. In fact, in Italy the vast majority of scholastic building and infrastructures belong to municipalities and provinces, and are currently underused. A way to improve adolescents' participation in physical activity could be involving them in extra-curricular activity carried out within the schools. As an example, childhood obesity prevention might be achieved considering a variety of interventions targeting built environment, physical activity, and diet. As suggested, some of these potential strategies for intervention in children can be implemented by targeting preschool institutions, schools or after-school care services as natural setting for influencing the diet and physical activity. In this sense, the outcomes will be useful to school administrators in their bid to bridge the gap between those children who are the most and least deprived.

1. **ISTAT**（意大利统计局）：The Italian National Institute of Statistics is a public research organization. It has been present in Italy since 1926, and is the main producer of official statistics in the service of citizens and policy-makers. It operates in complete independence and continuous interaction with the academic and scientific communities.

2. **Declaration of Helsinki**（赫尔辛基宣言）：The Declaration of Helsinki is a set of ethical principles regarding human experimentation developed for the medical community by the World Medical Association (WMA). It is widely regarded as the cornerstone document of human research ethics.

3. **SPSS**（"统计产品与服务解决方案"软件）：It is a computer program used for survey authoring and deployment (IBM SPSS Data Collection), data mining (IBM SPSS Modeler), text analytics, statistical analysis, and collaboration and deployment (batch and automated scoring services).

4. **Hosmer-Lemeshow:** It is a statistical test for goodness of fit for logistic regression models. It is used frequently in risk prediction models. The test assesses whether or not the observed event rates match expected event rates in subgroups of the model population. The Hosmer-Lemeshow test specifically identifies subgroups as the deciles of fitted risk values.

Unit 11　Extra-curricular Activities　课外活动

New words and expressions

1. remunerative [ri'mju:nərətiv]　　*adj.*　酬报的，报偿性的
2. inferable [in'fə:rəbl]　　*adj.*　能推理的，能推论的
3. variable ['vɛəriəbl]　　*n.*　变量
4. respectively [ris'pektivli]　　*adv.*　分别；各自；顺序为；依次为
5. validate ['væli,deit]　　*v.*　证实；确证；使生效；使有法律效力
6. municipality [mju,nisi'pæliti]　　*n.*　自治市；自治区；自治市或区的政府当局
7. degenerative [di'dʒenərətiv]　　*adj.*　退步的，变质的，退化的
8. sedentary ['sednteri]　　*adj.*　（人或动物）定居的；定栖的；不迁徙的

I　Vocabulary.

Fill in the blanks with the most suitable words. Change the form when necessary.

| degenerative | validate | inferable | sedentary | respectively |

1. People in _____ jobs need to take exercise.
2. The ticket has to be stamped by the airline to _____ it. I'm sorry I can't help you more.
3. My husband and I got pay rises of 8% and 10% _____. Let's celebrate!
4. _____ changes of the myocardium occur in many diseases.
5. Is the rightness of actions _____ from the goodness of their consequences?

II　Comprehension of the text.

Decide whether the following statements are true (T) or false (F) according to the passage.

1. The relationship between socio-economic status (SES) and physical activity has been investigated in several studies.　　　　　　　　　　　　　　　　　　　(　)

2. Students with mothers graduated with a Degree were more likely to practice extra-curricular physical activity and undertook physical activity, for more than three hours per week. (　　)

3. As demonstrated by some studies, higher family income is associated with higher alcohol and cigarette consumption and a higher level of sedentary behavior. (　　)

4. Families with high SES consider physical activity useful both in preventing chronic and degenerative diseases and for socialization, essential for the correct physical and psychological development of adolescents. (　　)

III　Translate the following sentences into Chinese.

1. In Italy there isn't an individual SES classification available, territorial data (ISTAT data) is based on personal economic consumption rather than income and education.
2. Concerning attitudes toward physical activity, it was asked if physical activity is considered useful in preventing obesity, in socializing, and in character-building.
3. Mother's educational level also seemed to considerably influence the determinants of the student's physical activity and the total number of extra-curricular weekly physical activity hours.
4. Studies on the relationship between physical activity and parents' educational level show that higher educational levels are determinant factors for children's physical activity.
5. In this sense, the outcomes will be useful to school administrators in their bid to bridge the gap between those children who are the most and least deprived.

▶▶ Useful phrases and expressions ◀◀◀◀◀

课外活动　extra-curricular activity
兴趣培养　interest development
健康状况　health status
心理健康　mental health
情绪健康　emotional health
个人空间　personal space
人际关系　interpersonal relationship
社会行为　social behavior
社区参与　community involvement.
个人竞争力　Individual competitiveness

Unit 11　Extra-curricular Activities　课外活动

Activities organized outside of the regular school day, curriculum or course intending to meet learners' interests can help learners become more involved in their school or community and can help them to develop social and soft skills and to promote well-being.

为满足学习者兴趣而组织的课外活动或课程可以帮助学习者更多地参与到学校或社区活动之中，帮助他们提高社交能力和软技能，促进他们的健康发展。

An extra-curricular activity is any club, creative outlet, volunteer opportunity, or job that doesn't give you school credit but show colleges your interests, skills, impact, and community involvement.

课外活动可以是任何社团活动、创意活动、志愿者活动或工作体验，这些活动不会给你带来学分，但可以向高校展示你的兴趣、技能、影响力和社区参与度。

The first place to look for extracurricular activities is your high school which gives you and your peers many chances to develop interests, invest energy, and display talent.

课外活动的第一来源是你的高中，它为你和同龄人提供很多培养兴趣、投入精力，以及展示才能的机会。

Extracurricular activities show a personal side—what you're interested in or passionate about. Joining clubs, volunteering, or holding a job shows your attachment to your community and desire to help others, as well as your sense of responsibility and time management.

课外活动展示了你个性的一面——你感兴趣或热衷的东西。参加俱乐部、志愿服务或从事某种工作可以体现出你对社区的依恋以及帮助他人的愿望，更可以展现出你的责任感和时间管理意识。

To develop the various facets of personality of children and students, curricula must be supplemented with extracurricular activities which help in the development of intellectual, emotional, and moral development.

为了促进儿童以及学生个性各个方面的发展，课程体系中必须增设课外活动来进行补充，因为课外活动有助于智力、情感和道德发展。

All-round development as well as intellectual development is not the domain of curriculum, these characteristics can be judiciously fulfilled by extracurricular activities.

全面发展以及智力发展并不是课程体系的专属领域，这些特点可以通过合理的课外活动来实现。

Insertion of extracurricular activities on resume strengthens your bio-data when you lack adequate work experience. If you switch over your career or changes your job, even in such conditions, insertion of extracurricular activities in your resume played an effective role.

如果你工作经验不足，在简历中添加课外活动可以为你的履历增彩；即使是在你转行或换工作的情况下，在简历中加入课外活动也可以起到有效的作用。

It's important to note that not all hobbies count as extra-curriculars. Basically, recreational activities that you do for your own enjoyment don't make the cut because extra-curriculars need to involve some concerted effort and contribute to your personal development.

需要注意的是，并非所有的爱好都算作课外活动。基本上以个人享受为主要目的的娱乐活动不能算作课外活动，因为课外活动需要涉及一些协同努力，并且应该有助于你的个人发展。

However, extra-curriculars fall to the wayside here as more emphasis is placed on quantitative data, like GPA and test scores, because these require less time on the part of the admissions committee.

然而，在这里课外活动被搁置一边，因为更多的是强调定量数据，比如 GPA 和考试成绩，因为这些对招生委员会来说需要的时间更少。

Having extra-curriculars on your resume, no matter where you apply to, helps you present a robust application that helps the admissions officers gain an overall deeper understanding of the type of person you are. This can make or break their decision to accept you into their university.

将课外活动体现在你的简历上，无论申请什么学校，都可以使你的申请更加强有力，帮助招生人员全面深入地了解你是什么样的人。这可以使他们决定是否接受你进入他们的大学。

Unit 12 School Management
学校管理

Text A What is School-based Management?

导读：School-based Management 是何种管理方法？为什么会被引进学校？相比于旧式的管理方法，它有哪些优势，有哪些注意点？引入此种管理机制的学校又该如何提高学校的"产出"？本文将为你解答这些疑问。

Despite the clear commitment of governments and international agencies to the education sector, efficient and equitable access to education is still proved to be elusive for many people around the world. Girls, indigenous peoples, and other poor and marginalized groups often have only limited access to education. These access issues are being addressed with great commitment in international initiatives, such as Education for All, in which resources are being channeled to low-income countries to help them to achieve the Millennium Development Goals for education. However, even where children do have access to educational facilities, the quality of education that is provided is often very poor. This has become increasingly apparent in international learning tests such as Trends in International Mathematics and Science Study (TIMSS), in which most of the students from developing countries fail to excel. There is evidence that merely increasing resource allocations will not increase the equity or improve the quality of education in the absence of institutional reforms. Governments around the world are introducing a range of strategies aimed at improving the financing and delivery of education services, with a more recent emphasis on improving quality as well as increasing quantity in education. One such strategy is to decentralize education decision-making by increasing parental and community involvement in schools—which is popularly known as school-based management (SBM). The argument in favor of SBM is that decentralizing decision-making authority to parents and communities fosters demand and ensures that schools provide the social and economic benefits that best reflect the priorities and values of those local communities. Education reforms in Organization for Economic Co-operation and Development (OECD) countries tend to share some common characteristics of this kind, including increased school autonomy, greater responsiveness to local needs, and the overall objective of improving students' academic performance. Most countries whose students perform well in international student achievement tests give local authorities and schools substantial autonomy to decide the content of their curriculum and the allocation and management of their resources.

An increasing number of developing countries are introducing SBM reforms aimed at empowering principals and teachers or at strengthening their professional motivation, thereby enhancing their sense of ownership of the school. Many of these reforms have also strengthened parental involvement in the schools, sometimes by means of school councils. Almost 11 percent of all projects in the World Bank's education portfolio for fiscal years 2000-2006 supported school-based management, a total of 17 among about 157 projects. This represents $1.74 billion or 23 percent of the Bank's total education financing.

The majority of SBM projects in the Bank's current portfolio are in Latin American and South Asian countries. In addition, a number of current and upcoming projects in the Africa region have a component focused on strengthening school-level committees and SBM. There are also two Bank-supported SBM projects in Europe and Central Asia and one each in East Asia and the Pacific (the Philippines), and in the Middle East and North Africa (Lebanon). The few well-documented cases of SBM implementation that have been subject to rigorous impact evaluations have already been reviewed elsewhere. Here we focus on the concept of SBM and its different forms and dimensions and present a conceptual framework for understanding it. We define SBM broadly to include community-based management and parental participation schemes but do not explicitly include stand-alone, or one-off, school grants programs that are not meant to be permanent alterations in school management.

SBM programs lie along a continuum in terms of the degree to which decision-making is devolved to the local level. Some devolve only a single area of autonomy, whereas others go further and devolve the power to hire and fire teachers and authority over substantial resources, while at the far end of the spectrum there are those that encourage the private and community management of schools as well as allow parents to create schools. Thus, there are both strong and weak versions of SBM based on how much decision-making power has been transferred to the school.

The World Bank's World Development Report 2004 presented a conceptual framework for SBM. The WDR argues that school autonomy and accountability can help to solve some fundamental problems in education. While increasing resource flows and support to the education sector is one aspect of increasing the access of the poor to better quality education, it is by no means sufficient.

The SBM approach aims to improve service delivery to the poor by increasing their choice and participation in service delivery, by giving citizens a voice in school management, by making information widely available, and by strengthening the incentives for schools to deliver effective services to the poor and by penalizing those who fail to deliver.

SBM is the decentralization of authority from the central government to the school level. It is said that School-based management can be viewed conceptually "as a formal alteration of governance structures, as a form of decentralization that identifies the individual school as the primary unit of improvement and relies on the redistribution of decision-making authority as the primary means through which improvement might be stimulated and sustained. Thus, in SBM, responsibility for, and decision-making authority over, school operations are transferred to principals, teachers, and parents, and sometimes to students and other school community members. However, these school-level actors have to conform to or operate within a set of policies determined by the central government. SBM programs exist in many different forms, both in terms of who has the power to make decisions and in terms of the degree of decision-making that is devolved to the school level. While some programs transfer authority only to principals or teachers, others encourage or mandate parental and community participation, often as members of school committees (or school councils or school management committees). In general, SBM programs transfer authority over one or more of the following activities: budget allocation, the hiring and firing of teachers and other school staff, curriculum development, the procurement of textbooks and other educational materials, infrastructure improvements, and the monitoring and evaluation of teacher performance and student learning outcomes.

Good education is not only about physical inputs, such as classrooms, teachers, and textbooks, but also about incentives that lead to better instruction and learning. Education systems are extremely demanding of the managerial, technical, and financial capacity of governments, and, thus, as a service, education is too complex to be efficiently produced and distributed in a centralized fashion. Most of the incentives that affect learning outcomes are institutional in nature, and three can be identified in particular: (i) choice and competition; (ii) school autonomy; and (iii) school accountability. The idea behind choice and competition is that parents who are interested in maximizing their children's learning outcomes are able to choose to send their children to the most productive (in terms of academic results) school that they can find. This demand-side pressure on schools will thus improve the performance of all schools if they want to compete for students. Similarly, local decision-making and fiscal decentralization can have positive effects on school outcomes such as test scores or graduation rates by holding the schools accountable for the "outputs" that they produce. The World Development Report 2004, Making Services Work for Poor People, presents a very similar framework, in that it suggests that good quality and timely service provision can be ensured if service providers can be held accountable to their clients.

In the context of developed countries, the core idea behind SBM is that those who work in a school building should have greater control of the management of what goes on in the building. In developing countries, the idea behind SBM is less ambitious, in that it focuses mainly on involving community and parents in the school decision-making process rather than putting them entirely in control. However, in both cases, the central government always plays some role in education, and the precise definition of this role affects how SBM activities are conceived and implemented. SBM in almost all of its manifestations involves community members in school decision-making. Because these community members are usually parents of children enrolled in the school, they have an incentive to improve their children's education. As a result, SBM can be expected to improve student achievement and other outcomes as these local people demand closer monitoring of school personnel, better student evaluations, a closer match between the school's needs and its policies, and a more efficient use of resources. For instance, although the evidence is mixed, in a number of diverse countries, such as Papua New Guinea, India, and Nicaragua, parental participation in school management has reduced teacher absenteeism.

SBM has several other benefits. Under these arrangements, schools are managed more transparently, thus reducing opportunities for corruption. Also, SBM often gives parents and stakeholders opportunities to increase their skills. In some cases, training in shared decision-making, interpersonal skills, and management skills is offered to school council members so that they can become more capable participants in the SBM process and at the same time benefit the community as a whole.

Unlike in developed countries where SBM is introduced explicitly to improve students' academic performance, how school decentralization will eventually affect student performance in developing countries is less clear. This section tries to define the ways in which SBM can increase participation and transparency and improve school outcomes.

First, the SBM model must define exactly which powers are vested in which individuals or committees and how these powers are to be coordinated to make the plan workable within both the school culture and the available resources. However, the structure of authority needs to remain flexible enough to enable school managers to deal with any unexpected events, which always seem to emerge during implementation.

Second, the success of SBM requires the support of the various school-level stakeholders, particularly of teachers. Also vital to the success of SBM is for school principals to support the decentralization reform. This is not a foregone conclusion, as principals will remain personally accountable for the performance of their school but will no longer have complete control over its management. In effect, they are being asked to give up some authorities without a corresponding decrease in personal accountability. Once SBM is in place, principals can no longer blame the policies of the school district when things go wrong.

The support of both local and national governments is also required. SBM by definition requires these governments to surrender some power and authority to the school level, but they retain the right and ability to reverse their earlier decision in favor of SBM if they feel their power is being usurped.

The final and most important source of necessary support is from parents and other community members. It is important, however, to distinguish between parents and other community members. While parents are always part of the community that surrounds a school, school councils do not have to include parents as members. For instance, in the United States, many schools are locally controlled in the sense that a school board of local residents officially sets policy, but there may be no parental participation in these schools. In some cases, wealthy individuals in a community may be members of a school council simply because they financially support the school.

Particularly in developed countries, parental participation as members of school councils or of the group that is implementing SBM is distinct from community participation. However, in developing countries, in particular in isolated small or rural communities, parental participation tends to be synonymous with community participation, since in these small communities almost everybody has a family member in school.

The expectation underlying SBM is that greater parental involvement will mean that schools will be more responsive to local demands (for example, for better teaching methods or more inputs) and that decisions will be taken in the interests of children rather than adults. A further hope is that involved parents will become unpaid or minimally paid auxiliary staff who will help teachers in classrooms and with other minor activities. Furthermore, even if parents are too busy working to help in the classroom, they can still encourage their children to do their homework and to show them, in this and other ways, that their family really values schooling and academic achievement. Since parents are networked in various ways with community leaders, the further hope is that parental support for SBM will encourage local community leaders to put schools higher on their political agendas and thus provide the schools with more material resources.

Once the nexus of autonomy-participation and accountability has been defined and a realistic management plan has been drawn up that has the support of all stakeholders, then it becomes possible to expect better school outcomes. Thereafter, the hope is that the school climate will change as the stakeholders work together in a collegial way to manage the school. However, there is little evidence that this really happens in practice. Also, the possibility exists that teachers and principals will come to resent being constantly monitored by parents and school council members, which will cause relations within the school to deteriorate.

At the same time, the teaching climate of a school is predicated on, among many other factors, how motivated teachers are to teach well, whether they know how to teach well, how good the various curricula are, how eager pupils are to learn, and how much parents actually support their children's learning in whatever ways are practical for them. Any school that wants to improve its academic record will have to work actively on some or all of these factors. Sometimes, the obstacles to improve the quality of instruction are motivational, sometimes they are cognitive in the sense of what teachers know, and sometimes they are social in the sense of petty personal matters that can prevent teachers from behaving professionally. Ideally, under SBM, because those who run the school are intimately acquainted with the individuals who work there, they will be able to identify the specific problems that need to be fixed and use their authority to find and implement solutions.

Some caveats must be mentioned about SBM. Decentralization or devolution does not necessarily give more power to the general public because it is susceptible to being captured by elites. As for the relationship between decentralization, proper growth, and reduced corruption, the evidence is mixed. Some scholars suggest that there may be numerous reasons why local control over resource allocation or decision-making may not yield the desired outcomes. First, local democracy and political accountability are often weak in developing countries and can lead to capture of governance—at the various levels—by elite groups. Second, in more traditional and rural areas with a history of feudalism, the poor or minorities may feel the need for a strong central authority to ensure that services are delivered to them and not just to the more powerful local citizens. Third, and related to this, is the issue that there may be no culture of accountability within communities, meaning that no one would think to question any actions taken by the group running the school. This can be a problem in places where the teacher is regarded as the ultimate authority by the virtue of being the only "highly" qualified individual in a community. Finally, those given the responsibility for managing the school may not have the capacity to do so, which points up the need to build the capacity of education stakeholders at the grassroots level to ensure that SBM reforms do not fail in their execution.

These caveats help to strengthen our understanding of the pattern of SBM in developing countries (as discussed above). In particular, the caveats strengthen the notion that the specific type of SBM introduced in any given country depends (or should ideally depend) on the political economy of the particular country. For instance, strong SBM reforms have been introduced, and have been quite successful, in those countries where communities have been forced by some calamity such as war or a natural disaster to come together as a group to find ways to deliver basic services, including education.

1. **Education for All**（全民教育）: The Education for All movement took off at the world conference on Education for All in 1990. Since then, governments, non-governmental organizations, civil society, bilateral and multilateral donor agencies and the media have taken up the cause of providing basic education for all children, youth and adults.

2. **Millennium Development Goals**（千年发展目标）: The Millennium Development Goals are eight international development goals that all 193 United Nations member states and at least 23 international organizations have agreed to achieve by the year 2015. They include eradicating extreme poverty, reducing child mortality rates, fighting disease epidemics such as AIDS, and developing a global partnership for development.

3. **Trends in International Mathematics and Science Study**（国际教育评价研究和评测活动）: The Trends in International Mathematics and Science Study (TIMSS) is an international assessment of the mathematics and science knowledge of fourth-and eighth-grade (Year 5 and Year 9) students around the world. TIMSS was developed by the International Association for the Evaluation of Educational Achievement (IEA) to allow participating nations to compare students' educational achievement across borders. The IEA also conducts the Progress in International Reading Literacy Study (PIRLS). TIMSS was first administered in 1995, and every 4 years thereafter. In 1995, forty-one nations participated in the study; in 2007, 48 countries participated. Another similar study is the Programme for International Student Assessment.

4. **Organization for Economic Co-operation and Development**（经济合作与发展组织）: It is an international economic organisation of 34 countries founded in 1961 to stimulate economic progress and world trade. It is a forum of countries committed to democracy and the market economy, providing a platform to compare policy experiences, seek answers to common problems, identify good practices, and co-ordinate domestic and international policies of its members.

New words and expressions

1.	indigenous [in'didʒənəs]	adj.	土产的，土著的
2.	marginalize ['mɑːdʒinəlaiz]	v.	使局限于社会边缘；排斥；忽视
3.	portfolio [pɔːt'fəuliəu]	n.	投资组合
4.	spectrum ['spektrəm]	n.	系列；范围；幅度
5.	incentive [in'sentiv]	n.	刺激；鼓励；动机
6.	auxiliary [ɔːg'ziliəri]	adj.	辅助的，备用的
7.	accountability [ə,kauntə'biliti]	n.	负有责任；应作解释；可说明性
8.	caveat ['kæviæt]	n.	警告

Unit 12   School Management   学校管理

I   Vocabulary.

Fill in the blanks with the most suitable words. Change the form when necessary.

| marginalize   incentive   auxiliary   spectrum   caveat |

1. The _____ units are called in only when the main force has been overtaxed.
2. We must not _____ the poor in our society.
3. There is a wide _____ of opinions on this question.
4. But there is a crucial _____: how much worse might the politics get.
5. The child has no _____ to study harder because his parents cannot afford to send him to college.

II   Comprehension of the text.

Decide whether the following statements are true (T) or false (F) according to the passage.

1. Increasing resource allocations will increase the equity or improve the quality of education in the absence of institutional reforms.
2. Good education means merely physical inputs, such as classrooms, teachers, and textbooks.
3. How school decentralization will eventually affect student performance in developing countries is apparent.
4. In developed countries, parental participation as members of school councils or of the group that is implementing SBM is the same as community participation.
5. The specific type of SBM introduced in any given country depends (or should ideally depend) on the political economy of the particular country.

III   Read the text and answer the following questions.

1. What's School-Based Management?
2. What are the benefits of SBM?
3. What does SBM need to improve school outcomes?
4. Apart from the benefits, SBM may fail to achieve school outcomes. What's the major caveat about SBM?

Text B Comparative Case Study on School Management Practices in Two Schools in the United States and Türkiye

导读：全球化和信息革命使得各个国家和地区的学校管理制度趋于一致，但是在这种大的趋势下，有些地区的学校管理方法却是截然不同的。本文选取了美国和土耳其这两个国家各一所学校，对比两者的学校管理制度以及两者在教学上的效率，希望给现在的学校一些管理上的参考。

The issue of centralized-decentralized governance structures and their influences on education systems has received a great deal of attention in recent decades. National education systems show great variation in certain respects because of the dissimilar historic paths they have followed. On the other hand, many believe that world education systems are converging because of increasing learning capabilities of systems from each other. Globalization and information revolution have brought the continents closer, along with making the educational practices less different. The American and the Turkish school systems, for example, are clearly distinct and have indicated signs of moving in opposite directions. The education system in Türkiye is centralized, which means that the policy-making function is in the hands of the Ministry of Education that has power over all educational matters. The Ministry determines the personnel policy and arranges training, certifying, appointment and salary schedules of teachers. On the other hand, the public school system in the U.S. is governed by an open decentralized system. State legislatures are responsible for public education. Their task is to authorize funding and give legislative support for the schools. All states have state boards of education, which deal with policy development, personnel recruitment, budgeting and the law.

Here we attempted to examine and compare Turkish and American school administrative processes and practices shaped by the national political traditions by using two schools, one in each country, as research sites. The two national political traditions correspond to two administrative paradigms: the Napoleonic tradition which connotes centralization and the Anglo-Saxon tradition which connotes decentralization. The researchers believed that looking at the administrative processes in the two schools, one in Türkiye and one in the U.S., would provide some insights into how the administrative processes supported or impeded the change process in both systems.

Turkish school: the case study in Türkiye was conducted at a state basic education school (grades 1–8). At this school there are 62 teachers, five administrators (one principal and four assistant principals), two counselors, one secretary, two cleaning personnel and 1,750 students. The school covers an area of 9,361m^2 and has 52 classrooms with one computer laboratory and a music room. This school was founded in 1967 and became a Curriculum Laboratory School in 1994. These were organized with the collaboration of the World Bank and established in the 23 provinces of Türkiye. New educational approaches are piloted in these schools before they are put into general practice. This school was also selected to be a CLS, among other schools, by the Ministry of Education in order to try out new educational approaches with the aim of raising Turkish education to the OECD standards. In line with this aim, a working team called the School Development Committee was involved in initiating strategic planning and total quality management activities at the school. This committee was under the guidance of the Ministry of Education.

American school: the case study in Madison, the Wisconsin state capital, was conducted in an elementary school founded in the fall of 1958. It is located in a prosperous neighborhood on the southwest side of Madison, where upper and upper middle class families reside. The school shares the building with a middle school and uses the rooms and grounds on the building's east side.

This school has a total K-5 enrolment of approximately 300 students and 31 regular classroom teachers. Because the school has fewer than 500 students, there is only a school principal, but no assistant principal. In the school there are two custodians, one kitchen staff and one librarian, two nurses, one "outreach" person, and three administrative staff. Recently the school was involved in a five-year School Improvement Plan (SIP). SIP activities are monitored by a facilitator from the Metropolitan Madison School District. The goals and objectives of the SIP plan were mainly to increase students' proficiency in literacy and mathematics.

Sample

Neither case schools involved are "average schools". They are both located in prosperous neighborhoods and are involved in undertaking change initiatives as part of the recent reform activities in the education systems of both countries. Despite the atypical characteristics of these schools, the researchers believe that this comparative case study manages to build a holistic description of activities and situations under investigation. Therefore, this research is significant for depicting the administrative styles and practices of both schools in relation to managing educational reform.

The participants comprised 14 teachers and four administrators (one principal and three assistant principals) in the Turkish case, and 10 teachers and one principal in the American case. The researchers chose the maximum variation as a sampling strategy which is proved to be helpful for researchers to select a small sample with great diversity. This sampling strategy will yield two kinds of findings: (1) high-quality, detailed descriptions of each case which are useful for documenting uniqueness, and (2) important shared patterns which cut across cases and which derive their significance from having emerged out of heterogeneity. The maximum variation sampling strategy enabled the researchers to work with teachers with different demographic characteristics (such as working experience, their subject areas, and gender).

Data collection and analysis procedures

Two of the questions in the schedule were:

(a) What can you say about your motivation and that of your teacher colleagues at work?

(b) Please identify some of the factors that helped or hindered your motivation.

The researchers collected data through semi-structured interviews. The interviews took on average 30-35 minutes. The researchers tried to elicit information about the participants' perspectives on the administrative processes (motivation, decision-making, leadership communication, organizational change) practiced in their school.

The Turkish version of the interview schedule was reviewed by three experts, experienced in qualitative studies, from the Department of Educational Sciences at the Middle East Technical University in Ankara. The draft interview schedule was later piloted with three teachers from a school that is equivalent to the case school. The instrument was revised in the light of the comments and the pilot study.

For the American school the researchers translated the interview schedule into English. In the U.S., feedback on the translated interview schedule was obtained from two experts from the Department of Educational Administration, University of Wisconsin-Madison.

The researchers transcribed the tape-recorded interviews verbatim. Content analysis was used to determine where the greatest emphasis was placed in the interview data. The data were broken down into manageable categories followed by thematic coding. Coding categories for both Turkish and English versions of the interview schedules emerged after the review of the relevant literature. The data collection during the first week of the interviews generated new categories and the coding was revised accordingly.

Findings

The Turkish school

The results related to "motivation" as perceived by teachers and administrators showed that some external factors such as poor physical conditions of the school, excessive paperwork, the education system, and the excessive involvement of parents and of the central authorities in the school's affairs and low enthusiasm for their work affected the teachers' motivation negatively. The administrators complained about the lack of autonomy and responsibility to undertake initiatives, and stated that school staff attempted participatory and collaborative work. This was interrupted by bureaucracy and centralization. The principal said:

"The impossibilities that arise from poor physical conditions, poor communication within the administration, the education system, and the environment affect us negatively. We have efforts for collaboration, sharing, but there is no implementation. Why? Because centralized structure forms barriers to it, on one hand, it is said that the principal administers the school; on the other hand, I am deprived of autonomy. To say the least, whatever I want to do, I need to get permission from the central authorities."

The results concerning "decision-making" at the Turkish school showed a trend towards participatory decision-making. All administrators and teachers said that they made decisions through some committees concerning school issues such as strategic planning and total quality management. Yet most teachers complained that their decisions were not considered. They added that they were allowed to make decisions collaboratively, yet the principal still acted as the highest decision-making authority. Some teachers related this situation to the bureaucratic structure of the Turkish education in which administration was seen as the power base that can override participative decisions. On the other hand, the administrators complained about the reluctance of teachers in taking an active role in decision-making and avoiding taking responsibility in the application of the decisions.

Concerning the third administrative process, "leadership", most of the teachers viewed their administrators as effective leaders. They had sufficient administrative knowledge and experience to administer the school. However, administrators felt they lacked resources. The principal, for instance, complained about the system which, he said, did not provide the school with the financial resources or physical environment to take part in and use in-service training. Administrators stated that in the leadership process they had financial problems because insufficient budgets provided by the Ministry for their school led to them asking for financial contributions from parents. This is illegal since public schools are free of charge in Türkiye. The three administrators saw their needs of in-service training to keep up with new development in the administrative field.

Results related to "communication" indicated that most of the teachers complained about the lack of communication between teachers and administrators for various reasons. Two related this problem to the hierarchical structure of the school. The principal was the highest decision-making authority. Although teachers did participate somewhat in decision-making through reform initiatives, some saw this as lip service rather than an indication of real participative management. Some teachers complained that the administrators rarely visited the teachers' room and did not know what was happening in the school building. The principal mentioned that hierarchical tradition of Turkish school management formed barriers to communication.

He complained that the principal was seen as the highest authority in the school and was expected to do everything.

Concerning communication at this school, we saw the traces of the authoritative administrative system. The principal knows everything. In fact the principal does not have to know everything. Ninety percent of what the principal knows should also be known by other administrators.

The administrators highlighted the hierarchical and centralized structure of the system which caused communication problems between the school and the Ministry of Education. They added that communication through the "grapevine" was sometimes more effective and reliable than official communication channels.

With respect to the last process, "organizational change", respondents emphasized the strategic planning and TQM efforts that school committees were currently undertaking as required by a CLS. Some saw these activities as positive reform attempts that were failing because of the ineffective cooperation between the central government and the school. One assistant principal stated:

"These activities are conceptually very useful. Yet they do not have concrete results. In other words, the people who represent the decision-making authority for these activities do not encourage the others towards an effective collaboration. They do not do it intentionally. These things are only done for the sake of doing it, not to get any results or to improve anything. No-one keeps track of these activities or prepares a convenient setting for them."

The principal supported strategic planning and TQM efforts but they failed because teachers did not seem to understand that they are also partners in this process. They assumed that the principal was responsible for everything at the school. One assistant principal said that these reforms should be site-based and planned according to the needs of that particular institution. Another assistant principal also stated that these reforms should be decentralized to the local educational directories and financed by the municipalities. The general conclusion that could be drawn from the participants' comments would be stated as such that reform initiatives which were undertaken at this school failed because of the centralized character of the education system in Türkiye.

The American school

The following results relate to administrative processes at the American school. The data concerning "motivation" revealed that all teachers at the American school seemed willing to work hard, and look for new ways and methods to help children learn. Some teachers related their high morale to the in-service training opportunities provided for them. They enjoyed the in-service classes where they could learn new things and share them with their co-workers. One said:

> "One thing that helps us become motivated is the fact that we have many in-service classes so we are introduced new things and we get to try them. We also have some book clubs that, when there are new programs coming, we can discuss them and we try things in the classroom and we try to share our professional experiences."

The American principal also said that he was happy to work hard, especially for children, the environment was comfortable, and he had good relationships with his staff.

Concerning "decision-making" processes, all teachers said this was promoted by committees (vision committee, data gathering committee, best practices committee, and leadership committee), each established for the recent reform initiatives undertaken at the school. Every teacher had a voice in decision-making, and their opinions and input were sought by the principal before he reached final decisions. Yet they stated that whatever decisions they made at the staff meetings, the principal made the final decision in line with what he had in mind. Participants added that their committee decisions and activities were controlled by the district office. This was similar to the Turkish school where staff complained about the bureaucratic central office control over the school.

Teachers were content with the shared decision-making process fostered through the committees that they sat on. Some complained that certain factors hindered decision-making. Five thought that during this process everybody gave their opinion but it was difficult for them to sift the ideas and reach consensus. The principal saw the master bargaining agreement between the union and the school as the greatest factor that hindered the decision-making process. This agreement decreased his autonomy in making decisions about certain educational issues.

The master bargaining agreement is between the union and the school. This is an agreement that we have to follow with teachers. It tells things like how much time the teacher must use as planning time or how often the school should hold staff meetings. They also set rules on job postings. This limits my decision-making in the school.

Findings concerning "leadership" showed that all the teachers perceived their administrators as hardworking, diligent, receptive to new ideas, open to criticism, friendly and approachable. He visited homes of the students in crisis, tracked their progress and dealt with their behavioral problems. One teacher said that he was enthusiastic about learning new things, building on his knowledge by attending some classes as part of the professional development program. However, the principal saw some weaknesses in himself as an administrator. He said that after the summer holiday he would give teachers a chance to evaluate him.

As regards results concerning the "communication" process, most of the teachers complained that they did not have enough time for communication. Teachers said that, due to the recent mandates from the district office, they had little time to speak to each other. Yet all teachers said that communication among teachers teaching the same grade level was good. Teachers would come together, sharing their classroom materials, handouts, and their classroom experiences either at the grade level meetings or through visits to each others' classrooms. All teachers were content with the communication tools that the principal used. Among these tools were e-mail, newsletters, bulletins, voice-mail, and telephone. Teachers said that the principal was always accessible through these and by appointment.

Teachers did not know how communication took place between the central district office and the school. Three teachers mentioned a move in the education system towards centralization and standardization which would limit their freedom in their classrooms. They also complained that because of the new governor, the state had far more weight in making educational decisions. The principal was also concerned about increased centralization and bureaucracy:

Unit 12   School Management   学校管理

We operate under the guidelines of the School District. Our SIP (School Improvement Program) committee submits things to my supervisor for approval. We report to the assistant superintendent. Federal government barriers to what we do, making mandates. In Madison, 20 years ago it was pretty much a local building business. It became much more centralized in the last five years. Our teachers do not like that. Now everything is decided by the school district. There used to be 30 report cards for 30 different schools. Now there is one that everybody should follow.

This made it clear that increased centralization and bureaucracy in the American education system made communication between the district and the school more centralized and hierarchical.

Findings about the administrative process of "change" revealed that all the American teachers were very positive about the new initiatives the school has recently undertaken. The biggest organizational change attempt in the school was the SIP program designed by a committee. This year's plan was different because it had a five-year planning and implementation process. Most teachers agreed that although SIP was mandated by the district office, schools had autonomy in designing the organization and the components of their own improvement plan. But the principal said that the SIP was strategic planning developed by the district, so each school's plan had to fit in with the district's strategic planning. One teacher said that, outside the SIP, the school was involved in other activities which also contributed to school improvement:

> There are other things we do. We had family fun night that did not come up under SIP where we invited parents to come and do activities with their kids.
> We do plan reading days when we devote all of our day and we invite guest readers to come in, especially on Dr. Seuss' birthday. So there are other things that are done outside SIP.

The interviews concerning the change process revealed that most participants were quite positive about the change process. They believed that the change initiatives undertaken at the school were going to be successful over the next five years.

1. **Kentucky**（肯塔基）: The Commonwealth of Kentucky is a state located in the east-central

United States of America. As classified by the United States Census Bureau, Kentucky is a Southern state, more specifically in the east-south-central region. Kentucky is one of four U.S. states constituted as a commonwealth (the others being Virginia, Pennsylvania, and Massachusetts). Originally a part of Virginia, in 1792 it became the 15th state to join the Union. Kentucky is the 37th largest state in terms of total area, the 36th largest in land area, and ranks 26th in population.

2. **Wisconsin**（威斯康星州）：It is a US state located in the north-central United States and is considered part of the Midwest. It is bordered by Minnesota to the west, Iowa to the southwest, Illinois to the south, Lake Michigan to the east, Michigan to the northeast, and Lake Superior to the north. Wisconsin's capital is Madison, and its largest city is Milwaukee. As of 2010 the state has 5,686,986 residents. The state contains 72 counties.

3. **TQM**（全面质量管理）：Total quality management or TQM is an integrative philosophy of management for continuously improving the quality of products and processes. It is used around the world. TQM functions on the premise that the quality of products and processes is the responsibility of everyone who is involved with the creation or consumption of the products or services offered by an organization. In other words, TQM capitalizes on the involvement of management, workforce, suppliers, and even customers, in order to meet or exceed customer expectations.

New words and expressions

1.	paradigm ['pærədaim]	n.	范例，师范，典范
2.	connote [kə'nəut]	v.	意味着，隐含，暗示
3.	impede [im'pi:d]	v.	防止，阻碍
4.	verbatim [və:'beitim]	adj./adv.	逐字的（地），一字不差的（地）
5.	bureaucratic [ˌbjuərəu'krætik]	adj.	官僚的，繁文缛节的
6.	grapevine ['greipvain]	n.	小道消息
7.	mandate ['mændeit]	v./n.	命令，指令，要求
8.	bulletin ['bulitin]	n./v.	公告，公示

Unit 12　School Management　学校管理

I　Vocabulary.

Match the word in Column A to the correct definition in Column B.

Column A
1. bureaucratic　　2. impede
3. mandate　　　　4. verbatim
5. bulletin

Column B
A. to order sb.to behave, do sth. in a particular way
B. to delay or stop the progress of sth.
C. exactly as spoken or written
D. involve complicated official rules which may seem unnecessary
E. an official statement about sth. important

II　Read the text and answer the following questions.

1. What are centralized-decentralized governance structures' influences on education systems?
2. What do you think has contributed to the lack of autonomy and responsibility to undertake initiatives?
3. Why do most teachers in America think the Sip program is helpful?

Useful phrases and expressions

参与式管理　participatory governance
教育管理权下放　decentralization of educational administration
学校本位管理　school-based management
社区本位管理　community-based management
政府管理　government management
学校自治　school autonomy
学校问责　school accountability

有效服务 effective services
预算分配 budget allocation
教师雇佣与辞退 the hiring and firing of teachers

Over the past decades, education systems all over the world have been evolving from largely centralized structures to more decentralized ones.

在过去的几十年里，世界各地的教育体系一直在从高度集中化的结构向更加分散化的结构演变。

To promote quality education, a school should adopt a model of teaching and learning and a management framework that best suit the needs of the students and the community.

为推动优质教育发展，学校应采用最适合学生以及社会发展需要的教学模式和管理架构。

Education institutions require management to plan, organize, direct, control and evaluate day to day activities to accomplish education goals through coordination education personnel and allocated budgets.

为实现教育目标，教育机构要求管理层通过协调教育人员及预算分配，来对日常活动进行计划、组织、指导、控制和评估。

Governments around the world are introducing a range of strategies aimed at improving the financing and delivery of education services, one of which is to decentralize education decision-making by increasing parental and community involvement in schools, which is popularly known as school-based management (SBM).

世界各国政府正在引入一系列策略，以期改善教育服务的融资和具体实施状况，其中之一便是通过提高家长和社区对学校事务的参与度来下放教育决策权，这就是当下广泛流行的校本位管理（SBM）概念。

The argument in favor of school-based management is that decentralizing decision-making authority to parents and communities fosters demand and ensures that schools provide the social and economic benefits that best reflect the priorities and values of those local communities.

支持校本位管理的论点是，将决策权下放给家长和社区可以刺激需求，同时确保学校提供的社会和经济效益能够最大程度上反映当地社区的优先事项和价值观。

Education reforms in Organization for Economic Co-operation and Development (OECD) countries tend to share some common characteristics of this kind, including increased school autonomy, greater responsiveness local needs, and the overall objective of improving students' academic performance.

经济合作与发展组织（OECD）成员国的教育改革通常共有此类特征，包括增加学校自主权，对当地需求作出更大回应，以及提高学生学习成绩的总体目标。

Most countries whose students perform well in international student achievement tests give local authorities and schools substantial autonomy to decide the content of their curriculum and the allocation and management of their resources.

在国际学生成绩测试中学生表现良好的大多数国家，通常会给予地方当局和学校很大的自主权，来决定其课程内容以及资源的分配和管理。

It is essential to introduce a participatory governance framework involving the school sponsoring body, the principal, teacher(s), parent(s), alumni and independent community member(s), as direct participation in school decision making and different input of these key stakeholders help enhance transparency and accountability of school governance and contribute to more effective school operation.

必须引入参与式治理框架，让办学团体、校长、教师、家长、校友和独立的社区成员参与进来，因为让这些关键利益相关者直接参与学校决策并提供不同意见，有助于提高学校治理的透明度和问责性，进而有助于提高学校运作的效率。

The implementation of school-based management brings the education system of Hong Kong into a new era to tie in with global developments, with the aims to contribute to the personal growth of students; build a competent workforce to sustain the social, economic and cultural development of Hong Kong; and further enhance our competitiveness on the world stage.

校本位管理的实施将香港的教育制度带入一个新时代，使其可以紧跟全球发展步伐，其目的是促进学生的个人成长；组建高能工作团队，以维持香港的社会、经济和文化发展；并进一步提高我们在世界舞台上的竞争力。

Given the financial flexibility available under school-based management, an effective internal control mechanism has to be installed to prevent malpractices for selfish ends and to ensure proper use of resources in accordance with the relevant regulations and guidelines.

鉴于校本位管理在财务上的灵活性，学校必须设立有效的内部控制机制，防止徇私舞弊，并确保资源按照有关规例和指引妥善使用。

Unit 13 Teaching Methods
教学方法

Text A   Refuting Misconceptions about Classroom Discussion

导读：长期以来，小组讨论法被普遍认为是一种能培养学生批判性思维、小组合作精神，提高学生理解能力的有效教学手段。但是，在现实教学情景下，受到一些条件的限制，小组讨论法经常被误用，以至于达不到理想的效果。本文探讨了四个对课堂小组讨论法的错误性认知，并对这些错误观点进行反驳，减少教学者对采用这种教学法的顾虑。

Social studies educators advocate discussion as an influential instructional method to encourage students to apply knowledge and develop higher-order thinking and understanding. Because firstly, telling students about something does not necessarily ensure their comprehension, but discussing a topic helps students strengthen and extend their existing knowledge of the topic and increase their ability to think about it. Secondly, discussion promotes students' involvement and engagement. Researcher, as well as the wisdom of experienced teacher, demonstrates that for true learning to take place students must take responsibility for their own learning and not depend solely on a teacher. Using discussion is one means of doing this. It gives students public opportunities to talk about and play with their own ideas and provides motivation to engage in discussion beyond the classroom. Thirdly, discussion is used by teachers to help students learn important communication skills and thinking process. Because discussions are public, they provide a means for a teacher to find out what students are thinking and how they are processing the ideas and information being taught. Discussions thus provide social settings in which teachers can help students analyze their thinking process and learn important communication skills such as stating ideas clearly, listening to others, responding to others in appropriate ways, and learning how to ask good questions.

In classroom reality, however, teachers only use the discussion method sparingly. Instead, teachers predominantly use a quasi-discussion form called recitation to involve students in demonstrating their knowledge of subject matter. The problem is compounded by the fact that teachers generally refer to all major interaction sessions with students in the classroom as "discussions" when, in reality, they are recitations. Although both forms of interaction are effective in achieving their intended purposes, discussion is vastly more appropriate and effective in developing in students the widely endorsed citizenship competencies associated with rational and humane decision making and problem solving necessary for the common good.

Social studies teachers do not use discussion in their classrooms for many reasons, including a lecture-recitation instructional tradition, a long tradition of discipline-based curriculum design, emphasis on speedy and superficial coverage of content, fact-based textbooks and the limited availability of issue-based materials. It is hypothesized that one reason teachers avoid discussion is that they are relying on common misconceptions about the discussion method to make judgments about its use. Those misconceptions diminish the role that discussion can play in the classroom to help achieve the purpose of social studies. Logically, we can further assume that reflective and conscientious teachers might consider using discussion more often if their misconceptions were refuted with accurate and practical information. Possessing reliable and up-to-date information is the first step teachers need to consider when evaluating discussion as a viable instructional method.

Discussion misconception 1: A discussion consists of a teacher asking questions and students answering them.

If we substitute the word recitation in place of discussion, that statement would not be a misconception. A recitation does consist of a teacher asking questions and students answering them, but a discussion is much more. Therefor, a recitation is not a discussion; it is, at the most, a quasi-discussion.

The traditional recitation method emphasizes on finding out whether students know certain fact, often to prepare them for objective tests. As an instructional method, the use of the recitation method is very effective in achieving goals related to knowing content. It has been the dominant interaction form in classrooms throughout the past century, and it is characterized by the interaction pattern of a teacher question, usually at the lower cognitive levels, followed by a student response, and then a teacher evaluation. This procedure is referred as the IRE (teacher initiation, student response, teacher evaluation) pattern. One reason the pattern has persisted in the classroom is that it helps teachers manage and direct the flow of interaction. Teachers continuously need to reaffirm their authority when dealing with groups of twenty to thirty students, many of whom are reluctant learners.

Discussions physically look and sound different from recitations. Discussion has a different purpose, interaction structure, and cognitive focus. It has as it emphasizes that students should apply what they have read or learned through the oral exploration of ideas, issues, and problems. A teacher's interaction with students aims at encouraging students to make connections between the new content and their past knowledge and perspectives. The general goal is for students to understand the material more fully. Key to achieving that is the use of authentic questions that request new information rather than memorized facts from the text. The interaction pattern is much more variable than the pattern of a recitation with teacher and students asking and answering questions and making comments. A discussion more closely approximates natural conversation than recitation because it is slower paced and not driven by the questions or evaluations of one person. It is an educative conversation with and among students. For example, a teacher might initiate a discussion with a higher cognitive-level question and may redirect that question to several students who have different perspectives on the issue being discussed. The teacher may probe one or more of the students for clarification of their responses and for elaboration or extension of their thinking. Students may converse with one another, sharing or questioning perspectives, and asking for evidentiary support for perspectives. It is not uncommon during genuine discussions for students to assume discussion leadership at various points.

Discussion misconception 2: Teachers cannot get students involved in discussions if the students do not want to participate.

This misconception applies to reluctant students, not to those students who adamantly refuse to participate in class for whatever reason. That is an extreme behavior. Teachers can get students involved who appear apprehensive, who do not raise their hands, who say "I don't know." who sit in the back of the room, who appear disinterested, and who are silent most of the time.

The classroom climate a teacher creates is very important in encouraging student participation. Some researchers find that teachers tend to control discussions excessively by moving discussions back to themselves. They inadvertently do this by reacting in one way or another to almost every student response, question, or comment. Instead, they should only intervene with a comment or question at key points during the discussion and encourage more student-student interaction. Teachers who use those discussion techniques will give students more freedom to converse.

Teachers can employ many questioning techniques to encourage students to participate, including probing students' initial responses, redirecting questions to several students, and calling on non-volunteering students. During discussions, students sometimes lack the skill and confidence to express themselves at the higher cognitive levels. Resulting responses to questions can be ambiguous and incomplete. Teachers find that probes are useful follow-up questions to encourage students to complete, clarify, expand, or support their answers, especially with younger students as they begin to articulate the basics of reflective thinking during discussions. Questions such as "Why?", "What evidence do you have?", and "How can you support your view?" are common in discussions about societal issues and problems. A teacher leading students in discussion will need to be particularly diligent in listening to students' initial responses to follow-up with appropriate probes. Another useful approach to stimulate student participation in discussion is to direct one question to several students. The redirection could be prompted by an unanswered question or a desire to get additional responses to the same question and can involve volunteering and non-volunteering students.

Another questioning approach to stimulate participation during discussions is to have students formulate questions. Students ask few information-seeking questions so they need to be prompted to formulate questions related to the issue or problem being discussed. For example, a teacher might ask that all students write one question in response to the request, "If you had an opportunity to participate in a presidential press conference, what question would you ask him related to his policy on terrorism?" A question of this type will encourage all students to think and get involved. Having students ask questions of each other is another approach to consider because students tend to respond in more complex ways to each other than to teachers' questions.

The key to encouraging students to get involved in discussions is to create the conditions under which they want to contribute to discussions. The most obvious one is to rearrange students from seating in rows facing the teacher to seating them in a circle or semicircle to face each other, thereby facilitating communication. Another seating arrangement is referred to as the parliamentary style with two sets of rows facing each other. Establishing a positive social-emotional climate where students' responses, comments, and questions are respected, encouraged, and supported by both teacher and students is essential. Rules might be established by the teacher or the students to create discussion-behavioral expectations and guide the development of students' civic behaviors.

Other approaches to encourage participation include "pump priming" techniques such as having students write a response to a question first before answering, using a "think-pair-share" approach to get them to test a response with a peer first rather than with the whole class, or using small groups of two to three students to have them reflect on questions related to issues and problems. The key is getting students to discuss with each other, which they find is much less threatening than having to "be on stage" in front of the whole class. A student's "stage performance" will improve after having presented "off-Broadway" first.

There are many other instructional activities to get students to think and contribute responses to higher-order questions that can then be used as a base for a discussion:

1. Response cards. Pass out index cards and ask for anonymous answers to your discussion questions. Then group the responses to structure a class discussion or identify an issue for the class to explore through discussion;
2. Polling. Use a verbal survey by asking for a show of hands on positions related to an issue. Then follow up the diagnosis of group sentiment with a discussion based on support for positions;
3. Whips. Go around the group and obtain each student's point of view or a random sample of views. Use whips when you want to obtain something quickly from each student. The information might be used to form small groups representing different perspectives on an issue or solutions to a problem;
4. Informal panel. Invite a small number of students to present their views in front of the entire class;
5. Discussion chip. Distribute the same number of chips or pennies (three to five) to each member in a small group of students. Tell them that they are to use one chip for every answer, comment, or question as part of a discussion. Students need to use up all their chips before the discussion is completed or redistribute another equal number of chips for the discussion to continue;
6. Talking ball. Toss a small foam ball to a student with the understanding he or she must provide an answer to the discussion question, make a comment, or ask a question. That student then tosses the ball to another student, and so on.

Discussion misconception 3: Teachers are unbiased when encouraging students to make discussion contributions.

Although social studies teachers claim they take student diversity into account when involving students in discussion, observation of their discussion practices suggests a differentiated approach. In an in-depth study of five social studies teacher, Larson found that student diversity is a factor teachers said they consider when deciding whether to engage their students in discussion. Components of this factor are cultural background, ethnicity, gender, race, learning styles and ability. Students representing different backgrounds were perceived as potentially valuable for discussion because an opportunity was provided to have a variety of viewpoints represented on an issue.

Evidence had shown that teachers, generally, expose low ability students to an "impoverished curriculum", which translates to limited and repetitive content, emphasis on factual recitation rather than on lesson-extended discussion, stress on drill and practice tasks rather than application and higher-level thinking tasks. In other research, it was also found that male students were given more time to talk in classrooms and received more remediation, praise and criticism than female students.

Discussion misconception 4: Teachers cannot objectively evaluate students' contributions during classroom discussions.

Through the use of rubrics, teachers can assess more objectively the quantity and quality of students' verbal contributions during classroom discussions. During the past decade, there has been a movement toward integrating assessment of students' learning with instruction. One of the trends is the emphasis on moving away from what have been, until recently, the "tried and true" means of assessing student achievement and skills—traditional objective tests. In the old paradigm, the primary and major evaluation, usually a test was something that followed instruction to determine if students had learned the lesson material. Today, alternative and authentic assessment is more closely linked to instruction so that assessment becomes the means and ends of instruction.

Instruction involves formative and summative assessment of students by using authentic approaches or approaches that reflect the real world. Discussion is considered to be one such alternative and authentic instructional approach because it is how we communicate in many different venues—schools, works, communities, and families, for example. And, we can measure and assess discussion in terms of the content of the discussion and the process of discussing.

Over the past ten years, new techniques can help teachers to assess students' contributions during discussions more objectively. One such technique is a discussion rubric, which is a description of the teacher's requirements for varying degrees of student performance as the students attempt to meet the established criteria for an effective discussion. Harris created a rubric for assessing classroom discourse about civics that is based on standards and criteria. The teacher's goal in assessing each student engaged in a small group discussion of an issue is to judge the extent that a student's contribution to clarifying the issue under consideration and assisting the group toward an understanding and resolution of the issue. Students are assessed on substantive criteria aiming at evaluating students' understanding of the issue and procedural criteria that focus on students' ability to engage one another in discussion about the issue. The procedural criteria include positive (e.g. "inviting contributions of others" and "summarizing points of agreement and disagreement") and negative (e.g. "irrelevant distracting statements" and "personal attack") components. Three elements of performance focus the assessment: Whether or not the student has presented accurate knowledge related to the policy issue, employed skills for stating and pursuing related issues, and engaged others in constructive dialogue.

Off-Broadway [在纽约市戏院区以外的戏院上演的戏剧（多半是非主流，制作费较少，或实验剧）]: It is a term for a professional venue in New York City with a seating capacity between 99 and 499, and for a specific production of a play, musical or revue that appears in such a venue, and which adheres to related trade union and other contracts. These theatres are smaller than Broadway theatres.

New words and expressions

1.	compound ['kɔmpaund]	vt.	混合，调和；使严重；私了
2.	diminish [di'miniʃ]	vt.	减少，减损，贬低
		vi.	变少，逐渐变细
3.	viable ['vaiəbl]	adj.	能生存的，可行的
4.	reluctant [ri'lʌktənt]	adj.	不情愿的，勉强的
5.	adamantly ['ædəməntli]	adv.	坚决地，顽固地
6.	inadvertently [,inəd'və:təntli]	adv.	不注意，疏忽的，非故意的
7.	ambiguous [æm'bigjuəs]	adj.	模棱两可的，含糊不清的
8.	remediation [ri,mi:di'eiʃən]	n.	纠正，补习
9.	rubric ['ru:brik]	n.	种，类，题目，标题，注释
		adj.	红色的，用红色写的
10.	paradigm ['pærədaim]	n.	范例，示范，典范

Unit 13 Teaching Methods 教学方法

Exercises

I Vocabulary.

Fill in the blanks with the most suitable words. Change the form when necessary.

| compound   diminish   reluctant   ambiguous   paradigm |

1. He's _____ to begin, but when he does you should see him go into action.
2. We were lost into bewilderment due to his intentionally noncommittal or _____ statement.
3. Several unpopular decisions _____ the governor's popularity.
4. The painting provides us with one of the earliest _____ of the use of perspective.
5. He _____ various ingredients into an effective drug.

II Comprehension of the text.

Decide whether the following statements are true (T) or false (F) according to the passage.

1. Instead, teachers predominantly use a quasi-discussion form called recitation to involve students in demonstrating their knowledge of subject matter.   (   )
2. A discussion more closely approximates natural conversation than recitation because it is quicker paced and driven by the questions or evaluations of one person.   (   )
3. To encourage students to get involved in discussion, it is essential to create the conditions under which they want to contribute to discussions.   (   )
4. It was found that male students were given more time to talk in classrooms and received more remediation, praise, and criticism than female students.   (   )
5. Response cards, polling, and informal panel are used to help teachers to objectively evaluate students' contributions during classroom discussions.   (   )

III Translate the following phrases into Chinese.

communication skills   _____
up-to-date information   _____
substitute A in place of B   _____
integrate...with...   _____
meet criteria   _____

Text B Brainstorming: a Creative Way to Learn

导读：头脑风暴这一问题解决方法不仅在商业、政府机构、工业等领域大受推崇，也在教育界成为一种教学手段。本文从使用这一教学手段该遵守的原则，以及在课堂实践中实施的具体步骤两方面入手，引导教育工作者最有效率地使用该方法。

Man is a highly creative creature who prefers to learn by doing, exploring, testing, questioning, and modifying ideas. However, the traditional school has not usually found it "economical" to foster learning by a process that is so natural to students. Education for today and the future must be relevant and meaningful. It must equip each student with a process by which he may solve many complex problems that will eventually evolve. Brainstorming is a creative problem solving technique that has been used successfully in business, government, industry, and to a limited degree in the field of education. In the classroom, brainstorming can provide a student the means by which early contact with peers becomes a stimulating and challenging experience. Children might be asked to solve practical problems that arise during the day or to solve problems that might be proposed by the teacher or students during a social studies lesson. Researchers have found that even first grade children can profitably use the brainstorming technique.

Small group interaction has long been cited as an effective teaching technique. This interaction is of importance because the pupil has the opportunity to become actively involved in the process of learning. Developing a positive self-concept by active participation would be one of the major benefits derived from group brainstorming. Educators often promote brainstorming as a useful technique in gifted education. There are many who claim that in a search for ideas there can be no implicit techniques, and rightly so, if the technique means a rigid set of rules. Any attempt to lay down hard-and-fast methods would be nothing but terminology masquerading as technology, but, there can be and are certain principles in the form of guides to procedure.

Brainstorming principles

Alex F. Osborn, the father of modern day brainstorming outlined four basic principles for effective brainstorming:

1. Critical judgment is ruled out; criticism of ideas must be withheld until later. Many creative thoughts have been lost simply because a person doubted that others

would think his ideas insignificant and of no value. Many students start out their question with "This may be a stupid question, but…" Education and experience have trained most children and adults think critically rather than creatively, and this preface to a question is an example.

As a result, they tend to impede their fluency of ideas by applying their critical power too soon. By deferring judgment during a brainstorming session, children will be able to conceive a large number of creative ideas.

2. "Free-wheeling" is welcomed. The wilder the idea, the better; it is easier to tame down that to think up.

3. Quantity is wanted. The greater number of ideas the more likelihood of potential solutions. Practically all the experiences with group brainstorming confirm the principle that quantity helps breed quality.

4. Combination and improvement are sought. In addition to contributing ideas of their own, participants should suggest how ideas of others can be turned into better ideas, or how two or more ideas can be combined to make one.

Steps to successful brainstorming in the classroom

1. Description of brainstorming and statement of instructions. Explain to the children that brainstorming is a way of stating the greater number of ideas in a limited amount of time. Emphasize the idea of spilling out ideas as quickly as possible while applying the deferred judgment principle. A short practice session can be attempted by asking the children to write a list of as many items as possible under the heading, "things we do at school." After several minutes, stop the listing and compile the number of different ideas on the chalkboard. You may wish to discuss with the children the following questions: Did each of you contribute some ideas? Were you able to avoid being critical of each others' contributions? This deferred judgment principle must be accomplished before effective brainstorming can take place.

2. Divide the class into brainstorming groups. Beginning groups seem to function well with 3 to 11 members. The groups can be all boys, all girls, or mixed. An odd number in the group might assure the availability of a majority, and thus avoid the danger of a split between two children of equal number. It will help if the teacher selects a few individuals who serve as self-starters for each group. With proper planning and guidance the whole room can brainstorm a problem or just one individual can use this technique. Several groups can be brainstorming at one time within the classroom.

3. Selection of a group leader and secretary. Each group should have a leader who

would present the problem and keep the group actively engaged in the brainstorming process. The function of the secretary would be to write in brief form all ideas as they are presented. At times the ideas may tumble out so fast that even a shorthand expert would have difficulty recording them. It may be necessary to have two secretaries, each one jotting down every other idea. A tape recorder can also be utilized with transcription of the tape to the made layer.

4. Selection of the problem. The problem to be brainstormed should be one that will arouse student interest. This may not be easy to do, but a way usually can be found to make the problem relevant to many interests. Many times a functional problem, like what to do during the upcoming party could be used as a starting point. After the technique is refined, problems dealing with academic topics could be brainstormed. Students should assist in the selection process.

5. Statement of the problem. Problems can be presented that will encompass several areas of study. Social studies is a particularly good area in which children can brainstorm. The major objective in selecting a problem and stating the problem properly is to make sure that it is specific, not general.

The guiding principle is that a problem should be simple rather than complex. Failure to narrow the problem to a single target can seriously mar the success of any brainstorming session. Sometimes a session can be conducted to break down broad problems into their specific components. But in the normal course of events, make sure the problem is simple and specific.

Another principle to be considered is that the problem must be one that lends itself to many possible answers. If there are just a few possible solutions to the present one, then it would be wise to select another problem.

6. The brainstorming session begins. The problem should be explained, and the group leader should then discuss the four basic principles. Placards stating these principles could be displayed to act as a constant reminder to the children.

After these preliminaries are completed, the leader then calls for suggestions on how the problem could be solved. What happens if all of the children's hands go up? If this occurs the group leader could simply go around the table and let each person present one idea in turn. One student should present only one idea at a time. The fun is just beginning! If a child has some idea that is directly related to the previous statement, he can snap his fingers to be recognized by the leader. The leader should give priority to the finger snappers and thus make the most of the power of association. The students will find this exciting and challenging! Throughout this entire procedure the secretary should be taking brief notes. However, a tape recorder works very well with elementary school children.

Past experiences indicated the optimum time for beginners using brainstorming is about ten minutes. As their experience in this activity increases so can the time period.

As the children's brainstorming skills become more sophisticated with time, new variations can be tried. After a brief amount of time on a problem, the leader can stop the session and ask the group members to keep the problem on their minds until the next day when they will be asked for their afterthoughts. Maybe you can come up with some new variations.

7. Evaluations of the presented ideas.

After the brainstorming session has been completed, the secretary of the group should prepare a list of all ideas suggested during the session. At this point the teacher has to make a decision: Should the ideas be evaluated by the group of students who think up the ideas or by an entirely different group? It is usually wise to have the final evaluation done by those directly responsible for the problem. This may or may not be the group that does the brainstorming. The teacher has a great deal of latitude when choosing the method of evaluation. To facilitate this evaluation, it is often advisable to prepare a check-list of criteria by which students and teachers can evaluate the ideas. The following criteria could be used to evaluate each idea: Is it feasible? Is the idea simple enough? Is it timely? Is it appropriate? Is it efficient? Is it an improvement?

It is important that the criteria are appropriate for the problem being brainstormed. With each new problem you may need to create a new check-list. The entire class can work together to determine the relative worth of the presented ideas. This evaluation process usually develops into a most effective and meaningful type of group interaction. During the final evaluation, the students should attempt to apply the final ideas to the problem to determine whether or not the ideas are applicable.

If application is not feasible, the children can conduct a debate or continue with class discussion on the relative worth of the ideas.

At this point a very important concept must be noted. In many areas of instruction, particularly in the social studies, there is not a "right" or "wrong" answer. From this type of learning experience students will have the opportunity to discover the dichotomies in our society. It is important that students find out how the real world operates and how to evaluate real problems. The teacher should integrate the final evaluated ideas into his teaching lesson.

Most practitioners of group brainstorming recommend that brainstorming groups be assisted by trained facilitators. These facilitators can ensure that group members follow the rules for effective brainstorming. For example, they might remind group members not to criticize or evaluate each other's ideas. Facilitators can also keep groups from drifting into issues or topics not directly related to the central problem being discussed. Group members who do not actively participate because of fear or lack of motivation can be encouraged to contribute to the group effort. When groups hit dry spells, the facilitator can suggest some areas or angles they have not considered and encourage them to keep trying by mentioning high performance levels attained by other groups. Several studies have shown that facilitators that use these strategies can in fact help brainstorming groups attain relatively high levels of performance.

It is often not feasible to have a facilitator work with each brainstorming group. Teachers who divide their classes into groups for brainstorming sessions cannot effectively monitor and facilitate each one of these groups. It is also difficult and expensive to provide facilitators for group brainstorming sessions in organizations. A more useful strategy is to train students to be effective group brainstormers. Experience in group brainstorming with an effective facilitator greatly enhances group brainstorming in subsequent sessions without facilitators.

Computers also appear to be useful in facilitating group brainstorming. Many corporations and university laboratories employ a group decision support system that allows participants to exchange ideas by means of a computer network. Ideas can be entered in the lower section of the computer screen while ideas generated by others in the group network are shown in the top of the screen. Studies have shown that this type of group brainstorming is as effective as individual brainstorming. It appears to be especially useful when dealing with large groups of 12 or more, in part because participants do not experience the interference of conventional group brainstorming. They can type their ideas at any time and do not have to wait until others have expressed their ideas. Unfortunately, this type of computer-based brainstorming requires equipment and software not easily available in most educational contexts. However, simply having students in a group type their ideas on computers as they share them aloud appear to be an effective alternative. Even though there is still some potential distraction from hearing others generate ideas, one does not have to wait one's turn to generate ideas. Moreover, there is a record of each person's ideas which should minimize the tendency to loaf in groups.

Unit 13　Teaching Methods　教学方法

1. **Brainstorming**（头脑风暴）: a group creativity technique, by which a group tries to find a solution for a specific problem by gathering a list of ideas spontaneously contributed by its members.
2. **Alex F. Osborn (May 24, 1888-May 13, 1966):** was an advertising executive and the author of the creativity technique named brainstorming.

New words and expressions

1. foster ['fɔstə]	vt.	领养，培养，促进，鼓励，抱有（希望等）
2. derive [di'raiv]	v.	获取，得自，起源
3. rigid ['ridʒid]	adj.	严格的，固执的，刻板的
4. impede [im'pi:d]	vt.	妨碍，阻止
5. free-wheeling		单向转动
6. spill out		溢出
7. tumble out		乱七八糟地倒出来
8. encompass [in'kʌmpəs]	vt.	围绕，包围，包括，完成
9. preliminary [pri'liminəri]	adj.	初步的，预备的，开始的
	n.	初步行动，准备，初步措施
10. optimum ['ɔptiməm]	adj.	最佳的，最适宜的
11. sophisticated [sə'fistikeitid]	adj.	老练的，精密的；复杂的，久经世故的
12. dichotomy [dai'kɔtəmi]	n.	两分，分裂，二分法
13. distraction [dis'trækʃən]	n.	分心，分心的事物，注意力分散

I Vocabulary.

Fill in the blanks with the most suitable words. Change the form when necessary.

derive   encompass   rigid   optimum   sophisticated

1. She enjoys doing yoga because she can not only keep fit but also _____ happiness from it.
2. In the _____ college entrance exam, he stood out and was admitted into Peking University.
3. Nowadays, iphone enjoys immense popularity because it is very _____.
4. Both the weather and also the market offered _____ conditions for the sale of this product.
5. The general arts course at the university _____ a wide range of subjects.

II Comprehension of the text.

Decide whether the following statements are true (T) or false (F) according to the passage.

1. Brainstorming is a creative problem solving technique that has been used successfully in business, government, and industry, but not in the field of education.   (   )
2. Researchers have found that even first grade children can profitably use the brainstorming technique.   (   )
3. The greater the number of ideas the more likelihood of potential solutions.   (   )
4. Beginning brainstorming groups function well more than 11 members.   (   )
5. Assisted by trained facilitators, it is more likely that group members will follow the rules for effective brainstorming.   (   )

III Translate the following sentences into Chinese.

1. Man is a highly creative creature who prefers to learn by doing, exploring, testing, questioning, and modifying ideas.
2. Critical judgment is ruled out; criticism of ideas must be withheld until later. Many creative thoughts have been lost simply because a person doubted that others would think his ideas insignificant and of no value.

3. In addition to contributing ideas of their own, participants should suggest how ideas of others can be turned into better ideas, or how two or more ideas can be combined to make one.
4. The function of the secretary would be to write in brief form all ideas as they are presented. At times the ideas may tumble out so fast that even a shorthand expert would have difficulty recording them.
5. Ideas can be entered in the lower section of the computer screen while ideas generated by others in the group network are shown in the top of the screen.

Useful phrases and expressions

一带一路倡议 the Belt and Road Initiative
改革是教育事业发展的根本动力 reform as the mainspring of educational development
深化教育领域综合改革 deepen comprehensive reform in education
打造"留学中国"品牌 build a strong brand of "Study in China"
促进中外教育人文交流 promote people-to-people exchange in education
推动教育合作 promote educational cooperation
积极参与全球教育治理 participate in global governance of education
推进人才培养模式创新 promote innovation in talent cultivation modes
树立正确的人才培养观念 establishing the right concept on talent training
扩大世界影响力 enhance its global influence

Align education with the reality of China.
中国的教育必须按中国的特点和中国的实际办。
Bolster confidence in education rooted in China.
坚定扎根中国大地办教育的自信。
Tell China's stories well and make its voice heard.
讲好中国故事，传播好中国声音。
Innovate teaching methods and improve the quality of talent training.
创新教育教学方法，提高人才培养质量。
We should have confidence in the path, theory, system, and culture.
要坚定道路自信、理论自信、制度自信、文化自信。
We will strengthen people-to-people and cultural exchanges with other countries, giving prominence to Chinese culture while drawing on other cultures.
加强中外人文交流，以我为主，兼收并蓄。

Draw on advanced international experiences in running schools and conducting academic research, and coordinate efforts to serve inbound and outbound study programs.

吸收借鉴世界先进办学治学经验，统筹出国留学和来华留学工作。

Support overseas studies, encourage returns, guarantee the freedom of leaving, and promise a role to play.

支持留学、鼓励回国、来去自如、发挥作用。

Be committed to cooperation among strong partners to introduce high-quality educational resources and enhance China's educational strength and capacity for innovation.

坚持强强合作，引进优质教育资源，提升我国教育实力和创新能力。

Invigorate education through reform and innovation to further open up education to enhance its global influence.

深化教育改革创新以激发教育事业发展活力，以扩大教育开放提升我国教育世界影响力。

Unit 14 Materials & Test
教材与考试

Text A Materials and Media

导读：随着社会进步和科学技术的发展，教材与教学媒体也经历着一次次重大的变革。本文从教材与教学媒体的定义和分类，外语教学发展历程中教材与教学媒体的演变和改革，以及为此教师面临的挑战几方面入手，呼吁教师在使用教材与教学媒体时，要善于扬长避短，结合学习者的学习方式和学习需求，营造一个理想的教学情境。

Throughout the history of foreign language teaching, theorists and practitioners have tried to support the language learning process as best they can. To that end, foreign language teachers and material developers have introduced a variety of aids, materials and media. Whatever supportive means are chosen, their conception and format to a large extent determine the layout of a foreign language course.

Developments in the understanding of what foreign language competence implies and what is required to achieve it, combined with technological innovations and shifts in social demands on education, have entailed changes in the way in which the foreign language teaching process is conceived and supported. Materials and media that were believed to be effective learning tools at one point in time are supplemented with or even supplanted by others, which may in their turn become marginalized.

The gradual increase in diversification of teaching materials and media, with the ensuing danger of overburdening teaching with them for their sheer availability, makes it an absolute necessity that teachers are able to perceive both strengths and weaknesses of available teaching aids, and can make well-considered judgments as to when, how and to what end they can most effectively be harnessed to particular learning or teaching tasks. Often such decisions are influenced by considerations beyond the control of the course designers and procedures. Questions of organization and coordination in any multimedia course will play an important role. In addition, materials and media deliberations must be made with respect to the abilities and needs of particular learner groups.

Definition and classifications

Materials and media are everything that can be used to support the foreign language learning process. In many foreign language classes today these aids will probably include the teacher's voice, tapes, worksheets, sets of task cards and objects (props, pictures, posters, food tins or labels, maps, wall charts and the like). Some teachers may also have an overhead projector with transparencies or even a video player with videotapes or films at their disposal. In some language classrooms, reference materials, such as dictionaries, grammar or phrase books, may also be permanently available. Schools may have foreign newspapers, periodicals, magazines, cultural background books or supplementary readers in their library. The large majority of teachers may not yet consider computers with foreign language learning software, CD-ROMs, DVDs or an internet connection common teaching aids. A minority of specialized language schools may have at their disposal a self-access centre, where a large variety of the above-mentioned media and materials are freely accessible to learners for self study. Still other materials and media which have at some point in time been introduced into foreign language teaching with more or less success could be mentioned here. They include the language laboratory, the flannel board, the epidiascope, the flipchart, flashcards, radio, television and even puppets.

This broad spectrum of teaching aids can be classified according to various perspectives. An obvious way to do so is to distinguish between aural, visual and audio-visual aids, with the last category having the advantage of combining sound and image. Another common way to classify materials and media is to do so according to their function. Thus a distinction can be made between teaching and learning materials, or between data, instruction, process and reference materials. Data materials are chunks of language that are presented to learners for exploration. Instruction materials typically include workbooks, exercise books and other materials designed for language practice. Process materials are those parts of a language course that mediate to learners how the course is to proceed. Reference materials and media may be referred to as either basic or supplementary, with the first category comprising materials and media that are considered essential parts of a particular language course, and the latter that can but need not be used on top of the basic materials to assist students to meet the requirements of a particular course or to further improve their language competence. Whereas course books, workbooks and course-related cassettes are now typically considered basic course materials, computer packages, slides and transparencies, videos, additional listening materials, set of games, simplified readers and the like, tend to be considered supplementary, although many multimedia courses attempt to integrate a large variety of different media and materials, and, consequently, might consider these aids to be basic, not supplementary. Fourth, materials may either be designed for use in the classroom or for self study. A final commonly used procedure is to classify materials and media according to the language components or skills they aim to practice. Thus, listening materials are distinguished from, for example, reading, writing, speaking or grammar practice materials. Some media are considered better suited to practice particular skills or deal with particular requirements of foreign language course than others. Thus, learners' listening skills may benefit most from aural aids, such as tapes, radio broadcasts or the teachers' voice. Cultural background information, on the contrary, may best be presented over video, television, films, transparencies, posters or pictures, or it may be taught via the internet or with the help of CD-ROMs.

Materials and media in the history of foreign language education

When looking at the history of foreign language education from the point of materials, a number of evolutions in their selection and design are noticeable. At various stages in the development of foreign language teaching, new media and teaching aids have been introduced, of which some have managed to establish themselves firmly, and continue to be used to date, whereas others have become marginalized or seem to have gradually disappeared from mainstream teaching altogether.

Shifts in the selection and conception of media and materials seem to have been dependent on a number of interrelated factors. Developments in the understanding of what competence in a foreign language entails and what is required to reach it, in theories about the nature of the language learning process and how it is best supported, combined with technological developments and the commercial exploitation of particular "teaching and learning machines", have to a large extent determined the way in which materials and media have been used in foreign language instruction. Thus, the need for the pupil to hear himself when practicing pronunciation was recognized early. No effective way of meeting the problem was found until the tape recorder was invented. The popularity of drill exercise in the audio-lingual foreign language teaching can in part be explained by the commercialization of a machine that was capable of doing these monotonous, unnatural and inhuman activities, i.e. the language laboratory. Television and video were acclaimed by foreign language education theorists of the communicative era for their capability of bringing "real life" into the language learning classroom and of communicating the total situation of language to the learner. Insights from cognitive psychology, notably that people learn best when several senses are simultaneously addressed, triggered efforts of the teaching profession to introduce all kinds of visual, audio-visual and even tangible aids into foreign language teaching, so as to complement or replace the predominantly written and aural materials.

Teaching practice and teachers' and learners' experiences with particular materials and media, too, contributed to their refinement and adaptation to particular educational needs. Thus, following teachers' unsatisfactory experiences with films and videos which tended to be quite long when they were first introduced into the foreign language classroom, a clear evolution towards shorter films has been noticeable replacing the input of large amounts of aural and visual data with shorter sequences, say of about four minutes, followed by careful exploitation. Learners' frustrating experience with monolingual dictionaries containing long entries formulated in a language too far above their level of competence incited publishers and researchers to develop learner dictionaries with clear definitions written in simple language, highlighting active words to be learnt first, providing study pages and grammar help boxes focusing on vital grammar points, building in a workbook section to develop students' dictionary skills, providing colorful illustrations with corresponding vocabulary practice exercises or usage notes designed to help learners avoid common errors.

Teacher frustration at the impracticability of certain media and materials proposed by theorists further determined their lifecycle. Whereas textbooks are very user-friendly "packages" of materials, because they are light, easily scanned, easily stacked and do not need hardware or electricity. Slide projectors or video machines are less so, also because in many institutions and schools the rooms where they are available have to be booked well in advance, which makes course planning more difficult. Some media can also be considered more flexible than others because they can be used for a variety of language practice activities, with various age groups and working arrangements. Thus, transparencies can not only be used by the teacher to capture class attention, they may also be used by pupils to report on group work results. They are easily wiped off and can be used in the context of almost any thinkable language practice activity. The language laboratory, on the contrary, appears more static and limited in use, seeming suitable foremost for individual pronunciation and drill practice, albeit those communicative group activities are not wholly excluded.

The selection of teaching materials and media is also partly dependent on the demands made by society at a given period in time. Computer literacy is now put forward as one of the aims which all teaching should pursue. In view of the explosion of knowledge and the fastness with which it is distributes, over the information highway and other media, society also demand that teachers and schools educate their children for independent, lifelong learning, providing them with the skills to find and evaluate information next to passing a body of well-structured knowledge on to them which can serve as a guiding framework. Since computers use language, it would seem logical to take advantage of them for language learning. Computers, moreover, enable independent individual work, since learners can progress at their own pace and many programs include a self-check facility, automatic contextualized feedback, the possibility to use reference materials in the screen, to listen to the spoken language, to watch pieces of video, to record one's own voice, or to interact on real time with native speakers of a foreign language, to name only a few advantages. The fact that young and adolescent learners in particular find the use of computers attractive and motivating is an added benefit.

These social demands urge a change in teachers' and learners' roles. Teachers have to become coaches rather than providers of information, since pupils can find their own texts and language data. Coaching entails the need to redesign many of the materials that have been developed for teacher-guided instruction and to consider seriously how individual differences in learning styles, needs, abilities and interests can best catered for in integrated powerful multimedia learning environments.

Debates and perspectives

With the boom of teaching media, interdisciplinary groups of social scientists, psychologists, educationists and technically oriented researchers started studying "educational technology". One of their major concerns was to investigate the possible surplus value of particular media over others in particular learning environments. A major problem facing this field of study is the fact that it is next to impossible to prove empirically the excess value of one medium over another, since each language learning situation is shaped by a complex whole of situational, relational, educational, cognitive and affective variables, which are hard to control and make a reliable comparison of two groups of learners-one working with a particular media remain largely based on assumptions, not on genera facts. It follows that authors, course designers and teachers alike have very little evidence upon which they can base any improvements to exciting media, materials or multimedia programs, or suggestions for new approaches in new materials.

It seems that, partly as a consequence of this, teachers have become skeptical and critical toward the hyperbole created around new teaching media. They tend to prefer to stick to what is familiar and most practicable, being ill-disposed toward devoting energy to changing teaching approaches that may well not lead to more effective learning. The fact that theorists and researchers often overlook the practical institutional or organizational constraints every teacher has to live with may further undermine teachers' belief in proposals made by non-practitioners.

On top of this, teachers may be afraid that new media may come to replace them as teachers, and therefore prefer not to cooperate in what to them seems a self-destructive process. However, since it is only when media and materials are used in a meaningful and pedagogically well-considered manner that they may make the learning process more effective, and since the teacher best qualifies for designing appropriate learning environments, the chance that teachers will disappear altogether is small. Certainly, if learners are to be provided with a large variety of learning experiences that promote independent learning, teacher whole-class instruction time may well have to be reduced. Rather than supplanting the teacher and the textbook, however, newer teaching aids will supplement and support them.

In view of the challenges that await teachers, teacher training intuitions have the responsibility to prepare teachers for an informed selection, adaptation and integration of available media and materials. It will be vital for teachers to perceive both the strengths and weaknesses of teaching media and materials, and to find ways to overcome shortcomings. The dangers that threaten teachers are those of over-burdening teaching with media for their sheer availability, and of falling prey to a naive belief in media's inherent capacities, without devoting sufficient attention to the quality of data input and instruction and process materials, or carefully considering learners' needs, learning styles, abilities, interests and levels of competence in designing learning environments.

Unit 14　　Materials & Test　教材与考试

1. **Epidiascope**（幻灯机片）：Epidiascope is a device which displays opaque materials by shining a bright lamp onto the object from above. A system of mirrors, prisms and/or imaging lenses is used to focus an image of the material onto a viewing screen.

2. **Flipchart**（活动挂图）：Flipchart is a stationery item resembling a whiteboard, typically supported on a tripod or four-legged easel.

3. **Cognitive Psychology**（认知心理学）：Cognitive psychology is a sub-discipline of psychology exploring internal mental processes. It is the study of how people perceive, remember, think, speak, and solve problems.

New words and expressions

1. entail [in'teil]	vt.	使必需，带来，限定继承
	n.	限定继承权
2. supplement ['sʌplimənt]	n.	增刊，补充物
	vt.	增补，补充
3. supplant [sə'plɑ:nt]	v.	取代，排挤
4. harness ['hɑ:nis]	vt.	利用，管理，控制
5. cassette [kə'set]	n.	盒式磁带，暗盒
6. periodical [ˌpiəri'ɔdikəl]	n.	期刊
	adj.	定期的
7. epidiascope [ˌepi'daiəskəup]	n.	幻灯机
8. spectrum ['spektrəm]	n.	系列，幅度，范围，光谱，[科]频谱
9. chunk [tʃʌŋk]	n.	厚块（片），相当大的量
10. tangible ['tændʒəbl]	adj.	可触摸的，实际的，有形的，确凿的
11. surplus ['sə:pləs]	n.	过剩，顺差，盈余
	adj.	过剩的，多余的
12. empirically [im'pirikli]	adv.	经验主义地
13. prey [prei]	n.	牺牲者，被掠食者
	vi.	掠夺，捕食，使……苦恼

I Vocabulary.

Fill in the blanks with the most suitable words. Change the form when necessary.

| entail | supplement | harness | periodical | chunk |
| tangible | supplant | surplus | spectrum | prey |

1. The project would _____ a huge increase in defense spending.
2. He retired, and was free. Every day he spent the whole morning reading _____.
3. Nowadays, solar energy _____ to better serve us.
4. The policy of apartheid is only a political _____ to an economic policy that depends on cheap native labor.
5. Instead of falling a _____ to the enemy, he committed suicide.
6. To better pursue his dreams, he spent _____ of time studying and finally became a scientist.
7. An efficient government should serve the people and bring more _____ benefits to common people.
8. The Commercial Press published a wide _____ of book.
9. I hate this writer's writing because his works is always heavy with _____ phrasing.
10. Machinery has largely _____ hand labor in making shoes.

II Comprehension of the text.

Decide whether the following statements are true (T) or false (F) according to the passage.

1. The broad spectrum of teaching aids can be classified according to various perspectives. ( )
2. At various stages in the development of foreign language teaching, some media and teaching aids have managed to establish themselves firmly, and continue to be used to date, whereas others seem to have gradually disappeared from mainstream teaching altogether. ( )
3. No valid facts have shown that people learn best when several senses are simultaneously

addressed. ( )

4. Computers support independent individual work because learners can progress at their own pace. ( )

5. Teachers may be afraid that new media may come to replace them as teachers, and therefore prefer not to cooperate in what to them seems a self-destructive process.
( )

III Complete the following sentences according to the text.

1. An obvious way to classify teaching aids is to distinguish between aural, visual and audio-visual aids, with _____ _____ having the advantage of combining sound and image.

2. Because of _____ _____ _____ _____ listening materials are distinguished from reading, writing, speaking and grammar practice materials.

3. When looking at the history of foreign language education from the point of materials, a number of _____ in their selection and design are noticeable.

4. With the boom of teaching media, _____ _____ is studied by groups of social scientists, psychologists, educationists and technically oriented researchers.

5. Textbooks are very _____ "packages" of materials, because they are light, easily scanned, easily stacked and do not need hardware or electricity.

Text B In Defense of Teaching "Outdated" Material

导读：虽然欧几里得几何学并不能完全解释我们生存的空间，但是许多学校仍然教授这一课程，因为如果不能了解欧几里得几何学，研究三角学、微积分则很困难。要想精通一门课程，了解这些所谓的"过时"的教材是非常有必要的。不能掌握一门课程的发展史，则充其量也只能是个门外汉。本文在呼吁重视一些经典教材时，要求教育者们培养学生在先前知识基础上，学会构建新知识的能力，而不只是做一个普通的信息接受者。

We all know that Euclidean geometry does not adequately explain the space in which we live. Our world is not that of the plane, as found in Edward Abbott's *Flatland*. Why, then, is Euclidean geometry still taught in schools? I suggest that without an understanding of Euclidean geometry, one would have difficulty understanding advanced concepts, such as trigonometry or calculus. As my college calculus teacher noted, calculus is just addition done with lines. Advanced concepts build on previous knowledge.

During my rhetorical criticism course, students sometimes wonder why we cover so much history. A similar issue is also raised in my rhetorical theory course, a survey course that begins with the pre-Socratics and ends with postmodern rhetorical theory. I openly state that some of the material that we cover is no longer useful from a methodological standpoint, but that there are reasons for teaching the material. I explain to the students that it is important to recognize not only current rhetorical theory and methods of criticism, but also the controversies, dead ends, and landmarks that brought us to the place we are today. Innovation is often the result of recognition of suboptimal processes or ideas. If we help students see where these shifts in method or theory occurred and what spawned these insights, and, more importantly, why previous generations held inaccurate understandings, we are more likely to have students who will likewise improve the discipline because they, too, can see potential ways to improve their craft.

Knowledge does not spring forth exnihility, and current knowledge is built on previous knowledge. But it is not enough to simply teach history. We must teach students how to use history. If we can teach students how to bind together previous knowledge with current knowledge, there will be little in any discipline that can truly be considered outdated.

Every subject has a history, including biology, physics, mathematics, literature, music and art... To teach, for example, what we know about biology today without also teaching what we once knew, or thought we knew, is to reduce knowledge to a mere consumer product. It is to deprive students of a sense of the meaning of what we know, and of how we know.

Too often we seek the most up-to-date material at the expense of the monumental works that defined a discipline. This is also structural. Publishers stop publishing groundbreaking books because there is no longer sufficient demand for them. For example, when I ordered Postman's Teaching as a Conserving Activity as part of the readings for my graduate pedagogy course, I was informed by the university bookstore that the book was out of stock indefinitely with the publisher and no longer available (despite the many potential sellers on Amazon and other such sites). Groundbreaking works in my field of rhetorical criticism, such as Edwin Black's Rhetorical Criticism: A

Study in Method, are only recently available through print-on-demand. With a seemingly constant flood of new books and knowledge, it is difficult enough to simply keep up, let alone delve into the archives.

We must, of course, stay up-to-date on current trends in our field. However, we must also remember that the insights of tomorrow are dependent on the knowledge of the past. Alfred Korzybski observed: The simple steel structure of a bridge, familiar to us in every day life, is a clear reminder to us all of the arts of Hephaestus and the bound-up knowledge of countless generations of smiths and mechanics, metallurgists and chemists, mathematicians and builders, teachers and engineers who toiled for many thousands of years to make possible the riveted steel beams which are the elements of modern structure. Korzybski referred to this process as time-binding, defining it thus: Human beings possess a most remarkable capacity which is entirely peculiar to them—I mean the capacity to summarize, digest and appropriate the labors and experiences of the past; I mean the capacity to use the fruits of past labors and experiences as intellectual or spiritual capital for developments in the present; I mean the capacity to employ as instruments of increasing the accumulated achievements of the all-precious lives of the past generations spent in trial and error, trial and success; I mean the capacity of human beings to conduct their lives in the ever increasing light of inherited wisdom; I mean the capacity in virtue of which man is at once the heritor of the by-gone ages and the trustee of posterity.

S. I. Hayakawa describes it more succinctly as "the ability to organize social cooperation at a distance and to accumulate knowledge over generations of time through the use of symbols" (emphasis in original). The simple fact that I am writing this essay using a system of symbols that I did not develop, and drawing on ideas created by a man who is now dead, is an example of time-binding. As Harry Weinberg observes, each of us "stands on the shoulders of the dead to peer into the future".

Yet, time-binding is not simply a matter of constantly revising and discarding the past. As Hayakawa notes, "The greater the area of cooperation between the living and the dead in the interests of those yet unborn, the better; the more people embraced in the cooperative enterprise, the better." We must make use of the past if we are to become effective time-binders ourselves and teach our students how to use the past if we are to also help them to become effective time-binders. Herein lays the problem with most uses of history: Rather than teaching the student to use history, many of us teach the student the history itself, as if it stood apart from contemporary practice. Perhaps the key term in time-binding is not time, so much as binding, at least where pedagogical practice is concerned. We must recognize that we are building knowledge from disparate elements and binding them together. Milton Dawes reminds us that "Whatever we think, say, feel, do, expect, plan for, want, or theorize about, is incomplete, because we have not included all." And we never can say it all. Michael McGee notes, "The only way to say it air in our fractured culture is to provide readers and audiences with dense, truncated fragments which cue them to produce a finished discourse in their minds. In short, text construction is now something done more by the consumers than by the producers of discourse". We must help students to become active participants in the construction of knowledge, rather than simply consumers of information.

Henry Giroux writes, "This is what the pedagogical struggle is all about—opening up the material and discursive basis of particular ways of producing meaning and presenting ourselves, our relations with others, and our relation to our environment so as to consider the possibilities not yet realized." But to help students recognize the possibilities not yet realized, we must inculcate a consciousness of their own time-binding nature. Dawes suggest: With time-binding consciousness we shift our notion of time-binding from a definition and classification, to a verb representing an action. We recognize time-binding as a psychological tool—a tool we can use to improve ourselves in any area we choose. With time-binding consciousness, we move from simply repeating "each generation can start where the former left off" to "self-consciously appreciating ourselves as time-binders". By helping students to make the connections between past and present understandings of the topic at hand, we can help them learn how to use the past. In other words, we can help them to become the self-conscious time-binders that Dawes proposes.

When we teach, we are not merely teaching content. We are teaching an orientation to a discipline, especially in upper-division courses and certainly in graduate programs. To know the current literature without an understanding of how we arrived there is much like entering a conversation at a bar and immediately joining in an ongoing heated debate. Without an understanding of the controversies and issues within a discipline, the student will likely have only a surface understanding of the material. The student will have a much greater understanding of the intricacies of a topic if he or she is aware of the ground that has already been covered by those before. This will help students avoid the pitfalls and dead ends that others may have already encountered. More importantly, the controversies in a field often persist and shape present understanding, knowing the contours of these arguments is an essential part of becoming a member of the discipline rather than simply an outside observer. Teaching the history of a discipline—any discipline—provides students with a greater understanding of how we have collectively arrived at the knowledge we currently hold. But we must teach this history with an eye focused on building conscious time-binders—those who can effectively use the history of a discipline to drive forward our understanding of the problems that face the world as a whole. After all, the ability to transmit knowledge across time and space is worth little if we are unable to use it well. Teaching students without providing a context in which to understand the discipline may well doom them to repeat the mistakes of those before them.

Despite our best efforts, many teachers still hold a bias toward current material, sloughing off old readings as we bring our reading lists and syllabi "up-to-date". Yet, recency of the scholarship does not necessarily equal relevance. After all, Plato has been read for almost 2500 years and his insights are still useful. Moreover, in our quest to teach current research, it is easy to lose sight of ideas to which we can bind that current scholarship. In the words of Ziggy Marley, "If you don't know your past, you don't know your future." But it is not enough to simply teach the insights that are still valid. A biologist teaching students that people used to believe that geese were generated from goose neck barnacles not only teaches a historical anecdote in biology, but also helps students understand how misguided thinking led to incorrect conclusions. Just because one thing looks similar to another does not mean that one becomes the other or that they have similar properties. It is just as important for the biologist of today to continually evaluate his or her patterns of thought that may likewise lead to incorrect conclusions. Such is the aim of general semantics.

History must also be critically assessed. After all, our representations of history are never as accurate as one may hope. Thus, we must take care when concerning how we transmit knowledge to students. Ben Hauck writes, "When the future listens, its understanding and success depends on our reports from the present. Time-binding is done individually and now, but the minutest choice of word can have cultural impacts and implications now and later." The practice of teaching is an exercise in creating the future out of the past. Gerald Savage notes that educators should transcend mere instrumental teaching and help students begin to re-conceive the profession as one that can be practiced in alternative ways that would permit them greater autonomy and professional integrity. This seems to be good advice for educators in any discipline.

Notes

1. **Euclidean Geometry**（欧几里得几何）: a mathematical system attributed to the Alexandrian Greek mathematician Euclid, which he described in his textbook on geometry: *The Elements*. Euclid's method consists in assuming a small set of intuitively appealing axioms, and deducing many other propositions from these.

2. **Trigonometry**（三角学）: a branch of mathematics that studies triangles and the relationships between their sides and the angles between these sides.

New words and expressions

1.	methodological [ˌmeθədə'lɔdʒikəl]	adj.	方法的，方法论的
2.	landmark ['lændmɑːk]	n.	陆标，地界标，里程碑，划时代的事
3.	suboptimal [sʌb'ɔptiməl]	adj.	未达最佳标准的，非最理想的，非最适宜的，非最满意的
4.	spawn [spɔːn]	vt.	产生，造成
5.	nihility [nai'hiliti]	n.	虚无，不存在，无效
6.	pedagogy ['pedəgɔgi]	n.	教育学，教授法
7.	delve [delv]	vi.	探究，挖掘，搜索
8.	archives ['ɑːkaivz]	n.	档案，档案馆
9.	metallurgist [me'tælədʒist]	n.	冶金家，冶金学者
10.	peculiar [pi'kjuːljə]	adj.	奇怪的，特殊的，独特的，古怪的
11.	succinctly [sək'siŋktli]	adv.	简明地，简洁地
12.	disparate ['dispərit]	adj.	不同的，异类的
13.	truncated [trʌŋ'keitid]	adj.	被截的，缩短的
14.	discursive [di'skəːsiv]	adj.	散漫的；不得要领的
15.	pitfall ['pitfɔːl]	n.	陷阱，隐患，想不到的困难
16.	contour ['kɔntuə]	n.	周线，轮廓，等高线，概要，电路
17.	slough [slau]	v.	蜕皮，摆脱

Exercises

I Vocabulary.

Fill in the blanks with the most suitable words. Change the form when necessary.

landmark	spawn	nihility	archive	sub-optimal
disparate	truncated	discursive	contour	slough

1. The invention of internet is a _____ in the development of human history.
2. His sudden resignation _____ many rumors.
3. Though the sweater and the coat are of _____ styles, he managed to wear in a fashionable way.
4. She could _____ off sadness and replace it by a hope.
5. He is a man of imagination and often thinks in a _____ style.
6. They were allowed to stay in the _____ to look for the information that they want.
7. He was angry because his original report had become a badly _____ one because of some trenchant but true words.
8. Nothing happens because of _____, and it happens of reasons.
9. I don't think now it is _____ for your investment, and the best time is yet to come.
10. Even having a glimpse of the _____ of Mount Tai is breathtaking.

II Comprehension of the text.

Decide whether the following statements are true (T) or false (F) according to the passage.

1. Innovation is often the result of recognition of sub-optimal processes or ideas. ( )
2. Time-binding is simply a matter of constantly revising and discarding the past. ( )
3. Time-binding consciousness enables us to move from simply repeating that "each generation can start where the former left off" to "self-consciously appreciating ourselves as time-binder". ( )
4. Students can learn how to use the past if they know the connections between past understandings and the present ones. ( )
5. Recency of the scholarship always equals relevance. ( )

III Choose the word or expression that has the similar meaning of the underlined word or expression.

1. To finish his paper, he <u>delved</u> in many libraries for that book and finally got it.
   A. searched   B. probed   C. read   D. questioned
2. The workers in that factory were exploited by the boss and <u>toiled</u> all through the night.
   A. worked hard   B. stayed up late   C. carried on   D. labored
3. His remarks are always <u>succinct</u> and pointed.
   A. complicated   B. easy   C. long   D. simple
4. Be careful. Don't fall into the <u>pitfalls</u> set up by the enemy.
   A. holes   B. traps   C. caves   D. wells
5. Teachers shouldn't <u>have a bias towards</u> these excellent students. They should treat them as equal.
   A. be fond of   B. be strict with
   C. have partiality for   D. admire

Useful phrases and expressions

开展高水平合作办学 carry out high-level collaboration in offering education programs
抓好教材体系建设 do a good job in course materials development
分类指定课程标准 develop the curriculum standards by category
充分利用现代信息技术 adopt information technology to
丰富并创新课程形式 enrich and innovate teaching methods
健全国家教材制度 improve the national textbook compilation system
科学规划课程 design the curricula well
借鉴先进的教育理念和教育经验 learn from advanced ideas and experience
切实保证教材的正确政治导向和价值导向 ensure a correct political orientation and values
坚持马克思主义在教育工作中的指导地位 uphold the guiding position of Marxism in education

Marxism makes China's education unique.
马克思主义是我国教育最鲜亮的底色。
Mechanisms and institutional innovations should be introduced in the compilation, distribution, and application of course materials.

Unit 14　Materials & Test　教材与考试

在教材编写、推广、使用上注重体制机制创新。

Course materials should be politically reliable, scientifically sound, up-to-date, systematic, and with Chinese characteristics.

增强教材编写、修订、审查、选用、退出机制。

Focus on the world's cutting-edge science and technology as well as domestic disciplines that are weak, absent, or in short supply.

聚焦世界科技前沿和国内薄弱、空白、紧缺学科专业。

Form a system that meets the requirements of socialist development, reflect the latest academic achievements and cover all subject areas.

形成适应中国特色社会主义发展要求，立足国际学术前沿，门类齐全的教材体系。

Conscientiously implement a responsibility system for ideological work, follow the guidance of Marxism, and integrate all constructive ides and cultures into our mainstream ideology.

引导广大师生坚定信仰、积极传播、模范践行社会主义核心价值观。

Marxist theory serves as the ideological foundation for students' lifelong growth.

以马克思主义理论教育为学生一生成长奠定科学思想基础。

Arm teachers and students with the latest theoretical achievements in adapting Marxism to China.

坚持不懈用马克思主义中国化最新理论成果武装师生头脑。

Take into consideration the characteristics of students in different stages of learning, and guide teachers and students to study this thought in an in-depth, systematic, and timely fashion.

结合不同学段学生特点，引导广大师生深入系统学、及时跟进学。

Course materials must be guided by Marxism and its adaptation to the Chinese context; they must reflect the national spirit and values, the Party's education policy, and the cultural achievements and innovation outcomes of humanity.

教材要坚持马克思主义指导地位，体现马克思主义中国化要求，体现中国和中华民族风格，体现党和国家对教育的基本要求，体现国家和民族基本价值观，体现人类文化知识积累和创新成果。

Unit 15 Educational Evaluation
教育评价

Text A Integration of Technology and Educational Assessment

导读：随着科学技术的发展，教育评价也走上了现代化的道路。对于学生评价体系也由单一向多维度转变。技术的发展让设计复杂的评价体系成为可能。

Across the disciplines, technologies have expanded the phenomena that can be investigated, the nature of argumentation, and the use of evidence. Technologies allow representations of domains, systems, models, data, and their manipulation in ways that previously were not possible. Models of population density permit investigations of economic and social issues. This move from static to dynamic models has changed the nature of inquiry among professionals as well as the way that academic disciplines can be taught. Correspondingly, a new generation of assessments is well on its way to transforming what, how, when, where, and why assessment occurs and its linkages to teaching and learning. Powered by the ever-increasing capabilities of technology, these 21st century approaches to assessment expand the potential for tests to both probe and promote a broad spectrum of human learning, including the types of knowledge and competence advocated in various recent policy reports on education and the economy.

Although early uses of technology in large-scale testing have focused on relatively straightforward logistical efficiencies and cost reductions, a new generation of innovative assessments is pushing the frontiers of measuring complex forms of learning. Computers' abilities to capture student inputs permit collecting evidence of processes such as problem-solving sequences and strategy use as reflected by information selected, numbers of attempts, approximation to solutions, and time allocation. Such data can be combined with statistical and measurement algorithms to extract patterns associated with varying levels of expertise. Research in the learning sciences is simultaneously informing the design of innovative, dynamic, interactive assessment tasks and powerful scoring, reporting, and real-time feedback mechanisms. When coupled with technology, such knowledge has propelled various advances in adaptive testing, including knowledge and skills diagnosis, the provision of immediate feedback to teachers and students accompanied by scaffolding for improvement, and the potential for accommodations for special populations. Technology also supports movement toward the design of more balanced sets of coherent, nested assessments that operate across levels of educational systems.

Information and communications technologies such as Web browsers, word processors, editing, drawing, simulations, and multimedia programs support a variety of research, design, composition, and communication processes. These same tools can expand the cognitive skills that can be assessed, including the processes of planning, drafting, composing, and revising. For example, the National Assessment of Educational Progress (NAEP) writing assessment in 2011 will require use of word processing and editing tools to compose essays.

In professional testing, architecture examinees use computer-assisted design programs as part of their licensure assessment. The challenge that such technology-based presentation and data capture contexts offers now lies in the design principles for eliciting complex learning, the analysis of complex forms of data, and their meaningful interpretation relative to models of the underlying components of competence and expertise. The area of science assessment is perhaps leading the way in exploring the presentation and interpretation of complex, multifaceted problem types and assessment approaches. In 2006, the Program for International Student Assessment pilot tested a Computer-Based Assessment of Science to test knowledge and inquiry processes not assessed in the paper-based booklets. The assessment included such student explorations as the genetic breeding of plants. At the state level, Minnesota has an online science test with tasks engaging students in simulated laboratory experiments or investigations of phenomena such as weather or the solar system.

Recently, a distinction has been made between assessments of the outcomes of learning, typically used for grading and accountability purposes (summative assessment), and assessments for learning, used to diagnose and modify the conditions of learning and instruction (formative assessment). Research has repeatedly shown the formative use of assessment to significantly benefit student achievement. Such effects depend on several classroom practice factors, including alignment of assessments with state standards, quality of the feedback provided to students, involvement of students in self-reflection and action, and teachers making adjustments to their instruction based on the assessment results. Technologies are well suited to support many of the data-collection, complex analysis, and individualized feedback and scaffolding features needed for the formative use of assessment.

In addition to assessment of student knowledge and skills in highly structured problems with one right answer, technology can also support the design of complex, interactive tasks that extend the range of knowledge, skills, and cognitive processes that can be assessed. For example, simulations can assess and promote understanding of complex systems by superimposing multiple representations and permitting manipulation of structures and patterns that otherwise might not be visible or even conceivable. Simulation-based assessments can probe basic foundational knowledge such as the functions of organisms in an ecosystem, and, more important, they can probe students' knowledge of how components of a system interact along with abilities to investigate the impacts of multiple variables changing at the same time. When well designed and implemented, classroom assessments that are used during instruction to monitor and improve progress and that are also administered following instruction to document learning and identify remaining needs can become credible components of a multilevel state assessment system. Technology-enhanced formative assessments during instruction can provide immediate, contingent feedback and adaptive coaching for reteaching of problematic knowledge and skills. Benchmark assessments following instruction can provide summative classroom-based assessments with technical quality that could be aggregated into the state accountability system. Moreover, because simulations use multiple modalities and representations, students with diverse learning styles and language backgrounds may have better opportunities to demonstrate their knowledge than are possible in text-laden print tests.

It is an exciting time in the field of assessment for several reasons. First, individuals have realized that there are multiple roles for assessment to play in the educational process and that one of the most valuable roles are the formative function of assisting student learning. Second, cognitive research and theory have provided us with rich models and representations of how students understand many of the key principles in the curriculum, how students develop knowledge structures, and how to analyze and understand simple and complex aspects of student performance. Third, technology makes possible more flexible, tailored presentations to students of a much wider and richer array of tasks and environments where students can learn and where they can show us what they know and how they know it. Thus, there is an interesting and powerful confluence among theory, research, technology, and practice, especially when it comes to the integration of curriculum, instruction, and assessment.

In numerous areas of the curriculum, information technologies are changing what is taught, when and how it is taught, and what students are expected to be able to do to demonstrate their knowledge and skill. These changes in turn are stimulating people to rethink what is assessed, how that information is obtained, and how it is fed back into the educational process in a productive and timely way. This situation creates opportunities to center curriculum, instruction, and assessment around cognitive principles. With technology, assessment can become richer, timelier, and more seamlessly interwoven with multiple aspects of curriculum and instruction. As discussed earlier, the most useful kinds of assessment for enhancing student learning emphasize knowledge integration and extended reasoning, support a process of individualized instruction, allow for student interaction, collect rich diagnostic data, and provide timely feedback. The demands and complexity of these types of assessment can be quite substantial, but technology makes them feasible. Diagnostic assessments of individuals' learning, for example, must involve collecting, interpreting, and reporting significant amounts of information. No educator, whether a classroom teacher or other user of assessment data, could realistically be expected to handle the information flow, analysis demands, and decision-making burdens involved without technological support. Thus, technology removes some of the constraints that previously made high-quality formative assessment of complex performances difficult or impractical for a classroom teacher.

Clearly, we are just beginning to see how to harness technology to support the formative and summative functions of assessment. We still need to learn a great deal about the quality and efficacy of systems operating at both the large-scale level and the small-scale level. Not the least of the concerns facing us is the integration of assessment tools and practices into the educational system and teachers' practices. But we must also take note of the fact that extremely powerful information technologies are becoming as ubiquitous in educational settings as they are in other aspects of people's daily lives. Technologies are almost certain to continue to provoke fundamental changes in learning environments at all levels of the education system. Many of the implications of technology are beyond people's speculative capacity. Little more than 15 years ago, for example, few could have predicted the sweeping effects of the Internet and social networking on education and other segments of society. The range of computational devices and their applications is expanding exponentially, fundamentally changing how people think about communication, collaboration, problem solving, connectivity, information systems, educational practices, and the role of technology in society.

We can, therefore, imagine a future in which the audit function of assessments external to the classroom would be significantly reduced or even unnecessary because the information needed to assess students, at the levels of description appropriate for various monitoring purposes, could be mined from the data streams generated by students in and out of their classrooms. A metaphor for such a radical shift in how one "does the business of educational assessment" exists in the world of retail outlets, ranging from small businesses to supermarkets to department stores. No longer do these businesses have to close down once or twice a year to take inventory of their stock. Rather, with the advent of automated checkouts and barcodes for all items, these enterprises have access to a continuous stream of information that can be used to monitor inventory and the flow of items. Not only can business continue without interruption, but the information obtained is far richer, enabling stores to monitor trends and aggregate the data into various kinds of summaries. Similarly, with new assessment technologies, schools would no longer have to interrupt the normal instructional process at various times during the year to administer external tests to students, nor would they have to spend significant amounts of time preparing for specific external tests peripheral to the ongoing activities of teaching and learning.

The design and deployment of even simple technology tools must ultimately rely on a technology infrastructure that connects the classroom to powerful database management and information retrieval systems that operate within and across schools and systems. This is especially true when the classroom assessment data are viewed as part of a coordinated system of assessment data that would potentially include curriculum-embedded assessment information, unit and end-of-course benchmark assessment data, interim cross-unit summative status checks, and state-level test data. Further work addressing issues of technology and the design of a comprehensive assessment system involves consideration of information and how it needs to flow through this system. For example, who needs to use assessment data? What questions need to be answered? In what timeframe do they need to be answered? What actions might they take based on these answers?

Extensive technology-based systems that link curriculum, instruction, and assessment at the classroom level might enable a shift from today's assessment systems, which use different kinds of assessments for different purposes, to a balanced design that would ensure the three critical features of comprehensiveness, coherence, and continuity. In such a design, for comprehensiveness, assessments would provide a variety of evidence to support educational decision-making, for coherence, the information provided at differing levels of responsibility and action would be linked back to the same underlying conceptual model of student learning, and for continuity, it would provide indications of student growth over time.

Technological advances will allow for the attainment of many of the goals that educators, researchers, policymakers, teachers, and parents have envisioned for assessment as a viable source of information for educational improvement. When we implement powerful technology-based systems in classrooms, rich sources of information about intellectually significant student learning will be continuously available across wide segments of the curriculum and for individual learners over extended periods of time. This is exactly the kind of information we now lack, making it difficult to use assessment to truly support learning. The major issue is not whether this type of innovative assessment design, data collection, and information analysis is feasible in the future. Rather, the issue is how the world of education anticipates and embraces this possibility, and how it will explore the resulting options for effectively using assessment information to meet the multiple purposes served by current assessments, and most important, to enhance student learning.

1. **Summative Assessment（or Summative Evaluation）**（终结性评价）：Summative assessment is the assessment of the learning and summarizes the development of learners at a particular time. After a period of work, e.g. a unit for two weeks, the learner sits for a test and then the teacher marks the test and assigns a score.

2. **Formative Assessment**（形成性评价）：Formative assessment is a reflective process that intends to promote student attainment. Cowie and Bell define it as the bidirectional process between teacher and student to enhance, recognize and respond to the learning.

New words and expressions

1. manipulation [mə,nipju'leiʃən]　　n.　操纵，控制
2. algorithm ['ælgəriðəm]　　n.　算法
3. simultaneously [saiməl'teinjəsli]　　adv.　同时地
4. propel [prə'pel]　　v.　推进，驱使
5. cognitive ['kɔgnitiv]　　adj.　认识的，认知的，有认识力的
6. elicit [i'lisit]　　vt.　引出，诱出，探出
7. alignment [ə'lainmənt]　　n.　排成直线，直线性；结盟
8. interactive [intər'æktiv]　　adj.　相互作用的，交互的
9. seamless ['si:mlis]　　adj.　持续的，无缝的
10. interwoven [,intə'wəuvn]　　adj.　交织的，混合的（动词 interweave 的过去分词）
11. audit ['ɔ:dit]　　n.　审计，查账
　　　　vt.　旁听，审计
12. aggregate ['ægrigeit]　　adj.　合计的，总的
　　　　n.　总计，进球总数，集料
　　　　v.　（使）聚集，总计
13. envision [in'viʒən]　　vt.　想象，设想
14. segment ['segmənt]　　n.　部分，弓形，瓣，段，节
　　　　vt.　分割

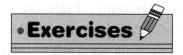

I　Vocabulary.

Fill in the blanks with the most suitable words. Change the form when necessary.

manipulate　simultaneous　cognitive　alignment　interactive

1. Hearing the good news, the crowds burst into applause _____.
2. Practice is based on the _____ elements of perception.
3. Intimate friends always have _____ effect on each other.

4. Having been in China for 4 years, Mr. Smith was able to _____ chopsticks with great dexterity.
5. A new _____ is rising in Mideast.

II Comprehension of the text.

Decide whether the following statements are true (T) or false (F) according to the passage.

1. Planning belongs to the rank of cognitive skills, while revising is not. ( )
2. Assessment used to diagnose and modify the conditions of learning and instruction is called summative assessment. ( )
3. Technology can now support the design of complex and interactive tasks that can assess students' learning. ( )
4. Technology information is changing the way in which knowledge is taught and the content of teaching. ( )
5. Technology removes some of the constraints that previously made high-quality formative assessment of complex performances difficult or impractical. ( )

III Choose the word or expression that has the similar meaning of the underlined word or expression.

1. Chop the stalks into short <u>segments</u> so that the animals can digest them easily.
   A. parts   B. sticks   C. circles   D. chunks
2. Though his plan is <u>seamless</u>, he still failed and got caught by the police.
   A. good   B. plain   C. tight and close D. clever
3. People in war all <u>envision</u> peace and a bright future.
   A. desire   B. look forward to C. call   D. fight for
4. <u>Propelled</u> by greed, he took away a large sum of money and went abroad.
   A. Stimulated   B. Seduced   C. Tormented   D. Asked
5. The audiences <u>aggregated</u> a million people.
   A. were less than B. were more than C. totaled   D. added

Text B Sustainable Assessment and Evaluation Strategies for Open and Distance Learning

导读：随着互联网的兴起，远程教育的发展方兴未艾。和传统的教育评价相比，远程教育的评价则比较棘手。本文列出了远程教育评价的一些策略，如创建题库、设计计算机化的考试系统等。

Distance Learning (DL) is the fastest growing form of domestic and international education today. In addition to the challenges of assessment in conventional institutions, distance learners are spread out geographically and physically from each other and from the instructor. Moreover, class sizes for DL courses are generally larger than those for traditional classes. These large numbers of students and numerous courses make assessment and evaluation very difficult and administrative nightmare at DL institutions. Yet, given large class sizes and their physical separation from students, many distance learning instructors feel they have few options for assessing students' performance.

Assessment is a systematic basis for making inferences about the learning and development of students. It is the process of defining, selecting, designing, collecting, analyzing, interpreting and using information to increase students' learning and development. In education, assessment may be thought of as occurring whenever one person, in some kind of interaction, direct or indirect, with another is conscious of obtaining and interpreting information about the knowledge and understanding, or abilities and attitudes of that other person. There are two distinct interpretations of assessment. The first is interpretation of assessment in terms of the routine tasks that students undertake in order to receive feedback on their learning and a mark or grade signifying their achievement. The second interpret assessment is applied to processes at the institutional level, for example, program evaluation.

There are various methods of assessment. The commonly used ones are objective questions, short answer questions, long answer questions and presentation. The method of assessment named objective questions derives its name from objectivity employed in marking the answers to the questions. The marking which is a simple mechanical process can be done by an individual or by a computer. Examples of objective type questions are true/false item; fill in the blanks item; multiple choice items; completion items and

Unit 15 Educational Evaluation 教育评价

matching items. Short answer questions may take different forms of answers such as one word/phrase; one sentence; completing a table/diagram; preparing a list or writing a paragraph. Long answer questions may also take various forms such as essay; reports or dissertations. The method of presentation is used to assess presentation skills. It requires appropriate assessment criteria for assessing the appearance of presenter; introduction of self; introduction of presentation; content of presentation; logic and order of presentation; eye contact; audibility; handling questions and use of visual aids. This method of assessment has high validity when the presentation is assessed by a group.

Assessment in ODL, unlike in the conventional system where students have a range of opportunities to demonstrate their learning periodically, depends on formal assessment tasks. The major characteristics of assessment in both settings are: For the conventional system, the learners are known through lectures, tutorials and individual consultations. They have a range of opportunities to demonstrate their learning—their interest, motivation, questioning and interaction. Moreover, they have opportunities to diagnose their errors before they go for formal assessment tasks and assessment activities have some flexibility.

On the other hand, ODL learners are at a distance, thus they rarely enjoy varied opportunities to communicate their learning depend much on formal task as they have less opportunity in which to diagnose their errors or mistakes before formal assessment task. Accordingly, assessment must be thoroughly planned, communicated and managed.

Validity is the extent to which an assessment measure does the job for which it is intended. The validity of an assessment can only be determined by reference to the assessment's stated purposes and its design specifications. For validity to be high the assessment must analyze student's performance on each objective and the assessment should provide the appropriate situation possible for measuring the specific abilities being measured. Reliability refers to consistency or precision or dependability of the assessment measurement and how consistent results are from one to another. The assessment is reliable if the results would be replicated on a subsequent occasion. Reliability is maximized when the assessment items are many, the items are not too easy or too difficult for the candidates and the marking is consistent.

Educators generally work with learners to review and support learning, and to make judgment regarding their merits and their achievements. In ODL, Self Assessment Questions, Tutor Marked Assessments and End of Semester Examinations are used. There is no immediate feedback and reinforcement. Self-Assessment Questions embedded in the course material enable distance learners to evaluate their progress frequently. Tutor Marked Assessments serve as the continuous assessment and the marks obtained carry about 25% to 30% weight which count in the final result of the course. End of Semester Examinations carries about 70% to 75% weight age of the final results. Distance learners are usually free to appear at any of these examinations either for specific courses or for all the registered courses provided that the minimum period of study prescribed for the relevant course is completed. Like in the conventional system, assessment in ODL can be both formative and summative. Formative assessment takes the form of Tutor Marked Assessments. It helps to identify the weaknesses and strengths in learning. It also helps to improve upon the process and the attainment of learning. Grading or scoring may be done in formative assessment. Summative Assessment takes the form of End of Semester Examinations.

A question bank is a planned library of test items pooled through cooperative efforts under the protection and support of an institution for the use of evaluators, academics and students in partial fulfillment of the requirements of the teaching learning process.

It is designed to fulfill certain pre-determined purposes namely to enrich the instructional aspect and to judge the distance learner. It offers a utility service with an inbuilt feedback mechanism for improvement of its questions. The number of questions needed for a course or a program which runs for a number of years is very large in a distance education institution. The academic staff are accordingly supposed to prepare a large number of quality questions on different topics of the prescribed courses or programs for learners self assessment, Tutor Marked Assessments and End of Semester Examinations. Most of these academics lack the adequate skill in test development and the time at their disposal is limited and they cannot be expected to develop a question pool of reasonable magnitude and quality within a specific time.

In the absence of a stock of ready made questions, the quality of question papers is liable to suffer. This necessitates the entrusting the preparation of quality items in different subjects to experienced teachers who are well conversant with the content and techniques of framing questions.

This strategy helps to build up ready made stock of items for Learners' Self Assessment, Tutor Marked Assessments and End of Semester Examinations. Such pool of item is of immense use if developed according to predetermined objectives. The types of questions making up a question bank are to depend entirely on the total framework of reference envisaged at the planning stage.

Running a question bank efficiently to sustain assessment necessitates careful planning. The objectives of such a bank should clearly be visualized and include: to increase the value of measurement; to increase the pedagogical value of evaluation; and more detailed specific objectives on special need for the question bank. The question bank should be located in such a place that it should be managed properly to provide utility services to all those who are interested. The planning of a question bank should take care of suitable place and equipment for storing, vetting and screening of items before depositing them in the bank, sorting and classifying items in the question bank, arrangement for subject wise assistance for efficient maintenance and an academic manager for question bank to direct the activities of the question bank. Carefully selected questions from the question bank can be used for instructional purposes. Various types of questions may be selected from the question bank for pre-testing, review and revision of a lesson. A question pool from a question bank can be utilized in the preparation of textual material and review exercises in course materials.

Learners can also use questions from question bank for self assessment of their learning outcomes for specific units or modules of a course since outline answers are provided in such questions. A question bank is evaluated at regular intervals at least once in three years, the questions are screened and the obsolete ones are discarded. As old and obsolete materials are discarded, new materials are continually added in line with the revision of course materials. Enrichment of questions by updating, replacing, discarding, modifying, adding new ones, regrouping and classification is an ongoing process aimed at giving the question bank a dynamic look. A well developed and efficiently used question bank is an asset to sustainable assessment.

Computer based tests are defined as test or assessments that are administered by computer in either alone or networked configuration or by other technology devices linked to the internet or World Wide Web (WWW). Computer based testing is recognized as a sustainable strategy for sustainable assessment for ODL because it can be more responsive to the needs of both the test provider or institution and distance learners. Where "on demand" testing of examinees is needed, the use of computer based testing is more helpful. Computer based testing works on a completely different model than paper and pencil administration and offers the benefits that the later cannot match. Smaller number of candidates can be tested throughout the year rather than large numbers several times a year. Study centers can offer different tests at the same time since examinations may be delivered on personal computers using local area network, and the computer selects test questions from a pool, so candidates taking the same examination will not be answering identical questions, which would enhance test security.

Computer based assessment allows for a diverse range of question types which is a better test of candidates competency. It can be offered at different times, locations or even different tests to different students. The computer selects test question from a pool, so candidates taking the same examination will not be answering identical questions. It eliminates the need for test booklets and answer sheets that increase the security levels. Self paced tutorials show candidates how to use a mouse and other testing tools, ensuring that even those without computer experience are comfortable. Candidates can use either paper and pencil or word processing for essay questions depending on their own preference. It improves the link between instruction and assessment, providing a profile of candidates' strengths and weaknesses, and matches questions and the order in which they are presented to the ability of each test taker.

Computer based examination system reduces the large proportion of workload on examination, training, grading and reviewing. The set of questions mostly used in computer based examination system are multiple choice tests that can be formally and easily evaluated online. Emphasis is now shifting to computer based tests and on-screen marking of essay questions in the developed world. Computer based tests are scored immediately or shortly after administration unlike the paper and pencil test result that takes several months to process. Fast scoring helps for publishing results quickly. It can be used to control inadequate examination halls.

Limitations of computer based testing attempts to grade students' essays online are now being explored in the on-screen marking is already being practiced by Cambridge Assessment. On-screen marking is much better than paper scripts. Although this process is already practiced by some institutions in the developed world, it is still at the fundamental stage. It is necessary that the question bank should be large enough to prevent high levels of repetition. Computer crashes sometimes occurs. Hence, there is need for contingency plan in case there are any technical faults in the middle of the examination period that may prevent student from completing the examination and disadvantage their results. Other limitations are related to resources required—a sufficient numbers of computers, a room to install them, appropriate software and adequate technology expertise.

Unit 15 Educational Evaluation 教育评价

University of Cambridge Local Examinations Syndicate（UCLES）（剑桥大学考试委员会）：University of Cambridge Local Examinations Syndicate is a non-teaching department of the University of Cambridge and is a not-for-profit organization. Cambridge Assessment is the brand name of UCLES.

New words and expressions

1. replicate ['replikeit]   v.   复制，模拟，折叠
2. reinforcement [,ri:in'fɔ:smənt] n.   增强，加固，强化物，增援力量
3. embed [im'bed]   v.   （使）插入，（使）嵌入，深留脑中
4. magnitude ['mægnitju:d]   n.   大小，重要，光度，（地震）级数，（星星）等级
5. entrust [in'trʌst]   vt.   信赖，信托，交托
6. immense [i'mens]   adj.   巨大的，广大的，〈口〉非常好的
7. envisage [in'vizidʒ]   vt.   面对，想象
8. pedagogical [pedə'gɔdʒikəl]   adj.   教学（法）的
9. configuration [kən,figju'reiʃən] n.   结构，布局，形态，格式塔心理完形，[计算机]配置
10. responsive to   对……起反应，对……敏感
11. contingency [kən'tindʒənsi]   n.   偶发事件，偶然

I Vocabulary.

Fill in the blanks with the most suitable words. Change the form when necessary.

replicate   magnitude   configuration   pedagogical   envisage

1. The board of this company _____ that there will be a high profit in producing this

kind of new product.
2. To be an excellent teacher, one should learn _____ techniques.
3. Due to the lack of space, the designer has to reduce the _____ of the building.
4. Twenty-four _____ texts are carried out to obtain reasonable statistics.
5. Though it is a small business computer system in its simplest _____, it managed to produce large quantities of products efficiently.

II Comprehension of the text.

Decide whether the following statements are true (T) or false (F) according to the passage.

1. Teaching assessment is the process of defining, selecting, designing, collecting, analyzing, interpreting and using information to increase student' learning and development.
2. ODL learners enjoy varied opportunities to communicate their learning and have more opportunity to diagnose their errors or mistakes before formal assessment task.
3. In the absence of a stock of ready made questions in question bank, the quality of question papers is liable to suffer.
4. Computer based assessment can be offered at different times, locations or even different tests to different students.
5. Computer based testing is recognized as a sustainable strategy for sustainable assessment for ODL because it can be more responsive only to the needs of distance learners.

III Choose the word or expression that has the similar meaning of the underlined word or expression.

1. I have <u>reinforced</u> the elbows of the jacket with leather patches.
   A. intensified   B. changed   C. minimized   D. beautified
2. Self Assessment Questions <u>embedded</u> in the course material enable distance learners to evaluate their progress frequently.
   A. excluded   B. list   C. covered   D. included
3. I <u>entrusted</u> him to sign the contract for me.
   A. authorized   B. asked   C. told   D. invited
4. China, as a trading market with <u>immense</u> potential and endless opportunities, has attracted many foreign funds.
   A. profound   B. huge   C. extensive   D. little
5. In case of future <u>contingencies</u>, one should get well prepared.
   A. problems   B. incidents   C. accidents   D. cases

Unit 15　Educational Evaluation　教育评价

▶▶▶ Useful phrases and expressions ◀◀◀◀

改革评价体系　remove evaluation systems
深化办学体制改革　deepen reform in school operation
分类考试　subject-specific examination
综合评价　comprehensive evaluation
多元录取　diversified admission criteria
解决教育评价指挥棒问题　use proper evaluation to steer education
多层次、多样化的教育需求　multi-layered and diverse educational needs
深化考试招生制度改革　deepen reform of examination and enrolment systems
用正确的立场方法分析问题　approach problems from correct perspectives and methods
培养学生解决问题的意识与能力　cultivate students' problem-solving awareness and ability

Knowledge and practice should be united, with knowledge guiding practice and practice generating new knowledge.
知行合一、以知促行、以行求知。
Serve the society and constantly improve the ability and level of service.
坚持面向社会、服务社会、不断提高服务意识、服务能力以及服务水平。
Improve the institution mechanisms to ensure fair and effective competition and supervision.
健全促进公平、科学选才、监督有力的体制机制。
Devise a lifelong learning system that connects all types and levels of education and recognize a wide range of learning outcomes.
构建衔接沟通各级各类教育、认可多种学习成果的终身学习立交桥。
Resolutely stop the practice of rewarding or penalizing schools of linking admission rates with the allocation of various resources.
坚决改变以升学率奖优罚劣的做法,坚决破除把升学率与各种资源分配挂钩的行为。
Extracurricular training institutions should be managed according to the law so that such training can perform its fundamental task of educating people.
依法管理校外培训机构,使校外教育培训回归育人正常轨道。
Further the reform of examination and enrolment systems to redress the deep-seated problems in educational evaluation.
以深化考试招生制度改革作为教育评价指挥棒问题的突破口。
Examination and enrolment systems are basic national education systems, which affect the forming of China's talent pool and its development plan.

考试招生制度是国家基本教育制度,是教育改革"牵一发而动全身"的重点领域和关键环节。

Overcome the deep-rooted problems of relying solely on grades, admission rates, diplomas, academic papers, and professional titles, and remove their excessive influence on the evaluation of education.

坚决克服唯分数、唯升学、唯文凭、唯论文、唯帽子的顽瘴气痼疾。

Whereas theory and practice should complement each other, teaching should relate to productive labor and social activities.

注重理论与实践相结合,坚持教育教学与生产劳动和社会实践相结合。

Keys to Exercises
练习答案

Unit 1

Text A

I. 1. corporal   2. hallmarks   3. monastery   4. slam   5. truancy
   6. reluctance   7. rampart   8. preliminary   9. compulsory   10. principality

II. compulsory education; convince; material/physical comfort; spiritual needs; supervise

III. 1. F   2. F   3. F   4. T   5. T

Text B

I. 1. E   2. A   3. H   4. C   5. F   6. I   7. D   8. B   9. G   10. J

II. freshmen; sophomore; junior sophister; senior sophister; academic institution; administrative regulations; unexpected changes; be destined to; be immune to; residential college

III. 1. F   2. T   3. F   4. F   5. T   6. F   7. T   8. F   9. T   10. F

Unit 2

Text A

I. 1. comprehensive   2. optimal   3. aptitude   4. encompass   5. inculcate
   6. compromised   7. interpret   8. integrate   9. disseminate   10. initiative

II. human capital; sustainable development; natural resources; rational thinking; take into account; living condition; physical infrastructure; consistent with; life long learning; social justice

III. 1. F   2. F   3. T   4. F   5. T

Text B

I. 1. B 2. E 3. H 4. F 5. C 6. A 7. I 8. D 9. J 10. G

II. Knowledge-based Society; bring light into; exclusive right; tertiary education; be bound to; vocational colleges; cultural norm; quality assurance; quality audit; cultural diversity; adapt to

III. 1. T 2. T 3. F 4. T 5. F 6. F 7. T 8. F 9. T 10. F

Unit 3

Text A

I. 1. cluster 2. probe 3. crucial 4. elucidate 5. intertwined 6. perception 7. thrive 8. propensity 9. intriguing 10. idiosyncratic

II. individual differences; educational environment; developmental process; academic potential; genetically identical; be aware; learning profiles; lay out; take up the challenge; build on

III. 1. T 2. T 3. F 4. T 5. F 6. F 7. F 8. T 9. T 10. F

Text B

I. 1. D 2. H 3. F 4. B 5. I 6. A 7. E 8. G 9. J 10. C

II. social skills; carry out; unconditional love; addict to; student-centered teaching method; be conscious of; secondary education; struggle for; obey rules; self-discipline

III. 1. T 2. F 3. T 4. T 5. F 6. F 7. T 8. T 9. T 10. F

Unit 4

Text A

I. 1. E-learning

2. Doing is the best learning way and E-learning is suitable for the modern educational system.

3. 听而易忘，见而易记，做而易懂。

4. Learning is a process of achieving certain competences that can be defined as a dynamical combination of cognitive and meta-cognitive skills, knowledge and understanding, as well as the development of social skills and growth in ethical values.

5. E-learning enhances the quality of educational process by enabling the practice of new roles in the process of learning. In addition, during this process, lifelong learning technologies are used.

Through E-learning, a new educational environment can be set and an environment can be constructed in the direction of interaction, processing information, researching and problem-solving. The students are asked to actively get involved, and often work in teams. The role of the professor is to design the methods of learning and help the student develop their talents and capabilities.

II. 1. B 2. D 3. C 4. B 5. D
III. 1. F 2. F 3. T 4. T 5. F

Text B

I. 1. A 2. C 3. B 4. B 5. B 6. B 7. A 8. C 9. D 10. A
II. 1. F 2. F 3. F 4. T 5. F
III. 1. 尽管联合国正在为到2015年实现全球儿童普遍基础教育而奋斗，但教育的不公平性一直存在，并且对全球的教育决策人、学者以及从业人员都是重大的挑战。
  2. 关于义务教育的法规，在中国，法律在决策制定中是一种解决特定教育问题的实用手段，也是对各级的政府负责提高教育的最终手段。
  3. 比尔顿证明，教育机会的平等需要确保让在学校的机会对每个相同能力的人都是一样的，无论其性别、种族、社会经济背景如何。
  4. 在《世界人权宣言》中，联合国声明每个人都有教育的权利，而教育至少在基础和基本阶段应该是免费义务教育。
  5. 结果，尽管一些如性别差异的问题存在，但世界儿童进入小学率从1999年到2005年增加了6%至688 000 000，而2005年儿童辍学率从1999年的96 000 000 降低到72 000 000。

Unit 5

Text A

I. 1. C 2. D 3. A 4. D 5. B
II. 1. exert   2. flourish/flourished   3. equipped   4. intuitive   5. priority
    6. abide   7. normative   8. talented   9. egalitarian   10. emphasized
III. 1. 教育应该使孩子们成为自主、自立的个体，能够对如何过自己的生活和如何为自己适应复杂的现代生活有很好的判断。

2. 教育应该为孩子们提供必要的技能和知识，使他们在经济中是有效的参与者，这样他们在劳动力市场中有大量不同的选择，必要的收入所得来繁荣市场经济。

3. 教育应该为孩子的成长发挥作用，使之成为独立参与经济活动的成年人。

4. 教育应该使孩子们成为好的公民——在政治生活中有责任感、能有效参与政治。

5. 当你对比有着同样才能、同样意愿努力的孩子们时，直觉告诉你说，当他们得到同样水平的教育资源，教育的公平会是令人满意的。

Text B

I. 1. C 2. D 3. D 4. A 5. B 6. B 7. C 8. A 9. D 10. B
II. 1. elusive   2. ample   3. upsurge   4. equitable   5. variations
    6. evading   7. straightforward   8. boost   9. warrant   10. assess
III. 1. T 2. F 3. F 4. F 5. T

Unit 6

Text A

I. 1. D 2. B 3. A 4. C 5. D
II. 1. ethnocentric   2. underscore   3. dogmatic   4. orthodox   5. attacked
    6. inculcate   7. articulate   8. constitute   9. filial   10. conquered
III. 1. Xunzi underscored the realistic and materialistic aspects of Confucian thought, stressing that morality was inculcated in society through tradition and in individuals through training.

2. He had many Confucian scholars killed and their books burned.

3. Zhu Xi

4. The works of Confucius were translated into European languages through the agency of Jesuit scholars stationed in China.

5. This passage talks about the development of Confucius thought.

Text B

I. 1. B 2. A 3. D 4. D 5. C 6. D 7. A 8. B 9. C 10. D
II. 1. T 2. T 3. F 4. F 5. F
III. 1. 教育是灌输自律的过程，这样思想和身体都会从对生活的关注中解放出来。

2. 以上天为中心和以尘世为中心的两种教育都在实践中作用于正规的教育系统，正规教育强迫儿童通过死记硬背记住古代作品，而年长的学生如学徒般或不拘小节地聚集在他们老师周围。
3. 希腊哲学思想认识到教育的目的是使人都要对无穷的,还有地球上的日常事务保持敏感。
4. 因此,他精确的教育设计被剥夺了强有力的目标,那些服务目标是在早期所使用的。
5. 从最广义上讲,作为地球上的生命的人放弃他的好奇心和寻求压倒一切可能未知的欲望是要认真地培育的。

Unit 7

Text A

I. 1. B 2. A 3. D 4. E 5. C
II. 1. F 2. T 3. F 4. T 5. F
III. 1. pre-independence system   2. expression through word and act
   3. social content and social goals   4. optimism and secularism
   5. the individual in society; the society.

Text B

I. 1. B 2. A 3. D 4. E 5. C
II. 1. F 2. T 3. F 4. F 5. T
III. 1. affective and psychomotor   2. demonstrable and measurable
   3. The sequencing of objectives   4. institutional or course goals
   5. Educational Objectives

Unit 8

Text A

I. 1. illiteracy   2. nonsensical   3. shudder   4. captivating   5. onus
   6. provoke   7. courtesy   8. zealously 9. trivial   10. blemish
II. 1. F 2. F 3. F 4. T 5. T
III. 1. The student   2. encourage   3. facilitator
   4. the absence   5. Building a foundation

Text B

I. 1. compelling   2. hostility   3. abhor   4. manifest   5. Concurrently
    6. assertiveness   7. maladaptive   8. assert   9. morale   10. hinder

II. 1. F   2. F   3. T   4. T   5. T

III. (1) negative teacher-student interactions
    (2) attachment
    (3) warmth and understanding
    (4) their behavior towards students
    (5) cognitive

Unit 9

Text A

I. 1. comprehensive   2. necessity   3. supervision   4. prescribe   5. contemporary
    6. priority   7. parental   8. intellectual   9. ethic/ethics   10. Admittedly

II. 1. F   2. T   3. T   4. T   5. T

III. 1. family
    2. cooperation between school and family
    3. disappointment and misunderstandings
    4. the family
    5. the district and state

Text B

I. 1. D   2. B   3. E   4. A   5. C

II. 1. F   2. T   3. T   4. F   5. T

III. 1. peer victimization   2. increases   3. developmental outcomes
    4. reduce   5. prosocial behaviors

Unit 10

Text A

I. 1. anthology   2. arbitrary   3. conspicuous   4. ethos   5. capstone

II. 1. F   2. F   3. T   4. T   5. F

III. Omitted.

Text B

I. d-b-c-a
II. 1. F 2. T 3. T 4. F 5. T
III. Omitted.

Unit 11

Text A

I. 1. correspond   2. Insofar   3. estimate/estimation   4. derived/derives   5. propensity
II. 1. F 2. T 3. F 4. T
III. 1. 因此,学生和毕业生们了解课外活动的影响,评估其在从高等教育到就业这一转变时期所可能扮演的角色是非常重要的。
2. 因此,被认为是高离职率人群的求职者面临着更为严格的就业标准,较低的工资,较少的面试机会;即使和其他的求职者一样的条件,他们也可能在招聘流程中被完全地排除在外。
3. 共涉及五个解释变量:课外活动的参与度,活动类型,参与活动花费的时间,参与的强度,以及活动情景。
4. 然而,整个的课外活动量应该控制在一个合理范围内:因为活动时间越长,获得管理职位的机会越少。
5. 此外,重新审视高等教育中课外活动的地位和认可度以及它和常规课程之间的联系可能对在高等教育市场中面临竞争的教育机构有莫大的好处。

Text B

I. 1. sedentary   2. validate   3. respectively   4. Degenerative   5. inferable
II. 1. F 2. T 3. F 4. T
III. 1. 在意大利,现在没有一个现行的个人 SES 分类,区域性数据来自个人经济消费水平,而不是收入和教育水平。
2. 关于对待体育活动的态度,主要调查体育活动在减肥、社会交往、性格形成方面是否有益。
3. 母亲的受教育水平也似乎相当大地影响学生体育活动的选择和每周课外体育锻炼总时间数。

4. 关于体育活动和父母受教育水平之间关系的研究显示，父母受教育水平的高低是孩子选择体育活动的决定性因素。

5. 从这个意义上讲，此次研究的结果对学校管理者如何去弥补贫富学生之间的隔阂是非常有用的。

Unit 12

Text A

I. 1. auxiliary　　2. marginalize　　3. spectrum　　4. caveat　　5. incentive

II. 1. F　2. F　3. F　4. F　5. T

III. 1. School-Based Management is a strategy which decentralizes education decision-making by increasing parental and community involvement in schools. it is the decentralization of authority from the central government to the school level. SBM programs transfer authority over one or more of the following activities：budget allocation，the hiring and firing of teachers and other school staff，curriculum development，the procurement of textbooks and other educational material，infrastructure improvements，and the monitoring and evaluation of teacher performance and student learning outcomes.

2. First of all，SBM helps to improve student achievement and other outcomes as these local people demand closer monitoring of school personnel，better student evaluations，a closer match between the school's needs and its policies，and a more efficient use of resources. Secondly，it reduces opportunities for corruption. In addition，it gives parents and stakeholders opportunities to increase their skills.

3. First，the SBM model must define exactly which powers are vested in which individuals or committees and how these powers are to be coordinated to make the plan workable within both the school culture and the available resources.

Second，SBM requires supports from the various school-level stakeholders，local and national governments. The support from parents and other community members is also needed.

4. The caveat is that the specific type of SBM introduced in any given country depends (or should ideally depend) on the political economy of the particular country.

Text B

I. 1. D　2. B　3. A　4. C　5. E

II. 1. The education system in Türkiye is centralized，which means that the policy-making function is in the hands of the Ministry of Education that has power over all educational matters. The Ministry determines the personnel policy and arranges training, certifying, appointment and salary schedules of teachers. On the other hand the public school system in the US is governed by an open decentralized system. State legislatures are responsible for public education. Their task is to authorize funding and give legislative support for the schools. All states have state boards of education, which deal with policy development, personnel recruitment, budgeting and the law.

2. Because centralized structure forms barriers to it, on one hand, it is said that the principal administers the school. On the other hand, the principle is deprived of autonomy. To say the least, whatever the principle wants to do, he needs to get permission from the central authorities. Some teachers related this situation to the bureaucratic structure of the Turkish education in which administration was seen as the powerbase that can override participative decisions.

3. Most teachers agreed that although SIP was mandated by the district office, schools had autonomy in designing the organization and the components of their own improvement plan. But the principal said that the SIP was strategic planning developed by the district, so each school's plan had to fit in with the district's strategic planning. One teacher said that, outside the SIP, the school was involved in other activities which also contributed to school improvement.

Unit 13

Text A

I. 1. reluctant 2. ambiguous 3. diminish 4. paradigms 5. compounded
II. 1. T 2. F 3. T 4. T 5. F
III. 沟通技能；最新信息；将 A 替换成 B；使结合，使合并；达到标准

Text B

I. 1. derive 2. rigid 3. sophisticated 4. optimum 5. encompasses
II. 1. F 2. T 3. T 4. F 5. T
III. 1. 人类是具有高度创造性的生物，喜欢通过对想法进行实践，探索，试验，质疑，纠正而学习。

2. 批判的评论必须略去，对别人想法的批评也应当延至最后。许多创造性的想法没有提出主要是因为提出者怀疑别人会认为他的想法不重要，或者毫无价值。

3. 除了提出自己的想法，成员们应当提出建议：其他人的想法怎样才能变得更好，两个或多个想法如何合并成一个？

4. 书记员的任务是把所有提出的想法简单地记下来。有时候组员们提出想法太快，即使是速记专家，记下这些想法也会有困难。

5. 成员们可以将自己的想法输入并显示在计算机屏幕的下方，而由其他成员提出的想法显示在屏幕的上方。

Unit 14

Text A

I. 1. entail   2. periodicals   3. is harnessed   4. supplement   5. prey
   6. chunks   7. tangible   8. spectrum   9. surplus   10. supplanted

II. 1. T   2. T   3. F   4. T   5. T

III. 1. audio-visual aids   2. what skills are practiced   3. evolutions
     4. educational technology   5. user-friendly

Text B

I. 1. landmark   2. spawned   3. disparate   4. slough   5. discursive
   6. archives   7. truncated   8. nihility   9. suboptimal   10. contour

II. 1. T   2. F   3. T   4. T   5. F

III. 1. A   2. A   3. D   4. B   5. C

Unit 15

Text A

I. 1. simultaneously   2. cognitive   3. interactive   4. manipulate   5. alignment

II. 1. F   2. F   3. T   4. T   5. T

III. 1. A   2. C   3. B   4. A   5. C

Text B

I. 1. envisage   2. pedagogical   3. magnitude   4. replicated   5. configuration

II. 1. T   2. F   3. F   4. T   5. F

III. 1. A   2. D   3. A   4. B   5. C

References
参考文献

[1] ABIDIN R R, KMETZ C A. 1997. Teacher-student interactions as predicted by teaching stress and the perceived quality of the student-teacher relationship//The Annual Meeting of the National Association of School Psychologists. Anaheim, C A.

[2] ADELMAN H S, TAYLOR L. 1998. Reframing mental health in schools and expanding school reform. Educational Psychologist, 33: 135–152.

[3] AIKEN L S, WEST S G. 1991. Multiple regression: Testing and interpreting interactions. Newbury Park, CA: Sage.

[4] ALTBACH P G. 2008. Globalization and forces for change in higher education. International Higher Education, 50: 2–4.

[5] ARROW K. 1973. The theory of discrimination//ASHENFELTER O, REES A. Discrimination in labor markets. Princeton, NJ: Princeton University Press: 3–33.

[6] BADDELEY A. 2003. Working memory: looking back and looking forward. Nature Reviews Neuroscience, 4: 829–839.

[7] BAGGEN P, TELLINGS A, VAN HAAFTEN W, et al. 1998. The university and the knowledge society.

[8] BAKER J A, TERRY T, BRIDGER R, et al. 1997. Schools as caring communities: a relational approach to school reform. School Psychology Review, 26: 586–602.

[9] BAKEWELL E B. 1988. Object, image, inquiry: the art historian at work. Santa Monica, CA: Getty Trust Publications.

[10] BEMMEL, BELL D. 1968. The measurement of knowledge and technology//SHELDON E B, MOORE W E. Indicators of social change. Concepts and Measurements Hartford, Connecticut: Russell Sage Foundation: 145–246.

[11] BEREITER C. 1999. Education and mind in the knowledge age [EB/OL]. http://csile.oise.utoronto.ca/edmind/edmind.html.

[12] BERNHARD A. A knowledge-based society needs quality in higher education. London, Paris: Concorde Publishing House.

[13] BLAU F D, KAHN L M. 1981. Race and sex differences in quits by young workers.

Industrial and Labor Relations Review, 34(4): 563–577.

[14] BOER. 2002. Academia in the 21st century: an analysis of trends and perspectives in higher education and research. Den Haag: AWT, 28.

[15] BOGLER R. 2001. The influence of leadership style on teacher job satisfaction. Educational Administration Quarterly, 37(5): 662–683.

[16] BOTSFORD D. 1993. Compulsion versus Liberty in education//Education Note: 5. London: Libertarian Alliance.

[17] BRATTESANI K, WEINSTEIN R, MARSHALL H. 1984. Student perceptions of differential teacher treatment. Journal of Educational Psychology, 76: 236–247.

[18] BREHM J W. 1966. A theory of psychological reactance. New York: Academic Press.

[19] BRENNAN J. 2004. The social role of the contemporary university: contradictions, boundaries and change//Ten Years On: Changing Education in a Changing World. Milton Keynes: The Open University: 22–26.

[20] BRIGHOUSE H. 2007. Educational justice and socio-economic segregation in schools. Journal of Philosophy of Education, 41(4).

[21] BROUILLETTE L. 1997. Who defines "democratic leadership"? Three high school principals respond to school-based reforms. Journal of School Leadership, 7: 569–591.

[22] BROWN A. CAMPIONE J. 1994. Guided discovery in a community of learners//MCGILLY. Classroom lessons: integrating cognitive theory and classroom practice: 229–270.

[23] BUTERA F, MUGNY G. 2001. Social influence and social reality. Seattle: Hogrefe & Huber Publishers.

[24] CALVIN J. 1962. Institutes of Christian religion. BEVERIDGE, translate. London: James Clarke.

[25] Canadian School Boards Association. 1999. Poverty intervention profile: partners in action.

[26] CENTRA J A. 1993. Reflective faculty evaluation: enhancing teaching and determining faculty effectiveness. San Francisco: Jossey-Bass.

[27] CHALL J S. 1996. Stages of reading development. 2 ed. Fort Worth: Harcourt Brace College Publishers.

[28] CHIAPPETTA E L, KOBALLA R Jr. 2002. Science instruction in the middle and secondary schools. Merrill Prentice Hall: Ohio.

[29] CHRISTMANN U, MISCHO C. 2000. The efficacy of communicative fairness and rhetorical aesthetics in contributions to argumentation. Language and Speech. 43: 229–259.

[30] COHEN L, MANLON L, MORRISON K R B. 2000. Research methods in education. London: Routledge.

[31] COLDING A, MEEK V L. 2006. Twelve propositions on diversity in higher education. Higher Education Management and Policy, 18(3): 31–54.

[32] COLTHEART M, RASTLE K, PERRY C, et al. 2001. DRC: A dual route cascaded model of visual word recognition and reading aloud. Psychological Review, 108: 204–256.

[33] CROWELL J A, FELDMAN S S. Mothers' internal models of relationships and children's behavioral and developmental status: a study of mother-child interaction. Child Development, 59: 1273–1285.

[34] DAMON. 2002. Bringing in a new era in character education. Stanford, CA: Hoover Institution Press.

[35] DAY C, ELLIOT B, KINGTON A. 2005. Reform, standards and teacher identity: challenges of sustaining commitment. Journal of Teaching and Teacher Education, 21: 563–577.

[36] DE DREU C K W, DE VRIES N K. 2001. Group consensus and minority influence implications for innovation. Oxford: Blackwell.

[37] DESJARDINS S L, DUNDAR H, HENDEL D D. 1999. Modeling the college application decision process in a land-grant university. Economics of Education Review, 18(1): 117–132.

[38] DFEE. 1996–2003. Pupil absence and truancy in England. London: the National Statistics, HMSO.

[39] DOISE W. 1982. L'explication en psychologie sociale. Paris: Presses Universitaires de France.

[40] DRVFOOS J G. 1990. Adolescent at risk: prevalence and prevention. New York: Oxford University Press.

[41] DUNCAN, G, BROOKS-GUNN J, KLEBANOV P. 1994. Economic deprivation and early childhood development. Child Development, 65: 296–318.

[42] ECCLES J S, BARBER B L, STONE M, et al. 2003. Extracurricular activities and adolescent development. Journal of Social Issues, 59(4): 865–889.

[43] ECCLES J S, GRUSEC J E, HASTINGS P D. 2007. Families, schools, and developing achievement related motivations and engagement. New York: Guilford Press.

[44] EHRI L C, SNOWLING M J, HULME C. 2005. Development of sight word reading: phases and findings//SNOWLING M J, HHLME C. The science of reading: a handbook. Oxford, UK: Blackwell Publishing. 135–154.

[45] EIDE E R, RONAN N 2001. Is participation in high school athletics an investment or a consumption good? Economics of Education Review, 20(5): 431–442.

[46] EL-KHAWAS E, DEPIETRO-JURAND R, HOLM-NIELSEN L. 1998. Quality assurance in higher education: recent progress; challenges ahead. Washington, D. C. : World Bank.

[47] ENDY D, BRENT R. 2001. Modelling cellular behavior. Nature, 409: 391–395.

[48] ENTWISLE D R, ASTONE N M. 1994. Some practical guidelines for measuring youth's race/ethnicity and socioeconomic status. Child Development, 65: 1521–1540.

[49] ERDOGAN I. 2002. Turkish education system towards a new millenium. Ankara: Sistem Publishing.

[50] EWELL P. 2007. The "quality game": external review and institutional reaction over three decades in the United States//WESTERHEIJDEN D F. Quality assurance in higher education: trends in regulation, translation and transformation. Dortrecht: Springer: 119–153.

[51] FEIGENBAUM H B. 1997. Centralization and national integration in France. Mediterranean Quarterly, 8(1): 60–76.

[52] FISCHER K W. 1980. A theory of cognitive development: the control and construction of hierarchies of skills. Psychological Review, 87: 477–531.

[53] FISCHER K W, BIDDELL T R. 2006. Dynamic development of action and thought. //DAMON W, LERNER R M. Theoretical models of human development. Handbook of child psychology: Vol. 1. 6th ed. New York: Wiley: 313–399.

[54] FISHER D, KENT H B. 1998. Associations between teacher personality and classroom environment. Journal of Classroom Interaction, 33(1): 5–13.

[55] FRITH U. 1986. A developmental framework for developmental dyslexia. Annals of Dyslexia.

[56] GAGER C T, COONEY T M., CALL K T. 1999. The effects of family characteristics and time use on teenagers' household labor. Journal of Marriage and the Family, 61(4): 982–994.

[57] GEORGE J M, JONES G R. 1996. Understanding and managing organizational behavior. TX: Texas A & M University.

[58] GERBER S B. 1996. Extracurricular activities and academic achievement. Journal of Research and Development in Education, 30(1): 42–50.

[59] GIBBONS M. 1994. The new production of knowledge: the dynamics of science and research in contemporary societies. London: Sage Publications.

[60] GIL R M. 2001. Human values and personal development: tutorships of secondary

education and schools of parents. Madrid, Spain: Spanish School.

[61] GLEMAN. 1995. Emotional intelligence: why it can matter more than IQ. New York: Bantam Books.

[62] GOEDEGEBUURE L, MEEK V L. 1997. On change and diversity: the role of government influences. Higher Education in Europe, 22(3): 309–319.

[63] GOLDSWORTHY R, SCHWARTZ N, BARAB S, et al. 2007. Evaluation of a collaborative multimedia conflict resolution curriculum. Educational Technology Research and Development, 55(6).

[64] GORNITZKA A, MAASSEN P. 2000. Hybrid steering approaches with respect to european higher education. Higher Education Policy, 13(3): 267–285.

[65] GRAHAM P A. 2005. Schooling America: how the public schools meet the nation's changing needs. New York: Oxford University Press.

[66] GROSS, JUVONEN, GABLE. 2002. Internet use and well-being in adolescence. Journal of Social Issues, 58(1): 75–90.

[67] HALL. 1995. The convergence of means. Educom Review, 30(4): 42–45.

[68] HAMMOND L D. 1993. Reframing the school reform agenda: developing capacity for school transformation. Phi Delta Kaplan, 74(10): 753–761.

[69] HANISH L D, GUERRA N G. 2000. Predictors of peer victimization among urban youth. Social Development, 9: 521–543.

[70] HARTELMAN P A, VAN DER MAAS H L J, MOLENAAR P C M. 1998. Detecting and modeling developmental transitions. British Journal of Developmental Psychology, 16: 97–122.

[71] HARTUP W W. 1996. The company they keep: friendships and their developmental significance. Child Development, 67: 1–13.

[72] HARVEY L, GREEN D. 1993. Defining quality. Assessment and Evaluation in Higher Education, 18(1): 9–34.

[73] HAWLEY P H. 2002. Social dominance and prosocial and coercive strategies of resource control in preschoolers. International Journal of Behavioral Development, 26: 167–176.

[74] HEYNEMAN, STEPHEN P, RANSOM, et al. 1990. Using examinations and testing to improve educational quality. Educational Policy, 4: 177–192.

[75] HIGH J, ELLIG J. 1988. The private supply of education: some historical evidence// COWEN. The theory of market failure. Fairfax, VA: George Mason University Press.

[76] HINDSON B, BYRNE B, FIELDING-BARNSLEY R, et al. 2005. Assessment and early instruction of preschool children at risk for reading disability. Journal of Educational Psychology, 97: 687–704.

[77] HLEBOWITSH P, TELLEZ K. 1997. American education: purpose and promise. California: Wadsworth Publishing.

[78] HOLUBOVÁ. 2010. Improving the quality of teaching by modern teaching methods. The 21st century, 25: 59.

[79] http://education. stateuniversity. com/pages/2246/Moral-Education. html.

[80] http://tigger. uic. edu/~lnucci/MoralEd/overview. html.

[81] http://en. wikipedia. org/wiki/Confucius.

[82] KACZMANREK P. 2002. Follow the leader. Washington D. C. : Education Reform Network, World Prosperity Ltd.

[83] KAZAMIAS A, EPSTEIN E H. 1968. Schools in transition. Massachusetts: Allyn & Bacon.

[84] KENDALL S, WHITE R, KINDER K, et al. Bedford, N. 2004. School attendance and the prosecution of parents: effects and effectiveness: final report. Slough: NFER.

[85] KENNEDY J H, Kennedy C E. 2004. Attachment theory: implications for school psychology. Psychology in the Schools, 41(2): 247–259.

[86] KNAPPER. 2001. Broadening our approach to teaching evaluation. New Directions for Teaching and Learning, Winter.

[87] KNIGHT C C, FISCHER K W. 1992. Learning to read words: individual differences in developmental sequences. Journal of Applied Developmental Psychology, 13: 377–404.

[88] KOZMA R. 1991. Learning with media. Review of Educational Research, 61(2): 179–212.

[89] KOZMA R. 1994. Will media influence learning? Reframing the debate. Educational Technology Research and Development, 42(2): 7–19.

[90] LANGFORD. 2010. Educational policy, housing policy, and social justice prospero, 16(2): 33–36.

[91] LAUGLO J, MCLEAN M. 1985. The control of education: international perspectives on the centralization-decentralization debate. London: Kogan Page.

[92] LAW, PAN SUYAN. 2009. Legislation and equality in basic education for all in China. Interchange, 40(4): 337–372.

[93] LAW. 2007. Major continuities and changes in the basic education law. Education and the Law, 19(12): 177–199.

[94] LEAHY S, LYON C, THOMPSON M, et al. 2005. Classroom assessment: minute by minute, and day by day. Educational Leadership, 63(3): 18–24.

[95] LESLIE N K, LO. 2002. The development of youth discussion on the educational role and functions of out-of-school education. Youth Studies (7): 29–38.

[96] LJOSA E, MANN K. 1995. EDEN: a growing garden. European Journal of Engineering Education, 20(2): 239–241.

[97] LUNCEFORD. 2009. In defense against outdated materials. Institute of General Semantics, Inc.

[98] LUNENBURG F C, ORNSTEIN A C. 2004. Educational administration: concepts and practices. California: Wadsworth/Thomson Learning.

[99] LUTHER M. 1962. To the councilmen of all cities in Germany that they establish and maintain Christian schools. Steinhaeuser A, Tr. Philadelphia: Fortress Press: 347–378.

[100] LUTHER M. 1967. Sermon on keeping children in school. JACOBS, Tr. Philadelphia: Fortress Press: 209–258.

[101] LYONS M. 1994. Napoleon Bonaparte and the legacy of the French revolution. New York: St. Martin's Press.

[102] MACCOBY E E. 1990. Gender and relationships: a developmental account. American Psychologist, 45: 513–520.

[103] MANTON. 2001. Filling bellies and brains: the educational and political thought of Frederick James Gould. History of Education, 30(3): 273–275.

[104] MARGINSON S, VAN DER WENDE M. 2007. Globalisation and higher education. OECD Education Working Paper (8).

[105] MARKWARDT J. 1997. Peabody individual achievement test-revised: normative update: manual. Circle Pines: American Guidance Service.

[106] MARSHALL C, ROSSMAN G B. 1999. Designing qualitative research. 3rd ed. California: Sage.

[107] MARTIN E, FEMFINDEZ I, ANDRS S., et al. 2003. The intervention for the improvement of the conviviality in the educational centers: models and areas. Infancy and Learning, Journal for the Study Education and Development, 26(1): 79–95.

[108] MASTEN A S, COATSWORTH J D. 1998. The development of competence in favorable and unfavorable environments: lessons from research on successful children. American Psychologist, 53: 205–220.

[109] MATTHEWS. The origins of distance education and its use in the United States. T H E Journal, 27(2): 54.

[110] MCLOYD V C. 1998. Socioeconomic disadvantage and child development. American Psychologist, 53, 185–204.

[111] MEANS B, OLSON K. 1997. Technology's role in education reform: findings from a national study of innovating schools. Washington, D. C. U. S. Department of Education, Office of Educational Research and Improvement.

[112] MILLER C, SMITH C, TILSTONE C. 1998. Professional development by distance education: does distance lend enhancement?. Cambridge Journal of Education, 28(2): 221−230.

[113] MORRIS C G, MAISTO A A. 2005. Psychology: an introduction. New Jersey: Pearson, Prentice Hall.

[114] MOSS C M, BROOKHART S M. 2009. Advancing formative assessment in every classroom: a guide for the instructional leader. Alexandria, VA: ASCD.

[115] NEAVE G. 1988. On the cultivation of quality, efficiency and enterprise: an overview of recent trends in higher education in western Europe, 1986−1988. European Journal of Education, 23(112): 7−23.

[116] NEWTON J. 2002. Views from below: academics coping with quality. Quality in Higher Education, 8(1): 39−61.

[117] NEWTON J. 2007. What is quality?//Bollaert L. 2006. Embedding quality culture in higher education. A Selection of Papers from the 1st European Forum for Quality Assurance, 23−25 November 2006, hosted by the Technische Universität München. (EUA Case Studies 2007).

[118] NICKELS L. 2002. Theoretical and methodological issues in the cognitive neuropsychology of spoken word production. Aphasiology, 16: 3−19.

[119] NOWOTNY H, SCOTT P, GIBBONS M. 2001. Re-thinking science: knowledge and the public in an age of uncertainty. London: Polity Press.

[120] O'CONNELL J, PEPLER D, CRAIG W. 1999. Peer involvement in bullying: insights and challenges for interventions. Journal of Adolescence, 22: 437−452.

[121] OKONKWO. 2010. Sustainable assessment and evaluation strategies for Open and distance learning. Turkish Online Journal of Distance Education (10).

[122] OWENS R G. 2000. Organizational behaviour in education: instructional leadership and school reform. Massachusetts: Allyn & Bacon.

[123] PATTON M G. 1987. How to use qualitative methods in valuation. California: Sage.

[124] PEDHAZUR E J. 1997. Multiple regression in behavioral research: explanation and prediction. New York: Harcourt Brace College.

[125] PELLEGRINO, QUELLMALZ. 2010. Perspectives on the integration of technology and assessment. Journal of Research on Technology in Education.

[126] PELLERT A. 1997. Die universität in der wissensgesellschaft zum verhältnis von forschung und lehre. Innsbruck/Wien: Studienverlag.

[127] PERRY K E, WEINSTEIN R S. 1998. The social context of early schooling and children's school adjustment. Educational Psychologist, 33: 177−194.

[128] ROBERT W. 2001. Brainstorming: a creative way to learn. Project Innovation, Inc.

[129] RUTTER M. 2000. Psychosocial influences: critiques, findings, and research needs. Development and Psychopathology, 12: 375–405.

[130] SANTIAGO P, TREMBLAY K, BASRI E, et al. 2008. Tertiary education for the knowledge society. OECD Thematic Review of Tertiary Education: Synthesis Report, 2.

[131] SCARDIMALIA M, BEREITER C. 1994. Computer support for knowledge-building communities. Journal of the Learning Sciences, 3(3): 265–384.

[132] SCOTT P. 2007. Back to the future? The evolution of higher education systems. // KEHM B. Looking back to look forward: analyses of higher education after the turn of the millennium. Kassel: INCHER: 13–27.

[133] SEIDLE T, RIMMELE R, PRENZEL M. 2005. Clarity and coherence of lesson goals as a scaffold for student learning. Learning and Instruction, 15: 539–556.

[134] SERCU. 2004. Language teaching and learning. London: Routledge.

[135] SIMONS R I, JOHNSON C, BEAMAN J J, et al. 1996. Parents and peer groups as mediators of the effect of community structure on adolescent behavior. American Journal of Community Psychology, 24: 145–171.

[136] SPENCER L M Jr, SPENCER S M. 1993. Competence at work: models for superior performance. New York: John Wiley & Sons.

[137] STEIN S, BOOK H. 2006. The EQ edge. Hoboken, NJ: John Wiley & Sons.

[138] STERNBERG R J. 1985. Beyond IQ: a triarchic theory of human intelligence. New York: Cambridge University Press.

[139] STIGGINS R J, ARTER J A, CHAPPUIS J, et al. 2009. Classroom assessment for learning: doing it right: using it well. Columbus, OH: Allyn and Bacon.

[140] STIGLITZ J E. 1999. Knowledge as a global public good. //KAUL I, GRUMBERG I, STERN M A. Global public goods. International cooperation in the 21st century. New York: Oxford University Press: 308–325.

[141] SUN CAIPING. 2004. Reflections on moral education from the dimensions of morality new thinking for the study of moral education in the context of social diversity. Journal of East China Normal University: Education Science Edition, 22(4). 17, 24, 37.

[142] SWANER L E. 2007. Linking engaged learning, student mental health and well-being, and civic development: a review of the literature. Liberal Education, 93(1): 16–25.

[143] TAYLOR S N. 2006. Why the real self is fundamental to intentional change. Journal of Management Development, 25(7): 643–656.

[144] TAYLOR, WARD. 1998. Literacy theory in the age of the internet. New York: Columbia University Press.

[145] THORNDIKE R L, STEIN S. 1937. An evaluation of the attempts to measure social intelligence. The Psychological Bulletin, 34(5): 275–285.

[146] THORNDIKE E L. 1920. Intelligence and its uses. Harper Magazine, 140: 227–235.

[147] TOMASEGOVIC, ELIAS, BARACIC, MRVAC. 2011. E-learning and evaluation in modern educational system. US-China Education Review, 8(2): 198–203.

[148] TROW M. 1973. Problems in the transition from elite to mass higher education. Berkley: Carnegie Commission on Higher Education.

[149] TROW M. 1976. Elite higher education: an endangered species? Minerva, 14(3): 355–376.

[150] TROW M. 1979. Elite and mass higher education: American models and European realities. //Research into Higher Education: Processes and Structures. Stockholm: National Board of Universities and Colleges: 183–219.

[151] TROW M. 1981. Comparative perspectives on access. //FULTON O. Access to higher education. Guildford: SRHE: 89–121.

[152] TROW M. 1994. Managerialism and the academic profession: quality and control. QSC Higher Education Report, 2.

[153] TROW M. 2000. From mass higher education to universal access: the American advantage. Research and Occasional Paper Series, CSHE, 1: 1–17.

[154] TROW, M. 2006. Reflections on the transition from elite to mass to universal access: forms and phases of higher education in modern societies since WWII. International Handbook of Higher Education, 18: 243–280.

[155] TUCKER M L, SOJKA J Z, BARONE F J, et al. 2000. Training tomorrow's leaders: enhancing the emotional intelligence of business graduates. Journal of Education for Business, 75: 331–338.

[156] VITARO F, BRENDGEN M, PAGANI L, et al. 1999. Disruptive behavior, peer association, and conduct disorder: testing the developmental links through early intervention. Development and Psychopathology, 11: 287–304.

[157] WARDEN R. 1995. Metaphor made real with an open mind. Times Higher Education Supplement (1197).

[158] WATTS W D, SHORT A P. 1990. Teacher drug use: a response to occupational stress. Journal of Drug Education, 20(11): 47–65.

[159] WERNER E E. 1993. Risk, resilience, and recovery: perspectives from the Kauai longitudinal study. Development and Psychopathology, 5: 503–515.

[160] WILLIAM W. 2004. Refuting misconceptions about classroom discussion. Heldref Publications.

[161] WILLIAMS W M, STERNBERG R. 1988. Group intelligence: why some groups are better than others. Intelligence, 12: 351–377.

[162] WORLD BANK. 2002. Constructing knowledge societies: new challenges for tertiary education. Washington, D. C. : World Bank.

[163] WORLD BANK. 2003. Lifelong learning in the global knowledge economy: challenges for developing countries. Washington, D. C. : World Bank.

[164] WÖβMANN. 2008. Efficiency and equity of European education and training policies. International Tax and Public Finance, 2: 200–201.

[165] YOON J S. 2002. Teacher characteristics as predictors of teacher-student relationships: stress, negative affect, and self-efficacy. Social Behavior and Personality, 30(5): 485–494.

[166] ZHANG M. 2004. Time to change the truancy laws? Compulsory education: its origin and modern dilemma. UK: Blackwell Publishing.

[167] ZIMMERMAN B J. 2001. Theories of self-regulated learning and academic achievement: an overview and analysis. //ZIMMERMAN B J SCHUNK D H. Self-regulated learning and academic achievement: theoretical perspectives. Mahwah, NJ: Erlbaum: 1–65.